Marvell
and the
Civic Crown

That candid Age no other way could tell
To be ingenious, but by speaking well.
. . .
These vertues now are banisht out of Towne.
Our Civill Wars have lost the Civicke crowne.

*To his Noble Friend Mr. Richard Lovelace*

# Marvell
## and the Civic Crown

*Annabel M. Patterson*

Princeton University Press

Copyright © 1978 by Princeton University Press
Published by Princeton University Press, Princeton, New Jersey
In the United Kingdom: Princeton University Press,
Guildford, Surrey

All Rights Reserved

Library of Congress Cataloging in Publication Data will
be found on the last printed page of this book

Publication of this book has been aided by a grant
from The Andrew W. Mellon Foundation

This book has been composed in linotype Janson

Printed in the United States of America
by Princeton University Press, Princeton, New Jersey

*To my Parents*

# Contents

# Plates

# Acknowledgments

With the increase and updating of editions, quoting from Marvell becomes more complicated all the time. There is an embarrassment of riches, which makes consistency undesirable. My basic source of reference is H. M. Margoliouth's superb two-volume *The Poems and Letters of Andrew Marvell*, now brought up to date by Pierre Legouis with E. E. Duncan Jones (Oxford, 1971). For the *Rehearsal Transpros'd*, I have of course referred to D.I.B. Smith's fine edition, *The Rehearsal Transpros'd and The Rehearsal Transpros'd: The Second Part* (Oxford, 1971); but for Marvell's other pamphlets the most convenient source is still A. B. Grosart's *Complete Works* (New York, 1875, reprinted 1966), IV.

However, because some aspects of Marvell's canon are still in dispute, one cannot rely entirely on modern editions. In particular, there are some parts of this book which reflect the growing importance of the so-called Popple manuscript acquired by the Bodleian Library in 1944 and catalogued as Eng. poet. d.49. This manuscript, which consists of a copy of the 1681 *Miscellaneous Poems*, with deletions, corrections, and substantial manuscript additions, is now recognized as the one presented to Captain Edward Thompson, Marvell's eighteenth-century editor, by a descendant of William Popple, Marvell's "beloved" nephew and perhaps his closest friend. I am indebted to the Curator of Western Manuscripts at the Bodleian for permission to consult this and other manuscripts which bear on Marvell's satirical canon. It is partly the authority of the Popple manuscript which persuaded me of Marvell's responsibility for the *Second* and *Third Advices to the Painter*, but for accessibility these poems are cited as from George de F. Lord's *Andrew Marvell: Complete Poetry* (New York, 1968).

Because the italicization of seventeenth-century texts, so

faithfully recorded in these editions, is often without significance and detracts from the markings of emphasis, I have always removed it, except where "foreign" words are involved. Wherever else you see italics now, they are mine.

This book is the result of an opportunity for contemplation provided by York University, who granted me an early sabbatical, and the Canada Council, who supported me with a Leave Fellowship. I am also grateful to Barbara Lewalski, Donald Friedman, Elsie Duncan-Jones, Warren Chernaik, and Heather Asals, who all provided the candid advice of which Marvell would have approved. Invaluable criticisms by Earl Miner and John Wallace have made revision its own reward. As always, my family forgave me.

In slightly altered form, part of Chapter 2 has already been published in *English Literary Renaissance*, and part of Chapter 5 in *Studies in the Literary Imagination*. I am grateful for permission to reprint.

For the illustrations, I acknowledge thanks to the Duke of Northumberland and to *Country Life Magazine*, for permission to reproduce Lely's portrait of Charles I and the Duke of York; the National Maritime Museum, Greenwich Hospital Collection, London, for permission to reproduce Lely's naval portraits; the National Portrait Gallery, London, for permission to reproduce the portraits of Marvell and Richard Gibson; the British Library, for reproductions of the broadside *The Dutch Boare Dissected*, and "Dutch Pictures" from Henry Stubbe's *Justification of the Present War Against the United Netherlands*; and Cambridge University Library, for the frontispiece to *Eikon Basilike*.

A.M.P.
January 1978

Marvell
and the
Civic Crown

# Introduction

I can think of no greater dissuasive from another book on Marvell than what he himself wrote as an introduction to the *Second Part* of the *Rehearsal Transpros'd*:

> Those that take upon themselves to be Writers, are moved to it either by Ambition or Charity: imagining that they shall do therein something to make themselves famous, or that they can communicate something that may be delightful and profitable to mankind. But therefore it is either way an envious and dangerous imployment. For, how well soever it be intended, the World will have some pretence to suspect, that the Author hath both too good a conceit of his own sufficiency, and that by undertaking to teach them, he implicitly accuses their ignorance. So that not to Write at all is much the safer course of life: but if a mans Fate or Genius prompt him otherwise, 'tis necessary that he be copious in matter, solid in reason, methodical in the order of his work; and that the subject be well chosen, the season well fix'd, and, to be short, that his whole production be matur'd to see the light by a just course of time, and judicious deliberation. Otherwise, though with some of these conditions he may perhaps attain commendation; yet without them all he cannot deserve pardon. For indeed whosoever he be that comes in Print whereas he might have sate at home in quiet, does either make a Treat, or send a Chalenge to all Readers; in which cases, the first, it concerns him to have no scarcity of Provisions, and in the other to be completely Arm'd: for if any thing be amiss on either part, men are subject to scorn the weakness of the Attaque, or laugh at the meanness of the Entertainment.[1]

[1] *The Rehearsal Transpros'd and The Rehearsal Transpros'd: The Second Part*, ed. D.I.B. Smith (Oxford, 1971), pp. 159-160.

3

It would be hard to produce a more painful account of the moral and professional hazards of the writer's trade, or one more relevant to that trade as now practiced by academics, who depend for their survival on the good-will of others toward their published work, but must often depend for their opportunities on the errors and omissions of their predecessors. As Marvell observed a few paragraphs later on (though specifically about the writing of satire), "it is a praedatory course of life . . . wherein all that stock of Credit, which an honest Man perhaps hath all his age been toyling for, is in an hour or two's reading plunder'd from him by a Freebooter." Moreover, the latecomer to a particularly well-explored territory experiences in an exaggerated form this vulnerability to reproach. Not only does it seem impudence to resume discussions on which so much superior intelligence has already been expended but, if one does find a space to work in, it cannot be defined without some reflection, however tactful, on the limits of the scholarship to which one is most deeply indebted.

Nevertheless (and this is a favorite conjunction in Marvell's own rhetorical strategy) the *Second Part* of the *Rehearsal Transpros'd* was written out of urgent concern to silence Samuel Parker and to do intellectual justice to the arguments for religious toleration. I, too, have been driven to write these essays by a desire to see justice done, to Marvell himself. Among all the persuasive accounts we have been given of the way he must have thought and felt, there is nothing which corresponds to the preoccupations of that opening warning paragraph. We have grown familiar with the images of incorruptible patriot, garden-loving poet, metaphysical wit, Neoplatonic savant, the man of Puritan conscience, the reasonable loyalist politician, the literary critic disguised as a lyric poet; but Marvell the Writer, who considered the motives, sanctions, quality, and results of *everything* he wrote, is not, as yet, a figure we recognize.

Beyond this possibility that some aspect of Marvell's own preoccupations may have been overlooked, there is also the sad fact that the images we already have of him are divisive. Some of them can only be made convincing if others are left out of account. It has not seemed possible to make a completely whole man out of this poet with too many personae, as Rosalie Colie called him,[2] except by excluding what will not fit our immediate focus. Eliot solved his problem of definition handily, by simply declaring that "of all Marvell's verse, which is itself not a great quantity, the really valuable part consists of a very few poems,"[3] and by proceeding to base his enormously influential judgments on the *Nymph complaining, To his Coy Mistress*, and the *Horatian Ode*.

The title and chapter headings of Legouis' great biography helped to develop the notion that the patriot and Puritan in Marvell were somehow separable from the poet, and that even the poet could be subdivided. The "lyrical poet" who wrote, it is assumed, most of his best pieces on Fairfax's estate at Nunappleton, was distinct in motive and artistic achievement from "Cromwell's Poet," and different again was the "Satirist in Verse" who wrote after the Restoration and allowed his talent to be "injured by carelessness."[4] Legouis initiated what is still a primary critical assumption: that by entering Cromwell's service and committing himself to a life of political action, Marvell abandoned the intellectual delicacy which was his greatest strength, and that everything that he later wrote was more or less clumsy in consequence. The modern editions in which his poems are now usually read tend to support this categorization, if not its value judgments. In Margoliouth's, the effect of the 1681 *Miscellaneous Poems* is changed to the extent that "satirical, commendatory, and political poems have been collected to-

[2] Rosalie Colie, *"My Ecchoing Song": Andrew Marvell's Poetry of Criticism* (Princeton, 1970), p. 3, n. 2.

[3] "Andrew Marvell," first printed in the *Times Literary Supplement*, 31 March 1921, pp. 201-202.

[4] Pierre Legouis, *Andrew Marvell* (Oxford, 1968), p. 192. Wherever possible I refer to the English condensation of this study, originally published in French in 1928.

gether and arranged in chronological order," and an assumption is made that pastoral lyrics belong together at the front of the volume.[5] George de F. Lord, whose edition continues and extends this policy, justified it in an article which divided Marvell's literary career into three phases: lyric detachment, political commitment, and satirical disillusionment.[6]

Recent major studies of Marvell have not been able to avoid these apparently natural boundaries, though some have tried. Donald M. Friedman broadened the meaning of "pastoral" as an intellectual construct to the point where it could almost encompass the later Cromwell poems.[7] Ann E. Berthoff invoked the *Rehearsal Transpros'd* in her account of Marvell's philosophy of time and necessity, but excluded the satires, in which one might have thought necessity to be dominant. Harold Toliver's account of *Marvell's Ironic Vision* touched on the satires but excluded altogether the ironies of the prose.[8] John M. Wallace succeeded, to my mind brilliantly, in reuniting the Marvell of the *Horatian Ode* with the Member for Hull, the Restoration satirist and the author of *An Account of the Growth of Popery and Arbitrary Government*;[9] but a final chapter on *Upon Appleton House*, which he was clearly unable to resist, only accented the gap between "political" and "literary" analysis. The clearest indication of where we presently stand was given by Isabel Rivers in a masterly synopsis of Marvell's whole career, which somehow managed to weld into a con-

[5] *The Poems and Letters of Andrew Marvell*, rev. ed., ed. Pierre Legouis (Oxford, 1971), I, 225.

[6] George de F. Lord, "From Contemplation to Action: Marvell's Poetical Career," PQ 46 (1967), 207-224. Lord's edition, *Andrew Marvell: Complete Poetry* (New York, 1968), adopts a fully generic principle of organization.

[7] *Marvell's Pastoral Art* (London, 1970).

[8] *The Resolved Soul: A Study of Marvell's Major Poems* (Princeton, 1970).

[9] *Destiny his Choice: The Loyalism of Andrew Marvell* (Cambridge, 1968).

sistent whole all of the best conclusions of her predecessors. But even here the three-phase theory of Marvell's work predominated: a lyric period of "intellectual exploration and play" was followed by "a different kind of poetry, assuming a direct relationship between life and art," as Marvell attempted to create viable myths in support of Cromwell's Protectorate. In his third period Marvell learned to use literature as a weapon and, though his satires in verse and prose were not without their counterideals, it was "inevitable that as the political situation deteriorated Marvell lost his interest in literature as such."[10] This study was called, significantly, "The Limits of Poetry" and, though it avoided the most obvious evaluative prejudices against Marvell's later work, it carried loud and clear the implication that end-oriented literature is based on an impure aesthetic.

My own work began in a mixture of delight and frustration over another book on Marvell which, while presenting a potentially integrating approach to his work, conspicuously declined a whole view. Reading Rosalie Colie's "My Ecchoing Song": Andrew Marvell's Poetry of Criticism, I wondered at the great silence it preserved on the subject of Marvell's political writing. Could it really be likely that a man so fascinated by the processes of his own mind and art would lose sight completely of those preoccupations for approximately twenty-five years, become uncritical, careless of how he wrote in the certainty of why, and then suddenly rediscover an analytical language of fine precision for his late poem, On Mr. Milton's Paradise Lost (1674)? In trying to answer that question, I found myself astonished by the results, discovering in the works uninteresting to Professor Colie exactly the same qualities of generic self-consciousness and inventiveness, the same redeployments of old topoi in intelligent new configurations, which she had found in Marvell's "garden" lyrics. The later poems on Cromwell appeared to examine conventions of panegyric and epicedion

[10] The Poetry of Conservatism 1600-1745: A Study of Poets and Public Affairs from Jonson to Pope (Cambridge, 1973), pp. 101-125.

with as much penetration as *Upon Appleton House* examined pastoral *otium, libertinage*, and meditation on the creatures. The *Last Instructions to a Painter* was, if anything, a better indication of Marvell's pictorial theory than *The Gallery* or the *Picture of Little T.C. in a Prospect of Flowers*. The *Rehearsal Transpros'd* proved to be full of quite explicit literary criticism and, in its *Second Part*, remarkably self-exploratory, even confessional, about the satirist's moral dilemma. Its problems were carried over and partially solved, again explicitly, in the later prose pamphlets, *Mr. Smirke* and the *Remarks* in defense of John Howe. In the apparently documentary *Account of the Growth of Popery*, it became clear, when one looked closely, that Marvell had gone to some pains to discuss with his audience the particular problem of decorum he there faced, and to relate his choice of a "naked narrative" both to generic decisions he had made in the past and to the nature of the governmental crisis which was then his subject.

By giving, in other words, the Protectorate and Restoration works the benefit of the doubt, the persona of the professional writer began to acquire real credibility. When the focus of interest was not poetry but poetics, another Marvell appeared, demanding serious attention. His identification with the writer's problems was clearly intensified, not canceled, by his decision to leave a purely reflective life; the interaction between his political motives and the literary aesthetics he inherited produced the very opposite of carelessness in his work. It could even be argued that, from a theoretical point of view, Marvell's political writings do not merely deserve a fair comparison with the "valuable" lyrics; if one is interested in the social function of literature as a cause of generic development, Marvell's political writings are documents of the first importance. Each time he made a marked shift in style or genre, his new method was generated not only by but *out of* a change in his political environment, to which his own conviction required him to respond, but for which the available literary traditions were less than entirely adequate. The execution of a king, the retirement of the head of the army in mid-career, the rule of a single man with all but monarchical power, an unholy alliance of England with a Catholic power against the Protestant Dutch, the threat of religious persecution on a wide scale, and finally a documented conspiracy to undermine the constitution and to cut off freedom of speech in Parliament itself— these were events which, if not entirely unprecedented in human history, yet put an enormous strain on standard literary resources. Because Marvell believed profoundly in the classical ideal of rhetoric as a politically significant force, he was not only required to respond but required to respond *effectively*. Ritual gestures were worse than useless; old forms had to be adjusted to make them relevant to new circumstances; and the element of surprise involved, of strenuous appropriateness rather than bland topicality, was the medium by which his writing was to carry his own convictions into other minds.

It is this aspect of Marvell's work which makes possible some degree of reconciliation between the reputation he achieved in his own generation and the one he presently holds. In the late seventeenth and early eighteenth centuries he was known and respected *politically* as the author of one or more of the satirical *Advices to a Painter*, the *Rehearsal Transpros'd*, and the *Account of the Growth of Popery and Arbitrary Government*. From the point of view of literary theory, it is these works, which developed the most significant formal innovations, that had the most influence on other writers prior to Eliot's reinstatement of Marvell as a formalist poet. Marvell's *Advices to a Painter* (and to a lesser extent the "Statue" poems) spawned a whole generation of imitators, including Dryden, who was probably the only one of them to perceive the theoretical relationship between the pictorial "conceit" and problems of political iconography. The *Rehearsal Transpros'd* initiated, as was

9

INTRODUCTION

recognized at the time, a new style of polemical repartee, of "raillery à la mode";[11] the *Account of the Growth of Popery* might equally be said to have initiated a new style of "literary" reporting, anticipating by three hundred years Norman Mailer's interest in the journalistic novel,[12] and leaving its mark, both for objectivity and partisanship, on eighteenth-century historians and on the Whig theoreticians of the next generation.

In this ability to respond to changing circumstances, and to make something powerful out of necessity, Marvell most closely resembled Milton, whose vast originality he understood so well, and of whose literary theories, as modified by twenty years of hard political experience, he was apparently well informed. However, while a close reading of all of Milton's work tends to reinforce the conventional three-phase theory of his career, from private to public and then back in disillusionment to creative privacy, a close reading of all of Marvell's work has, for me, broken down those convenient dividing lines. When one reads in their probable sequence the poems, the pamphlets, the letters to the Hull Corporation, the personal letters to friends, as well as what records we have of his activities in the House of Commons, the two- or even three-phase version of Marvell's career disappears. What appears instead is a pattern of alternating commitment and retreat, of rash involvement followed by self-doubt or apology, of changes of mind and direction. Marvell's political personality seems closely to resemble his "lyric" personality, as that was made most explicit in *Upon Appleton House*. Irony and detachment *about himself* remained his characteristic mode, and the

[11] Anthony à Wood, in his life of Samuel Parker, comments on the vogue for the "buffooning, burlesquing and ridiculing way and stile; in which fashion of writing, Marvell himself had led the way" (*Athenae Oxonienses*, London, 1691, pp. 618-619). See also Hugh Macdonald, "Banter in English Controversial Prose After the Restoration," *Essays and Studies* 32 (1946), 21-39.

[12] Norman Mailer's theory of the novel as documentary is made explicit in *The Armies of the Night* (1957).

ideal of intellectual privacy remained a personal temptation, to become no less real when books themselves became his chosen weapons.

Not unconnected with this, perhaps, was a trick of style developed in his personal letters, of speaking of himself in the third person, which is only partly explained by the need for secrecy. In a letter to Sir Edward Harley describing the reception of *Mr. Smirke* (1676), he wrote:

> the book said to be Marvels makes what shift it can in the world but the Author walks negligently up & down as unconcerned. The Divines of our Church say it is not in the merry part so good as the Rehearsall Trans-pros'd, that it runns dreggs: the Essay they confesse is writ well enough to the purpose he intended it but that was a very ill purpose . . . Marvell, if it be he, has much staggerd me in the busnesse of the Nicene & all Coun-cills, but had better have taken a rich Presbyterians mony that before the book came out would have bought the whole Impression to burne it. Who would write?

> (II, 346)

This strange circumlocution was presumably intended to keep his authorship of *Mr. Smirke* and the more controver-sial *Historical Essay touching General Councils* unknown, if not unguessed. Letters could always be intercepted. But there is as much irony here as caution. Marvell's recognition that he has once again achieved notoriety is mixed with hu-morous recognition that his methods have been misunder-stood. That cryptic and personal "Who would write?" re-calls the *Rehearsal*'s opening premise, that "not to Write at all is much the safer course of life," and confirms that such disclaimers were more than merely rhetorical.

Even in his letters to Hull, from which partisanship was most scrupulously excluded, these characteristics of Marvell the Writer occasionally made themselves felt. In this re-markable series of letters to his constituents, maintained, with only one unexplained hiatus, over twenty years, Marvell went out of his way to give only the most objective accounts of all debates in Parliament, and to avoid both value judgments and any indication of his own participatory role. And yet he still felt himself occasionally to have been indiscreet. In November 1670 he requested that the corporation would not "admit many inspectors" into his letters, since outsiders might put an "ill construction on his openesse . . . & simplicity of . . . expression" (II, 113). In May 1675 he thought it necessary to counteract some unusually emotive language in his account of the Shirley–Fagg dispute, that "unhappy misunderstanding" between Lords and Commons: "I dare write no more lest the Post leave me behind. And I have therefore exprest my self so hastily that I must advise you rather to diminish then heigten your conceptions of this matter" (II, 156). Style, as Marvell was always aware, has political responsibilities; it was the business of a Member of Parliament to keep his constituents informed, not to raise fears or start rumors. Still more revealing of his professional dilemma is a letter of 1675, which rebukes Mayor Shires for having broken his confidence. A certain Mr. Cresset has been told the contents of a previous letter. Marvell claims not to be concerned about the nature of the information so indiscreetly let loose, or about the character of the recipient: "yet seeing it is possible that in writing to assured friends a man may give his pen some liberty and the times are something criticall *beside that I am naturally and now by my Age inclined to keep my thoughts private*, I desire that what I write down to you may not easily or unnecessarily returne to a third hand at London" (II, 166). In the "criticall" environment of 1675 Marvell's thoughts must have been considerably less "green" than they were in the poems celebrating retirement, but the relationship between language and personal integrity had become more relevant than ever.

There is one other aspect of Marvell's work to which I found myself, in following his texts so closely, forced to pay attention. He had a habit of borrowing other men's words, a habit which has, since it was first discovered, been variously interpreted. The pamphleteers who replied to the *Rehearsal Transpros'd* not surprisingly regarded Marvell's borrowings from John Owen as a sign of incompetence: "The worthy Author, that he might not seem a Plagiary, doth with much modesty call his Book, *The Rehearsal*, willing to intimate, that, whatever may be accounted any thing in it, was taken from others."[13] Modern criticism has certainly discovered imitations of Cleveland, Waller, Jonson, Donne, Thomas May, Mildmay Fane, St. Amant, Hermann Hugo, Henry Hawkins, Crashaw, Cowley, and a host of less convincing likenesses. For J. B. Leishman, the only critic to deal systematically with a large number of these echoes, Marvell did not so much borrow as share, using a common and fashionable fund of conceits and topoi;[14] and essays on individual "sources," though often demonstrating a much more purposeful kind of imitation, have provided no general explanation of Marvell's indebtedness. For Rosalie Colie, however, the echoes we hear in *The Garden* and *Upon Appleton House* were part of Marvell's conscious strategy, a way of invoking traditions and contexts both for examination and consummation. I have found this to be just as true of the political poems where his critical impulses were supported by conviction, and what looks like imitation frequently turns out to be ideological parody. Marvell's mind, it seems, worked at all times by reflection and response. He found it easier to correct or modify other men's statements than formulate his own, to discover the ideal concept or metaphor behind its temporary aberrations, to base his differences from others upon a profound consensus of literary and political assumptions. He adjusted; and the art of adjustment that kept him writing under three radically different

[13] Anon., *A Common-Place Book out of the Rehearsal Transpros'd* (London, 1673), p. 1.

[14] J. B. Leishman, *The Art of Marvell's Poetry* (London, 1966), *passim.*

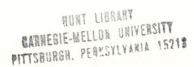

regimes allowed him to take what he found, in literature and politics, and literally make the best of it.

Despite the potential wholeness of this other Marvell, I have made no attempt to set him up as a replacement for the previous versions, and indeed have planned this book on the principle of trying only to fill the gaps. Where most has been said, there I have left well alone. Some of Marvell's best poems, therefore, are not discussed at all, and there are vast blocks of excellent criticism and scholarship to which I make no reference. I made myself a promise not to write a word on *The Garden*, a promise almost kept. As a consequence, this book will often seem to have dealt ponderously with writing which, in absolute terms, must be seen as very lightweight. In dealing with poetics and literary theory the criterion of selection cannot be evaluative; one must take seriously what the author himself seems to have taken seriously. If the resulting image of the writer now approaching his tercentenary is rather less elegant than some would like, it is, perhaps, not out of keeping with his view of himself and his profession.

# "*The times are something criticall*": Marvell's Reflective Politics

Few people argue nowadays about the shape of Marvell's political convictions, taken as a whole. Whether one calls it opportunism, loyalism, or conservatism, the tenacity of his belief in a mixed state and peaceful, constitutional government has been persuasively established,[1] and remains believable as a motivating principle behind all the strategic shifts and occasional compromises which political action required. Whether he was or was not consistently a monarchist (as distinct from a royalist), whether he ever desired that Cromwell should accept the crown, and for how long he really supported Charles II, are questions which continue to be controversial; because they also have considerable implications for Marvell's *literary* theories, I shall return to these questions in later chapters. Equally important for his poetics, and similarly to be postponed for detailed discussion, were Marvell's concomitant beliefs in freedom of conscience and freedom of speech, which not only motivated his hatred of Clarendon, of the Presbyterian majority in the Commons, and of Samuel Parker, all of whom threatened the survival of Puritan Nonconformity but also inspired his long campaign against, or defiance of, political censorship,

[1] By I. Caroline Robbins in her unpublished Ph.D. dissertation, "A Critical Study of the Political Activities of Andrew Marvell," University of London, 1926; John M. Wallace, *Destiny his Choice: The Loyalism of Andrew Marvell* (Cambridge, 1968); Isabel Rivers, *The Poetry of Conservatism 1600-1745* (Cambridge, 1973), pp. 101-125. Legouis' biography, which had proposed for Marvell a less consistent pattern of commitment, remains, of course, the essential source for the facts and dates of Marvell's career, and my debts to it are far greater than my occasional disagreements.

culminating in his most famous anonymous pamphlet, *An Account of the Growth of Popery and Arbitrary Government.*

What I am immediately concerned with here is Marvell's view of his own role in the political process. By offering a review of events and documents which are already largely well known, I hope to provide some psychological foregrounding, a shadowy outline of a personality which has always remained hidden because Marvell apparently wished it so. My argument is that, from a very early stage, Marvell perceived the role of a writer in his own period as a necessary compromise between the two venerable choices of commitment and retreat, political action and intellectual perspective, to which he pays homage in the opening lines of the *Horatian Ode.* The opening paradox of that poem has not always been noticed, but the "forward youth" who leaves his private study to write a political comment on the death of Charles I and the ascendancy of Cromwell can neither "forsake the Muses dear" nor leave the books behind. He needs his rhetorical training, he needs his Lucan (or rather, his copy of Thomas May's translation of Lucan) to give him perspective on such astonishing events. A classical education in itself provided a model for the political writer, whose role as mediator between the two worlds of thought and state had been defined by Cicero's precedent and authority.[2] Cicero's definition of the orator as public benefactor, legislator, and civilizer, on whom may depend the safety of the state and the civil liberties of its citizens (*De Oratore*, Loeb ed. I, viii, 31-32), was significantly balanced by his opening lament for the personal burdens of political activism, his own inability to live "vel in negotio

[2] The ideal of the orator as legislator by persuasion, and defender of civil liberties, was basic to the development of civic humanism in Quattrocento Florence. See Hans Baron, "Cicero and the Roman Civic Spirit in the Middle Ages and the Early Renaissance," *Bulletin of the John Rylands Library* 22 (1938), 72-97; and *The Crisis of the Early Italian Renaissance: Civic Humanism and Republican Liberty* (Princeton, 1966).

sine periculo, vel in otio cum dignitate" (I, i, 1-2), and his sense of having been born at the wrong time for a man of his intellectual yearnings:

> For in my early years I came just upon the days when the old order was overthrown; then by my consulship I was drawn into the midst of a universal struggle and crisis . . . But none the less, though events are thus harassing and my time so restricted, I will hearken to the call of our studies, and every moment of leisure allowed me by the perfidy of my enemies, the advocacy of my friends and my political duties, I will dedicate first and foremost to writing.
>
> (1, i, 3)

Much that Cicero said about himself in this moving preface to one of the great rhetorical textbooks is relevant also to Marvell's situation during the civil wars in England and the various crises of the Restoration Government; and everything that we do know or can deduce about Marvell's behavior from the late 1640s to the late 1670s is consistent with a belief in this most difficult compromise ideal.

About a year before the *Horatian Ode* was occasioned by Cromwell's return from the Irish campaign, Marvell had already written quite a subtle poem about the interdependence of literary and political values. *To his Noble Friend Mr. Richard Lovelace, upon his Poems* appeared in *Lucasta*, published in May or June 1649. The poem is not an expression of sympathy with the royalist cause,[3] but rather with one particular royalist whose literary career had run into trouble because of his own, perhaps rather rash, political involvement, especially in the Kentish Petition. Marvell attacks the official censorship which was in-

---

[3] Legouis' "presumptive evidence" that Marvell's political sympathies at this time "went to the Cavaliers" (*Andrew Marvell*, Oxford, 1968, pp. 12-14) depends mainly on George Clarke's ascription to Marvell of the violently royalist elegy for Francis Villiers (see Margoliouth, I, 432-433, on the value of this ascription).

stitutionalized under the 1643 Printing Ordinance, but which had recently, under the dominance of the Presbyterian House of Commons, developed into an irrational repressiveness. Lovelace's book had had difficulty with the censors. Even after license had been granted in February 1647/8, publication was delayed until the summer of 1649.[4] This delay was obviously connected to the "Sequestration" of Lovelace's estate to which the poem refers, and which was ordered by the Commons on 28 November 1648,[5] on the grounds that he was "delinquent," one who had taken up arms against the Parliament. But Marvell protests this wrongful, indeed absurd involvement of *Lucasta* in the argument, making irony of the notion that a book of poems, however Cavalier, could be seen as infringing on the "Houses Priviledge."

The real point of his poem, however, is that what these events stand for is a deep cultural loss, the disappearance, even from memory, of the age of classical rhetoric when the writer's trade was seen as a positive social and political force:

> That candid Age no other way could tell
> To be ingenious, but by speaking well.
> Who best could prayse, had then the greatest prayse,
> Twas more esteemd to give, then weare the Bayes:
> Modest ambition studi'd only then,
> To honour not her selfe, but worthy men.
> These vertues now are banisht out of Towne,
> Our Civill Wars have lost the Civicke crowne.

[4] Margoliouth assumed that the reference to "barbed Censurers" in l. 21 meant that the book was not *licensed* when the poem was written. But the delay between licensing and publication is surely a more significant motive for Marvell's poem.

[5] *JHC*, VI, 90. On 5 May 1649 Lovelace's name appears in the Journal in a list of delinquents whose cases were to be reconsidered with a view to mitigating their fines. *Lucasta* was registered for actual publication just over a week later.

He highest builds, who with most Art destroys,
And against others Fame his owne employs.[6]

What are missing from the present age are the virtues of candor and probity, which both guarantee the writer's objectivity and allow him to function constructively. "Modest ambition" allows a man to honor praiseworthy behavior in others, which in turn provides support for public ideals of conduct. What is also missing is the peculiarly Ciceronian complex of values implied by the term "ingenious"; natural talent, verbal wit, in the service of honest political suasion, Cicero's own *ingenium*, political genius. But in the political tensions of 1648/9 negative impulses predominate. Official policies of censorship and repression have sponsored a climate of unofficial destructiveness, the "Word-peckers, Paper-rats, Book-scorpions" who make up the literary underworld. Marvell himself, who has been suspected, he says, of belonging to "the rout" of Lovelace's critics, has risen to the defense both of his friend and of a better poetics, a plea for the art of "speaking well," itself a *double-entendre*; and his complimentary poem to someone from whom, perhaps, he differed in political affiliation, is itself a return to older literary values.

The problem of reconciling an ideal of literary objectivity with the writer's responsibility for upholding other ideals is not, of course, resolved in Marvell's poem to Lovelace; it is perhaps this dilemma, rather than political inconsistency, which emerges from the hints of his activity in 1649. If we suppose that Marvell, with his Puritan upbringing in Hull, would more naturally have sided with Cromwell and Fairfax than with the Cavaliers, the poem to Lovelace, which criticizes no group but the Presbyterians, raises no problems of contradiction. There are, in addition, other hints that Marvell was at this stage not clearly to be reck-

[6] The *Poems and Letters of Andrew Marvell*, rev. ed., Pierre Legouis (Oxford, 1971), I, 3.

oned among the royalists. Masson records a correspondence between Roger Williams and Mrs. Sadleir, Cyriack Skinner's aunt and benefactress of Marvell's family, in which the lady accused Marvell of assisting Milton in the preparation of *Eikonoklastes*, published in October 1649;[7] there is also a possibility, based on an ascription in Thompson's edition, that Marvell assisted Milton in the Latin version of the *Parliamenti Angliae Declaratio*, published by order of the House of Commons in 1649.[8] Whatever the validity of these rumors (and they are certainly not *less* to be trusted than George Clarke's ascription to Marvell of the Villiers elegy), they are not incompatible with the *Horatian Ode*. They raise instead the interesting proposition that Marvell was, in the year preceding the *Horatian Ode*, actively involved in the theoretical problems of the king's death, of which not the least important was the rhetorical nature of the king's image. The most significant literary event of 1649 was the publication of *Eikon Basilike*, which came hot off the press to coincide with the execution, and went through sixty editions in 1649.[9] No writer who had given any thought to the problems of political commentary could fail to realize the significance of the *Eikon*, which instantaneously created a legend and, by its symbolic frontispiece, showing Charles kneeling to accept a crown of thorns (Plate 1), conferred on a highly controversial and fallible human being the unambiguous status of a religious emblem.

Whatever his role in or knowledge of Milton's attempt to reverse this powerful icon, Marvell, I think, was moved to make his own comment upon it. *The Unfortunate Lover* is one poem which, on the basis of its echoes of *Lucasta*, has tentatively been assigned to this period.[10] It is also a

[7] D. Masson, *Life of John Milton* (London, 1881-1896), IV, 530.

[8] Robbins, "A Critical Study," p. 31.

[9] See Francis F. Madan, *A New Bibliography of the "Eikon Basilike" of King Charles the First* (London, 1950), pp. 2-4.

[10] J. B. Leishman, *The Art of Marvell's Poetry* (London, 1966), pp. 32-33.

1. Charles I, from the frontispiece to *Eikon Basilike*, 1649.

poem which, it has been suggested, derives some of its ex-
travagances from the emblem tradition.[11] Metaphors of violence derived from the pious hyperboles of Hermann Hugo
and Otto Van Veen are pushed in *The Unfortunate Lover*
to unprecedented extremes. But the poem's protagonist dif-
fers significantly from the suffering lover represented by
these emblematists. He is no winged Cupid surrounded by
the symbols of a self-inflicted passion. Rather, he is a man
born "by Cesarian Section," a phrase of at least historical,
and perhaps political, resonance into a world of "Storms and
Warrs." His nativity is celebrated by a "masque of quarrel-

[11] Ibid., pp. 33-34; Rosalie Colie, *"My Ecchoing Song": Andrew
Marvell's Poetry of Criticism* (Princeton, 1970), pp. 110-113.

ling Elements," a metaphor which reminds us both that masques are emblems in action, and that they were developed as a language to express the symbolic nature of rule. Far from remaining the spectator of his own masque, however, the Unfortunate Lover is drawn into its center, and becomes, by *double-entendre*, the very eye of the storm he has inherited, the "Orphan of the Hurricane." In another stage metaphor, he becomes the chief actor in a "spectacle of Blood" required by an "angry Heaven" which, from the emperor's seat, calls him to play "At sharp" with Fortune; and from this gladiatorial existence the only escape, we know, is death. But the main purpose of the poem, it appears, is to affirm the paradox that the Unfortunate Lover, passing through death to a peace he has never been allowed to experience, survives:

> [He] dying leaves a Perfume here,
> And Musick within every Ear:
> And he in Story only rules,
> In a Field Sable a Lover Gules.

If the poem was indeed written in the immediate aftermath of the king's execution, which was staged, largely by Charles himself, as a "great baroque tragedy"[12] designed to found a legend, Marvell could scarcely have failed to make some conscious connection between his emblematic victim-hero and the king who had performed so finely in his own "spectacle of Blood," the last of the Caroline masques. Charles on the scaffold had declared that he was going "from a corruptible to an incorruptible crown, *where no disturbance can be*" and, thanks to the author of *Eikon Basilike*, he too had died into art and returned to rule "in Story only," with perhaps greater effectiveness than he had ever ruled before.

It would be a mistake, however, to invoke the term "alle-

---

[12] J. P. Kenyon, *The Stuarts* (Glasgow, 1970), pp. 96-99. Kenyon's superbly readable history provides, incidentally, a useful counterbalance to this study, by putting, however judiciously, the Establishment rather than the Opposition viewpoint.

gory" for a connotative possibility of this kind. The analogy would be, rather, with *The Nymph complaining for the death of her Faun*, where most readers, alerted by the "wanton Troopers" who were responsible for the fawn's death, have sensed, but been unable to define, a political ambience. In that poem an experience of deep political sadness with sacrificial overtones has probably been completely transformed into an expression, not of erotic violence, but of erotic innocence and suffering. In neither poem is there any attempt to provide equivalencies of meaning in which one set of signifiers requires exegesis in terms of the other; but in each the quality and quantity of emotion involved seems somehow more appropriate if a political context is recognized.

Any feeling that there may be a political level of meaning in *The Unfortunate Lover* must, however, be strengthened by the discovery of unmistakable political connections in the last stanza. It has not been noticed before that the famous heraldic image on which the poem ends was in fact taken directly from a satire by John Cleveland on the Westminster Assembly. "The mixt Assembly" appeared in 1647 in *The Character of A London-Diurnall*, and is typical of Cleveland's attitude to the Puritan revolutionary movement, as a whole and in its various factions. The volume contains attacks on Presbyterians and Independents, on Cromwell and Fairfax, and in "The mixt Assembly" Cleveland directs his scorn at what he regarded as an unnatural alliance between different Puritan sects, as well as an unnatural confusion between secular and ecclesiastical authorities. He speaks of a "strange Grottesco" and includes in his catalog of grotesque comparisons a metaphor striking enough, it seems, to catch Marvell's attention:

> Strange Scarlet Doctors these, they'l passe *in Story*
> For sinners, half refin'd in Purgatory;
> Or parboyl'd Lobsters, where there joyntly *rules*
> The fading *Sables*, and the coming *Gules*.[13]

[13] John Cleveland, *The Character of A London-Diurnall* (London, 1647), p. 29.

It comes as something of a shock, on looking back to the "source," to see that Marvell's powerful heraldic color scheme originated in the "parboyl'd Lobsters" to which the Westminster divines were so rudely compared. But if Marvell reread, or at least remembered, Cleveland's poem in the context of the king's execution, its prophecy of the "coming Gules" would have carried its own appropriateness. Its transformation into Marvell's elegant icon is only stronger evidence of the power of art to confer dignity on troublesome experience, a theme which unites the Unfortunate Lover's heraldry to the Nymph's weeping statue.

But this does not complete the allusiveness of the last stanza. It has already been recognized that the prototype of the man whose death leaves behind him music and perfume was Josiah, the best king the Hebrews ever had.[14] Ecclesiasticus 49:1 provided this metaphor for the memory of a just and pious king, cut off in his prime. It would have been virtually impossible, however, at any time after Charles's execution, to allude to Josiah without summoning up the topical analogy, which was ubiquitous in elegies and commemorative sermons, both in 1649 and in the early years of the Restoration. One characteristic, anonymous poem, dated 11 March 1648/9, claimed that:

> our sad accents could out-tongue the Cryes
> Which did from mournful Hadadrimmon rise
> Since that remembrance of Josiah slain
> In our King's murther is reviv'd again.[15]

Another, *The Subjects Sorrow: or, Lamentations Upon the Death of Britaines Josiah, King Charles* (1649), reminds us that the imagery of fire and storm which define the Unfortunate Lover's predicament were also, thanks to the

14 By E. E. Duncan-Jones, in *Poems and Letters*, 1, 256, and in her fine "Reading of Marvell's *The Unfortunate Lover*" in *I. A. Richards, Essays in his Honour*, ed. Reuben Brower, Helen Vendler, and John Hollander (Oxford, 1973), pp. 211-226.

15 *An Elegy Upon the most Incomparable K. Charls the I* (London, 1649), p. 3.

*Eikon Basilike*, commonplaces for Charles's sufferings.[16] And one of the funeral sermons which developed the analogy between Charles and Josiah most tellingly was preached before the House of Commons on 30 January 1661/2, with Marvell probably in the audience. If he was there, it must have been with a peculiar sensation that he heard Nathaniel Hardy, the preacher appointed for the day of mourning, "take up the words of the son of Syrack concerning Josiah . . . the remembrance of Charles the First, is like the Composition of the perfume that is made by the Art of the Apothecary, it is sweet as honey in all mouths, and as musick to a banquet of wine; yet withall the remembrance of his death . . . cannot but be bitter as gall and wormwood."[17] If Marvell did indeed write *The Unfortunate Lover* in 1649, it was as a compromise, perhaps, between the image-makers and the image-breakers; but by 1662 the king's legend had won, and the iconoclasts had themselves been broken by history.

There are two ways of regarding the next eight years of Marvell's career, from 1650 to Cromwell's death in 1658. Sometime in 1650, after the Lord General Fairfax resigned his commission and retired to his country estate in Yorkshire, Marvell went to Nun Appleton to become language tutor to Mary Fairfax. In February 1652/3 Milton wrote to John Bradshaw recommending Marvell, as a competent linguist, for a political post, implying that his service to Fairfax was coming to an end, and the next thing we know of Marvell is that he was, in July 1653, acting as tutor to Cromwell's ward William Dutton, and staying with the

[16] *The Subjects Sorrow* (London, 1649), pp. 21, 23, comments on Charles's "matchlesse and kingly perseverance, even in the fornace of affliction, and hottest flames of adversity," and compares him to "a firme Rocke; which no stormes of popular rage, no swelling surges of the multitude, nor all the proud billowes of his insulting Adversaries, could alter or unsettle in his pious purpose."

[17] Nathaniel Hardy, *A Loud Call To Great Mourning: In a Sermon Preached On the 30th of January 1661 . . . Before The . . . Commons House of Parliament* (London, 1662), p. 35.

Puritan Oxenbridges at Eton. By September 1657 Marvell had acquired a junior position in the Latin secretariat, under John Thurloe and with Milton, in which position he made his first recorded contact with Dutch politics, writing to George Downing, English ambassador to the Hague (II, 307-308), and arranging for the reception, in 1658, of the Dutch ambassador William Nieuport. During this period he wrote three poems to or about Cromwell which we can date with some precision: the *Horatian Ode* on Cromwell's return from Ireland in May 1650; the *First Anniversary of the Government under O.C.*, which was advertised for sale in *Mercurius Politicus* in January 1655; and the *Elegy* for Cromwell's death, which occurred on 3 September 1658. He also wrote, presumably for Fairfax, three complimentary "estate" poems, *Epigramma in Duos montes, Upon the Hill and Grove at Bill-borow*, and *Upon Appleton House*, all (again presumably) before he left Fairfax's employment. On the basis of this evidence it has become customary to read Milton's letter to Bradshaw as a significant dividing line, indicating for the first time Marvell's wish for some kind of political post; three years of "detached" leisure and creative privacy are thus separated from five years of increasing commitment to Cromwell and decreasing literary significance. Not only the "pastoral" poems but the *Horatian Ode* are thus assigned to the Fairfax period, as a time when Marvell was gracefully free of partisanship.

The other way of considering Marvell's Protectorate poetry, and one I shall argue at length in the next chapter, is to see it as a whole, as a series of interdependent studies, if not exactly experiments, in the interpretation and evaluation of contemporary public figures. As an employee of both Cromwell and Fairfax, Marvell was in a position both of dependency and of peculiar privilege, as tutor to younger members of their families, a position which naturally carried the status of intellectual superiority. As a poet, he had a medium of communication with both men which carried its own sanctions, and allowed him, in the act of evaluation, to offer advice. Furthermore, pure political

chance had, as it were, offered him a subject of such classical dimensions that it is accepted even by those who would
force the Protectorate poems apart. Fairfax's resignation
from his generalship, and Cromwell's acceptance of leadership of the state, were not only interdependent politically
but were immediately recognizable as contrasting classical
archetypes of conduct. In evaluating these striking examples of political activism and contemplative retreat, Marvell
offers neither of them a ritualist's advocacy. His support of
Cromwell as the one strong man capable of settling the nation's divisions is heavily qualified by his dislike of Cromwell's use of violence; his respect for Fairfax, whose own
position was against the execution of Charles, carries with
it an equally serious reproach, that resignation at such a
time was indicative of selfish weakness. By a series of calculated echoes and contrasts between the two groups of
poems, Marvell created a formal but none the less urgent
dialectic about the events and issues involved and, in trying
to offer advice in a manner acceptable to his great subjects,
he developed some intelligent modifications of traditional
forms of praise.

These Protectorate poems, therefore, are vital evidence
of Marvell's political poetics. They also give us two of our
rare encounters with Marvell engaged in acts of self-defini-
tion, confirming that in his own eyes his own personality
was split. In *Upon Appleton House* we are shown the self-
indulgent tutor of Mary Fairfax, whose stance, if such a
word can be used of so recumbent a person, is that of the
"easie Philosopher," too lazy and too self-mocking to be
simply *libertin* or truly *savant*, but who can be recalled, at
least to attention, by the "discipline" embodied in his pupil.
In *The First Anniversary*, Marvell criticizes the kings of
Europe for their failure to support Cromwell's crusading
Protestantism, and makes for himself a strenuous commitment to write the epic of Cromwell's millennium:

> Unhappy Princes, ignorantly bred,
> By Malice some, by Errour more misled;

If gracious Heaven to my Life give length,
Leisure to Time, and to my Weakness Strength,
Then shall I once with graver Accents shake
Your Regal sloth, and your long Slumbers wake:
Like the shrill Huntsman that prevents the East,
Winding his Horn to Kings that chase the Beast.

(ll. 117-124)

This passage makes a significant contrast with Milton's expression, in *The Reason of Church Government*, of the
literary ambitions from which he was, in the 1640s, being
distracted by polemical engagement. Milton speaks of "in-
ward prompting," of the "labor and intent study" which he
takes to be his "portion in this life," and of the "strong
propensity of nature" to write, all of which allow him to
"covenant" with the reader for a great work to appear in
"some few years."[18] Marvell's disapproval of "Regal sloth,"
on the contrary, is accompanied by an admission of his own
"Weakness" which, however formally proposed, is partially
supported by the facts. Cromwell's epic was never written
in the three years before his death, and Marvell's monumental, as distinct from occasional, impulses were deflected
for over a decade.

To make an analogy with Milton who, for all his confidence, did not complete his great work until the Restoration
forced him out of public life, is to fall once again under
the shadow of the politics-literature dichotomy. But when
Marvell really began his own public career, as representative
for Hull in Richard Cromwell's Parliament, one cannot say
simply, as Milton said about himself, that he had become too
active in one sphere to attend to the demands of the other.
The record of his behavior for the next twenty years is itself a record of alternating commitment and retreat and,
when he moves forward, it appears he does so on both
fronts. Political involvement produced, in the mid-1660s,

[18] Milton, *Complete Prose Works*, ed. D. M. Wolfe *et al.* (New
Haven, 1953-   ).

the *Advices to the Painter*, in 1672 the *Rehearsal Trans-pros'd*, in 1676-1677 the *Account of the Growth of Popery and Arbitrary Government*. In between these very different (and differently motivated) achievements, there is evidence of absence, withdrawal, silence.

It seems clear that Marvell entered Richard's Parliament in a mood of optimism, and with a sense of being among the reasonable majority. Despite the resistance of the anti-Protectorate group, "it is to be hoped," he wrote in February 1658 to Downing at the Hague, "that our justice our affection and our number which is at least two thirds will weare them out at the long runne" (II, 308). He was active in committees in Richard's Parliament, and extremely so from June to December 1660 in the Convention Parliament, being appointed to thirteen,[19] and sometimes apparently taking leadership within them. On 27 November there is an unusually full and descriptive entry in the House of Commons journal (VIII, 193) showing Marvell reporting for a committee in which he might well have been particularly interested. It involved the religious climate of the universities, and their responsibility for endowing "impropriate" rectories; and, after reporting a series of amendments to the bill in question "which he read," says the journal, "with the Coherence, in his Place," Marvell transmitted "the desire of the said Committee, that this House would desire his Majesty, that he would be pleased to write his Letter to the Colleges in the Universities, that they would take into Consideration their respective Impropriations, and augment the Vicarages, or Curate Places, belonging thereto." The whole item carries a definite flavor, of competence combined with respectable enthusiasm; and a concern about impropriation was to remain with Marvell long after his initial hopes for the Restoration had disappeared.

[19] Marvell's appointments to parliamentary committees are, with one exception, conveniently listed and grouped under general headings, such as matters of religion, foreign policy, etc., in Robbins, "A Critical Study," Appendix IV.

Another most significant committee for him must have been that appointed to "settle the Militia," to work out some mechanism for controlling the army in the new conditions of peacetime. Marvell's own political views, as well as his temperamental preferences, are well expressed in a letter to his constituents in Hull written on 4 December 1660, reporting indirectly on the stormy reception which had greeted the Militia Bill when it first came forward from his own committee: "The Act for the Militia hath not been calld for of late," wrote Marvell, "men not being forward to confirme such perpetuall & exorbitant powrs by a law as it would be in danger if that Bill should be carryêd on. Tis better to trust his Majesty's moderation & that the Commissioners if they act extravagantly as in some Countyes should be liable to actions at law" (II, 7-8). What role he had played in the initial "forwarding" is not clear; but Marvell's position was now, and was to remain, opposed to a standing army, symbolic of violent intervention in the state, and therefore symbolically inconsistent with the new "moderation" expressed in Charles's Declaration of Breda. Though events had in the past and would again require Marvell to accept "forward" behavior in others and in himself, "moderation" and its concomitant term "modesty" were to remain his better values.

One such event has a special value for this study in that it signifies the reciprocity of Marvell's literary and political beliefs. In Marvell's connection with Milton there is more than friendship and certainly more than some points of analogy between their respective careers. Whenever he has something important to say, Marvell tends to quote from Milton, or allude to one of Milton's strategies, a process brought to fulfillment in his poem *On Mr. Milton's Paradise Lost*, which becomes the summative statement of his own values. In December 1660 Marvell spoke in the House of Commons in defense of Milton, an act which must have required considerable courage, since a few days earlier he had reported to Hull that the bodies of the chief regicides were to be publicly dishonored. Parliamentary history records that "the famous Mr. Milton having now laid long in Custody of the Serjeant at Arms, was released by Order of the House. Soon after Mr. Andrew Marvel complained that the Serjeant had exacted £150. Fees of Mr. Milton," a sum obviously in excess of what might have been expected. Others seconded the protest and, notwithstanding the assertion of Sir Heneage Finch "That Milton was Latin Secretary to Cromwell, and deserved hanging," the matter was referred to the Committee of Privileges and resolved somewhat more in Milton's favor.[20]

However, in the first years of the Restoration Parliament, the records (and the gaps in the records) present a very different picture. In those difficult months when the religious settlement was being negotiated, the bishops restored to the Lords, and the Nonconforming ministers ejected from their pulpits, Marvell made no speeches, although he was later to comment bitterly on those events in the *Third Advice to the Painter*. Instead, he was chiefly remarkable for his quarrel with Thomas Clifford in the House, which nearly resulted in his expulsion for breach of privilege. On 20 March 1661/2 the Speaker reported that "he had examined the Matter of Difference between Mr. Marvell and Mr. Clifford, and found, that Mr. Marvell had given the first Provocation, that begot the Difference: And that his Opinion was, that Mr. Marvell should declare his Sorrow for being the first occasion of this Difference; and then Mr. Clifford to declare, that he was sorry for the Consequence of it: And that Mr. Clifford was willing to yield to this Determination, but that Mr. Marvell refused."[21] The formality of the language does

---

[20] *Old Parliamentary History* (London, 1761), XXIII, 54; *JHC*, VIII, 209. Milton's nephew, Edward Phillips, also reported that Milton escaped punishment at the Restoration because of the intercession of Members of Parliament and the Privy Council: "Particularly in the House of Commons, Mr. Andrew Marvell . . . acted vigorously on his behalf." See Helen Darbishire, *The Early Lives of Milton* (London, 1932), p. 74.

[21] *JHC*, VIII, 391.

not conceal the heat of the incident, whose cause we do not know, nor the humiliating retreat which Marvell was forced to make when summoned with Clifford before the House which, upon receiving their apologies, withdrew the breach-of-privilege charge. Less than two months later, on 8 May 1662, Marvell informed the Hull Trinity House of his decision to go abroad and, although recalled from Holland by the fear of losing his seat, he soon found occasion for a further and longer absence to accompany the Earl of Carlisle on his embassy to Russia and Sweden.[22] He did not return to his seat in the House until February 1665, three years after his departure and one month before the Second Dutch War was officially declared.

This pattern was to be repeated. From late 1665 to early 1668 Marvell clearly found himself excited and outraged by the mismanagement of the war, the rule of the Cabal, especially of Clarendon, and the financial impasse between king and Parliament. He was appointed to several major committees of public inquiry, notably that directed to inquire into the "miscarriages" of the war,[23] and he made speeches on issues connected with those "miscarriages."[24] He also discovered a new connection between political and literary activity, which was more direct and certainly more dangerous than the role of poet-counselor to Cromwell and Fairfax.

[22] *Poems and Letters*, II, 37, 250. In the second of these letters Marvell spoke of "the interest of some persons too potent for me to refuse," which allows for another interpretation of his withdrawal.

[23] On 17 October 1667 (*JHC*, IX, 4), Marvell was also added on 25 October 1665 to the committee on the embezzlement of Prize goods from the war (*JHC*, VIII, 621), indicating early concern about corrupt administration, and, on 2 October 1666, to the committee appointed to investigate the Fire of London (*JHC*, VIII, 629, 654).

[24] On 31 October 1667, Marvell spoke in defense of Peter Pett, the naval officer who was being made the scapegoat for the disaster at Chatham, when the Dutch sailed up the Medway and burned the English fleet. See *The Diary of John Milward, Esq.*, ed. Caroline Robbins (Cambridge, 1938), p. 108. On 21 February 1667/8 he spoke against those responsible for paying seamen with tickets instead of money (ibid., p. 197).

In late 1666 and 1667, partly in response to Waller's ill-timed panegyric on the Battle of Lowestoft, there appeared a series of satirical poems that was far more than a commentary on the war. There is considerable evidence that these *Advices to the Painter*, as well as other attacks on, or appeals to, the Government, were the product of a vigorous Opposition underground press, which managed, in defiance of rigorous censorship, to print and circulate such pamphlets, sometimes in Westminster itself.[25] This form of publication was intended to influence policy, to apply pressure, not only on the king, to whom some of the *Advices* were formally addressed, but in Parliament; circulation, it appears, was timed to coincide with crucial parliamentary sessions. In this situation, an Opposition Member who also happened to be a writer of talent could, if he avoided discovery, perform an invaluable double function. Inside knowledge could, in effect, create an outspoken but anonymous lobby for positions which could only be held discreetly in the House. It is noticeable that when the temper of the Commons was for putting most of the blame for the war onto Clarendon, a position argued with violence in the *Second* and *Third Advices* and the *Last Instructions*, Marvell spoke three or four times in the House against impeachment,[26] perhaps to dissociate himself publicly from the satires. Later, when Clarendon had fled the country, Marvell sat on the committee ap-

[25] For example, on 12 February 1667/8, to coincide with the debate on "miscarriages," MPs received "several small printed papers in rhythm" (*Muddiman Newsletter*, 15 February), also identified as "printed books of verses, a down-right libel" (*HMRC*, VII, 486). On 20 October 1669 a prose pamphlet entitled *The Alarum* was distributed to MPs by name, as a surviving copy (SP Dom. 266, no. 152) addressed to Garroway and annotated by Williamson testifies. For fuller discussion of this situation, see Chapter 3.

[26] *Milward*, ed. Robbins, pp. 116, 328; Anchitell Grey, *Debates of the House of Commons from the year 1667 to the year 1694* (London, 1769), I, 14, 36. The contrast between these interventions, apparently on Clarendon's behalf, and Marvell's position in the satires has produced many puzzled comments.

pointed on 16 December 1667 to arrange for his banishment.[27]

However, in the spring of 1668 Marvell again committed acts of indiscretion, which marked the end of such strategic usefulness. On 15 February 1667/8, during the report of the committee on the miscarriages of the war, Marvell, as a member of that committee, spoke "somewhat transportedly" on the incompetence of Arlington, Secretary of State, accusing him of having bought an office for which he had no capacity, and thereby endangering the whole fleet for want of proper naval intelligence.[28] That Marvell had partially blown his cover, and that he tried to regain it, is suggested by a letter from Arlington himself to Sir William Temple two days later, referring to the incident as the most significant, from his point of view, in the whole debate: "The House of Commons are yet in their enquiry after miscarriages; I leave it to your other correspondents to tell you what Votes they have passed therein. But cannot forbear letting you know that Mr. Marvel hath struck hard at me, upon the Point of Intelligence . . . This Day he hath given me cause to forgive him, by being the first Man, that, in the midst of this enquiry, moved the taking into consideration of His Majesty's Speech."[29] A few weeks later, however, there are signs that Marvell was beginning to dissociate himself in a different way from his Opposition colleagues. On 13 and 30 March Marvell attacked the proposal, favored by the majority of the Commons, to renew the Conventicles Act preventing Nonconformists from holding religious meetings. On the second of these occasions, Marvell's was the only voice raised in opposition to the new bill.[30] Indignation against the Cabal for misgovernment had been diverted by indignation against the Commons for their intolerance; these speeches mark the beginning of Marvell's disillusionment

---

[27] *JHC*, IX, 41.     [28] Grey, *Debates*, I, 70-71.

[29] *The Earl of Arlington's Letters to Sir W. Temple*, ed. Thomas Bebington (London, 1701), I, 226.

[30] *Milward*, ed. Robbins, p. 238.

with the House of Commons and with his own role as participant.

In the remaining ten years of his career as Member for Hull, although he continued to do his share of committee work and to report regularly to his constituents, Marvell made only two speeches which have been recorded, although there *may* have been others which have vanished without trace. On 21 November 1670 he spoke briefly on behalf of James Hayes, under prosecution for attempting to subvert the Conventicles Act,[31] a single example of that "quintessence of arbitrary malice" which the Commons had unleashed upon the Nonconformists. However, in the same letter to William Popple in which the Conventicles Act is thus defined, Marvell made it clear that his disillusionment was caused by more than the toleration problem. The Commons have been intimidated by the king (whose new request for Supply was delivered, to Marvell's rhetoric-conscious ear, "*Stylo minaci & imperatorio*") and have abandoned their primary responsibility, which is to control government spending. The commissioners set up in the heat of December 1666 to inspect public accounts have been "continually discountenanced, and treated rather as Offenders than Judges." All of the advantages gained in the wartime crisis have been lost in cynicism and private interest, and the balance of power has shifted. "It is also my Opinion," Marvell wrote, "that the King was never since his coming in, nay, all Things considered, no King since the Conquest, so absolutely powerful at Home, as he is at present. Nor any Parliament, or Places, so certainly and constantly supplied with Men of the same Temper. In such a Conjuncture, dear Will, what Probability is there of my doing any Thing to the Purpose?" (II, 314-315.) It was not long before Marvell's reticence in the House became common knowledge. Samuel Parker, in

---

[31] Grey, *Debates*, I, 294. Compare Marvell's intense comment to Popple, 28 November 1670 (*Poems and Letters*, II, 318), that "The Lieutenancy, having got Orders to their Mind, pick out Hays and Jekill, the innocentest of the whole Party, to shew their Power on."

his *Reproof* (1673), imagined him as "fearful of speaking."[32] Another attack on the *Rehearsal Transpros'd* parodied Marvell's debating style: "Mr. Speaker—I, that spoke here but once before,/ Must now speak, though I ne'er speak more."[33] More interesting, perhaps, than these obviously hostile comments, is Marvell's apparent recognition of his own ambiguous position. Does not his silence make him complicit in the general weakness? Writing to Popple in April 1670, he comments on the spread of intimidation to the Lords, with the king in daily attendance at their debates: "The Parliament was never so embarassed, beyond Recovery. We are all venal Cowards, except some few" (II, 317).

How this retreat into backbench obscurity affected his writing is not so clear. The record, such as it is, consists of a number of satires of uncertain date and uncertain ascription, none of which, with the exception of the *Loyall Scot*, have any of the distinctive characteristics of the original *Advices to the Painter*.

Only in the *Loyall Scot* is there any evidence of constructive political intent, and there it seems partly dependent on Margoliouth's conjecture that the Cleveland framework and the appeal for English–Scottish unity were written to influence the debate in Parliament in 1669-1670, when political union of the two kingdoms was being considered. The text of the poem has been much disputed, particularly the validity of its long and vicious diatribe against the Anglican bishops; but the conclusion of the poem resembles the *Advices* in its return from satire to the expression of ideals ("One King, one faith, one Language and one Ile") and in its portrait of Charles as the "prudent Husbandman" who will be able to convert the strife of his "factious bees" into useful activity for the "Common Hive."

[32] Samuel Parker, *A Reproof to the Rehearsal Transprosed* (London, 1673), pp. 521-526. The idea was elaborated on in Parker's *History of His Own Time*, trans. Thomas Newlin (London, 1727), p. 335.

[33] Edmund Hickeringill, *Gregory, Father-Greybeard* (London, 1673), p. 14.

If, however, it was Marvell who wrote *The Kings Vowes* (1670), the first part of *Nostradamus's Prophecy* (1671), and the *Statue in Stocks-Market* (1672), he merely commented, in a variety of tones and formats, but in a comparatively superficial manner, on the major public scandals of the time: the king's mistresses, the attack on Sir John Coventry's nose and the subsequent royal cover-up, Colonel Thomas Blood's attempt to steal the crown from the Tower as a symbolic political protest, the defection of five leading "Country" MPs to the government side, and the closing of the Exchequer on 1 January 1671/2 against the king's creditors. The *Further Advice to a Painter* (1670) has a more detailed parliamentary focus, but its titular relationship to the original *Advices* only accentuates its total lack of a persuasive or lobbyist intent. Most of these events are also mentioned, with more interpretive comment, in Marvell's personal letters to Popple and to Thomas Rolt, the "friend in Persia" to whom Marvell wrote a long newsletter in the summer of 1671. This letter is more useful than any of the occasional satires for defining Marvell's view of his own role in the political process at this stage. He emphasizes to his friend the need for caution, "for in this World a good Cause signifys little, unless it be as well defended"; he repeats his fencing master's secret, "against which there was no Defence . . . to give the first Blow"; and he introduces what is in effect a prose satire of recent events in Parliament and the Court with the following significant disclaimer: "Now, after my usual Method, leaving to others what relates to Busyness, I address myself, *which is all I am good for*, to be your Gazettier" (II, 324). It is clear that in 1670 and 1671 Marvell's position is largely that of the observer, whose attitude is satirical detachment and whose medium is the private letter.

By the middle of 1672, however, Marvell had discovered another use for his talents. The combined occasion of Samuel Parker's attacks on the Nonconformists and Charles' Declaration of Indulgence offered him an opportunity to return both to the medium of print and to public statement, supported by his own strong convictions and without any of the disadvantages of party politics. By using a satirical exposé of Parker's style and temperament as the vehicle for a general appeal for religious toleration, Marvell was able to personalize his pamphlet, and only indirectly to encourage the king in what appeared to be a new lenience toward the Nonconformists on the church's left. The respectable genre of ecclesiastical dispute provided formal protection and, although there were some attempts at censorship, the second impression of the *Rehearsal Transpros'd* actually went out with the licenser's permission.[34] In a few weeks it made Marvell's reputation as a writer, and gave him recognition, if not practical success. The Declaration of Indulgence was voted by the Commons to be unconstitutional and was shortly withdrawn; but that Marvell's point had been well taken is indicated by the fact that no less than six hostile "answers" to his pamphlet immediately appeared.[35]

Even so, in the *Second Part* of the *Rehearsal*, Marvell claimed to have been only an unwilling participant in the dispute, which had really been taking place between Parker and John Owen. It took, he wrote, a very high level of provocation on Parker's part to "tempt [him] from that modest retiredness to which [he] had all his life hitherto been addicted" (p. 169). Although his intervention was more than justified by the dangerous implications of Parker's policies, the justice of his cause could not fully reconcile him to the methods he had been forced to use:

> Yet withall that it hath been thus far the odiousest task
> that ever I undertook, and has lookt to me all the while

[34] See D.I.B. Smith's account of the pamphlet's printing history, *Rehearsal Transpros'd*, xx-xxv.

[35] Henry Stubbe, *Rosemary and Bayes* (1672); *A Common-Place Book Out of the Rehearsal Transpros'd* (1673); Richard Leigh, *The Transproser Rehears'd* (1673); *S'too him Bayes* (1673); Edmund Hickeringill, *Gregory Father-Greybeard, with his Vizard off* (1673); and Parker's *Reproof to the Rehearsal Transprosed* (1673).

like the cruelty of a living Dissection, which, however, it may tend to publick instruction, and though I have pick'd out the most noxious Creature to be anatomiz'd, yet doth scarce excuse or recompense the offensiveness of the scent and fouling of my fingers.

(p. 185)

Theoretically, the *Second Part* of the *Rehearsal* (1673) was in part an act of reparation for the first, and full of evidence that Marvell had been thinking deeply about the problems of polemical engagement, even in defense of freedom of conscience. Having been "drawn in" to a level of argument which involved church history and doctrine,[36] he had become aware of the theoretical dilemma underlying all religious dispute: how may the methods of logomachia consist with Christian pacificism? In his later ecclesiastical pamphlets, *Mr. Smirke* and the *Remarks* in defense of John Howe's views of predestination, Marvell articulated his own solution to this dilemma, and retreated from satire and personal attack into a more dignified objectivity.

Meanwhile, the Declaration of Indulgence on 15 March 1671/2, and the declaration two days later of the Third Dutch War, had initiated a new phase of activity in Parliament in which Marvell seems to have played some part. Forced by financial necessity to recall a Parliament which had not been allowed to meet for nearly two years, Charles found himself compelled also to withdraw the Declaration of Indulgence and to accept instead a Test Bill designed to prevent Roman Catholics from holding office. As a result of the Test, Thomas Clifford resigned from his post of Treasurer and, in revenge against his all-too-flexible master, revealed to Shaftesbury (only recently made Lord Chancellor) the secret clauses in the Treaty of Dover whereby Charles had promised Louis XIV, his ally against the Dutch, his own public conversion to the Roman Catholic Church.

---

[36] Marvell's letter to Sir Edward Harley (*Poems and Letters*, II, 328-329) describes his motives for writing the *Second Part*.

Shaftesbury immediately went over to the Opposition in the Lords, where he was shortly joined by the Duke of Buckingham. In the Commons, the Opposition had already been strengthened by the defection of Sir William Coventry to the "Country" party. On the Government side, the rule of the Cabal was replaced virtually by that of a single man, Thomas Osborne, the new Treasurer, shortly to be created Earl of Danby. By the summer of 1675 Marvell was remarking caustically to Popple on the formation of a new "Episcopal Cavalier Party" (II, 341), an informal allegiance between Danby, Lauderdale (who was responsible for Scotland), and the Anglican bishops. In this invigorating context, where the lines between friends and enemies could be more clearly redrawn, Marvell was apparently able to reunite his convictions and coordinate his activities on several fronts. Abandoning the Declaration of Indulgence as an empty symbol, produced moreover in highly suspicious circumstances, he continued his literary campaign for toleration on increasingly theoretical grounds. By identifying Danby and Lauderdale as the new persecutors, he was also able to realign himself with the majority in the Commons whose strategy was, by withholding Supply, to acquire some measure of control over the king's prerogative in foreign policy. An anonymous ballad, the *Charge to the Grand Inquest of England 1674*, describes the activities of the Commons in the famous sessions from February 1673 to 1674, and focuses on the Committee of Privileges, of which Marvell was a member in 1673,[37] and which had been taking a legal interest in the whole matter of privilege and prerogative:

> But above all beat boldly everywhere
> For your just rights and privileges here;
> Find them out all, and more than ever were.
> Search the repositories of the Tower

[37] *JHC*, IX, 250. Altogether Marvell served on eighteen committees connected with parliamentary privilege or integrity. See Robbins, "A Critical Study," p. 377.

And your own brains to stretch your lawless power.
Ransack your Writers, Milton, Needham, Prynne.[38]

In the list of offenders, "Marvell, who yet wears his ears" becomes in effect a second William Prynne. On top of all this it appears that Marvell had been involved, to at least some extent, in undercover work for the pro-Dutch movement in England during the war. In May 1674 he was reported (by a Government spy) to have been sent on a secret mission to the Prince of Orange at the Hague.[39] Considering that he had spent a year from 1662 to 1663 staying at the Hague with George Downing, a contact from his work in Cromwell's Secretariat, and that he had so far identified with the Dutch in 1667 as to publish two of the *Advices* under a false "Breda" imprint, and to make De Ruyter one of the heroes of the *Last Instructions*, such a development is not surprising; it need not even be upsetting if one remembers how Marvell must have seen the war, as an unjustifiable attack of one Protestant country upon its nearest Protestant neighbor, and one which would primarily benefit an imperialist and Roman Catholic France. Even after Charles had officially withdrawn from the war in 1674, he maintained English troops in the French service, and completed a series of agreements with Louis XIV by which, in return for a subsidy paid by France, he agreed not to allow his Parliament to interfere.

When the thirteenth session of the same old Parliament was recalled on 13 April 1675 after a year's prorogation, it became clear that Danby's campaign to undermine parlia-

[38] Printed in George de F. Lord, *Poems on Affairs of State, 1660-1678* (New Haven, 1963), I, 220-227, with a valuable commentary.

[39] For Marvell's "inviolable Friendship" with Abraham van den Bempde, a Dutchman arrested on suspicion of espionage in 1673, see L. N. Wall, "Marvell and the Third Dutch War," *N&Q* 4 n.s. (1957), 296-297; Sir Gyles Isham, "Abram van den Bemde," *N&Q* 4 n.s. (1957), 461-463. K.H.D. Haley, in *William of Orange and the English Opposition 1672-4* (Oxford, 1953), pp. 57-59, cites documents that name Marvell among a group of pro-Dutch activists operating under Peter du Moulin.

mentary effectiveness was having results. This was the year of the notorious Non-Resisting Bill, a new test designed to eradicate all opposition to government or church policy for the foreseeable future. Promoted by the "Episcopal Cavalier Party," it was debated by the Lords in the spring, but interrupted in its progress to the Commons by the equally notorious Shirley-Fagg dispute, a quarrel between Lords and Commons over their respective legal jurisdictions. Bribery and conflict of interest were, if anything, on the increase. On 22 April 1675 Marvell was teller for the Yeas in a bill to prevent MPs taking paid positions with the Government, and he reported to Popple that an attempt to impeach Danby was "blown off at last by a great bribing" (II, 342). In October Shaftesbury and Buckingham called for a dissolution of Parliament and a new election, but instead of a dissolution they were given the Long Prorogation, which lasted for fifteen months, during which time Louis was able to campaign without interference against the Dutch.

The split between Lords and Commons, however disruptive of the nation's business, did not prevent communication between the Opposition members at both levels. Sometime in 1675 the satirical *Duke of Buckingham's Litany* accused Marvell of membership in a seditious group, the Green Ribbon Club, which was supposed to have formed around Buckingham, and which met, ironically, in the King's Head Tavern. Its members reportedly included Shaftesbury, Wharton (Marvell's friend and correspondent), Blood (one of Marvell's minor heroes), and Joseph Ayloffe (later the author of *Marvell's Ghost*). As the *Litany* put it:

> From changing old Friends for rascally new ones,
> From taking Wildman and Marvell for true ones,
> From wearing Green Ribbons gainst him gave us blue ones,
>
> Libera nos domine.[40]

[40] Robbins, "A Critical Study," pp. 249-258.

In December 1675 there had appeared also a satire from the other side, the *Dialogue between the Two Horses*, written or adapted in response to the royal edict for the suppression of coffee-houses, as potential meeting places for seditious groups. The crudely anti-Stuart, republican statements of the *Dialogue* have aroused suspicion that it was not written by Marvell, although it clearly belongs with the other two statue poems convincingly ascribed to him.[41] If collaborative authorship is invoked as an explanation, we have a further possibility that Marvell was once again working, as in 1667, with a "Company" of Opposition pamphleteers and poets.[42]

When the Houses met at last, in February 1677, after the Long Prorogation, the situation had changed still further for the worse. Arguing in the Lords that a prorogation for more than a year was illegal and had in effect dissolved the Parliament, the four peers, Shaftesbury, Buckingham, Salisbury, and Wharton, overstepped the bounds of discretion, and were committed by Danby to the Tower, thereby becoming for Marvell the first real political heroes of the Restoration. The Lords classified as seditious a range of pamphlets questioning the validity of the Long Prorogation and, while the Commons debated how to make the king withdraw all military assistance from France, John Harrington (not to be confused with James, founder of the Rota), was "newly committed close Prisoner," Marvell wrote to Hull, "while he negotiated the proof of things of that

---

[41] *The Statue in Stocks-Market* and *The Statue at Charing Cross*, both of which appear in the Popple manuscript of Marvell's poetry, Bodleian Ms. Eng. poet. d. 49. See discussions of authenticity in *Poems and Letters*, ii, 394, 408, 414; and also Marvell's letter to Popple (ibid., ii, 341), which describes the political motives behind the "Pageantry" of erecting these statues.

[42] The Gough manuscript, which is a printed copy of the satirical *Advices-to-a-Painter* (Bodleian Gough Ms. London 14), contains many important manuscript corrections matching the text of the Popple versions. On the title page is written: "London written for the Company of Poets. Anno. Dom. 1666."

nature lately done in Scotland" (II, 189). Ten days later, on 27 March 1677, Marvell made his first speech in the House for seven years. Two days after that he was involved in a scuffle in the House which, in curious reenactment of his earlier quarrel with Clifford, almost resulted in his expulsion. On both occasions he commented apologetically on his inarticulateness, observing that he had become, literally, unaccustomed to public speaking, and thereby confirming the rumors of his previous silence.

Both the speech and the fracas are worth consideration, not least because they seem to offer contradictory testimony of Marvell's state of mind. The speech was directed against a bill for "Securing the Protestant Religion" against the event of a Catholic succession, and Marvell's motives for opposing it are by no means clear. Perhaps he took the line that anything proposed by Danby must have a sinister motive. Perhaps he wished to establish a cover, a public position which defended the king, the Duke of York, and the royal prerogative in ecclesiastical affairs, so that he might with greater security launch an anonymous attack on a government which was beginning to look more and more like tyranny. Perhaps he was merely driven by frustration and sense of his own unhazarded immunity to join the braver spokesmen, to say *something* at a time when others were in prison for their conviction. One of the most striking characteristics of Marvell's speech, as reported, is its unmeditated quality; the other is its peculiar coloration by the language of passivity, a Solomonic emphasis on the vanity of human effort: "if we are to intermeddle in things of this consequence, we are not to look into it so early . . . There is none yet in sight, but whose minds are in the hands of God, 'who turns them like the rivers of water' . . . Whatever Prince God gives us, we must trust him . . . 'Sufficient to the day is the evil thereof.'" What was required of Parliament at this point, Marvell asserted, was not better legislation against popery but personal reform. MPs should "preserve the people in the Protestant Religion" by their own example: "If we do not practise upon ourselves, all these Oaths and Tests are of no use; they are but Phantoms."[43] The bill later died a quiet death in the committee of which Marvell was himself a member;[44] but its text was incorporated *in full* into his *Account*, where it assumes an importance quite disproportionate to other more relevant documents. This in itself might lead us to suspect that Marvell's speech on the bill was, for him, a moment of decision, the beginning of a new mission to regenerate Parliament and to redefine his own position within it.

Marvell's near expulsion, two days later, was promoted by Sir Edward Seymour, Speaker of the House, who had been offended by what he regarded as an indecorous metaphor in Marvell's speech. When Marvell stumbled over Sir Philip Harcourt's foot, and "seemed to give Sir Philip a box on the ear," Seymour thought it "his duty to inform the House of it." Although Marvell apologized for what he called a friendly tussle, he could not resist the observation that Seymour had been in breach of privilege by attacking his speech in his absence. His bold request that "as the Speaker keeps us in order, he will keep himself in order for the future" so far canceled the effect of his apology that he was forced to repeat it with a more expedient humility. The whole affair was an odd rumpus for a man in his fifties; even stranger was Marvell's later response to the criticism leveled at him that day. The weary protest of Sir Thomas Meres, that "by our long sitting together, we lose, by our familiarity and acquaintances, the decencies of the House,"[45] was retained in Marvell's memory and reappeared, in the *Account of the Growth of Popery and Arbitrary Government*, as part of his attack on his fellow parliamentarians:

> *By this long haunting so together* [the Members] *are grown too so familiar among themselves, that all reverence of their own Assembly is lost, that they live to-*

[43] Grey, *Debates*, IV, 321-325.     [44] *JHC*, IX, 407.
[45] Grey, *Debates*, IV, 331.

gether not like Parliament men, but like so many good fellows met together in a publick house to make merry. And which is yet worse, by being so thoroughly acquainted, they understand their number and party, so that the use of so publick a counsel is frustrated, there is no place for deliberation, no persuading by reason, but they can see one another's votes through both throats and cravats before they hear them.[46]

This was a Parliament which had outlived its ability for real debate, and whose members had consequently lost "all reverence of their own Assembly." If every man knew in advance which way he was supposed to vote, and how many votes could be expected on either side of an issue, the concept of "so publick a counsel" was nullified, and the Members might just as well have cast their votes at home. Those who believed deeply, like himself, in the value of a relevant deliberative tradition, might well (on occasion) behave with impropriety, but this remarkable echo of Marvell's own experience can hardly, in the circumstances, act as self-justification. If anyone but himself was expected to recognize it, the quotation from Sir Thomas Meres's rebuke must stand, rather, in lieu of personal confession, an admission of complicity in a decadent institution.

By Christmas of the following year the *Account of the Growth of Popery and Arbitrary Government* had been published, anonymously and with a false Amsterdam imprint. It was, for the last time, an attempt to influence Parliament directly; its publication was probably timed to anticipate by a few days the recall of Parliament in January 1678 and the opening debates on the three illegal adjournments imposed on the House by the Speaker Seymour at the end of 1677. Its theme was the destruction of parliamentary government in England, both by exterior coercion and interior corruption; its plea was for a regenerate (if not a

[46] *Complete Works*, ed. A. B. Grosart (New York, 1875, reprinted 1966), IV, 331.

new) Parliament, which would be strong enough to control the king, not only financially but in foreign policy also. The issue which had aroused the Commons during 1677 was Charles's increasingly suspicious dealings with Louis XIV of Roman Catholic France, an involvement which made the "growth of popery" inseparable from that of "arbitrary government" in England, and remained no less real when Charles engaged in double-dealing with Holland and France simultaneously. It was the Commons' demand for a league with Holland which had directly caused their illegal adjournment at the end of 1677, and when in December 1677 a formal treaty was concluded between England and Holland, following the king's arrangement of a marriage between William of Orange and his own niece, their suspicions were by no means allayed. The publication of the *Account* was an expression of those suspicions; it argued implicitly that a king who tried to prevent his Parliament from meeting, who refused to take them into his confidence, was not to be trusted. In the new session of 1678 a further attempt was made to pin Charles down by making the Supply contingent on declaration of war against France. On 30 April Marvell himself was appointed to a committee charged with getting from Williamson the *texts* of all foreign alliances.[47]

Once again he was to be disappointed. On 13 May Charles prorogued Parliament for ten days, a delaying tactic which had, as Marvell reminded his constituents, the same effect as a longer interruption: "always upon Prorogation whatsoever businesse was imperfect and depending is quite cut off and if the Parliament intend to proceede againe upon it, they must resume all from the very beginning." In a moment of candor unusual in his letters to Hull, he added: "I doubt not but many will reflect upon this Prorogation for other reasons. *But they that discourse the lest and thinke the best of it will be the wisest men and the best Subjects.* God in mercy direct his Majesty always to that which may most

[47] *JHC*, IX, 472.

conduce to his own and the Kingdomes happinesse" (II, 234). It does not necessarily follow that this was Marvell's personal response but, in the now obvious failure of the *Account* (his most ambitious act of political "reflection" so far), the Solomonic wisdom of silence may have seemed even wiser than usual.

Such, at any rate, is the inference to be drawn from Marvell's last surviving letter to William Popple, written in June 1678, two months before he died. The letter records, in the same oblique third-person manner employed for *Mr. Smirke*, the public reception of the *Account*. "There came out," Marvell wrote, "about Christmass last, here a large Book concerning *The Growth of Popery and Arbitrary Government*. There have been great Rewards offered in private, and considerable in the Gazette, to any who could inform of the Author or Printer, but not yet discovered. Three or four printed Books since have described, as near as it was proper to go, the Man being a Member of Parliament, Mr. Marvell to have been the Author; but if he had, surely he should not have escaped being questioned in Parliament, or some other Place" (II, 357). This dry invocation of the parliamentary privilege he had himself violated is, we may now fairly say, characteristic. Certain statements "being only proper within the walls of the Parliament house" (II, 165) are now, in breach of the rules of confidentiality, in the public domain; their publicist remains hidden behind the protective surface of his own rhetorical intelligence. This was a man in whom discretion and indiscretion, detachment and involvement, were so inscrutably mixed that even for his own much-loved nephew he became, finally, a politic irony, a figure of speech.

The most fitting conclusion to this inquiry, this doomed attempt to provide a coherent psyche for a man who insisted on traveling incognito, is the conclusion that Marvell himself wrote to an earlier letter to Popple. On 21 March 1670, after a long catalogue of governmental failures and abuses, and a clear statement of his own ineffectiveness ("In such a

Conjuncture, dear Will, what Probability is there of my doing any Thing to the Purpose?), Marvell turned to Virgil for what is, in effect, his own epitaph:

> Disce, puer, Virtutem ex me verumque Laborem,
> Fortunam ex aliis.

(II, 316)

In the twelfth book of the *Aeneid* (ll. 435-436), in the middle of the final battle, Aeneas bestows on Ascanius as his patrimony both the example of his own courage and the integrity of effort, and the devout hope that he will have a different kind of life, a better fortune. Marvell, who like Cicero has been unable to locate himself "vel in negotio sine periculo, vel in otio cum dignitate," hands on to his nephew (and indeed to anyone else who cares for it) the permanent value of his own heroic classicism.

# "*So with more Modesty we may be True*": Experiments in Praise

## EPIDEICTIC THEORY

By the accidents of literary history, Marvell's poems to Cromwell and Fairfax have been forced into separate camps. The discovery of the *Horatian Ode* by the school of Eliot led away from, not toward, the poems committed to Cromwell's regime, which for several decades were neglected as failed poetry.[1] That the *First Anniversary* (though not the *Elegy*) has recently recovered from such neglect may be attributed largely to different instincts; it has been the exponents of Marvell's political thought who have considered it worth the effort of close analysis.[2] On the other hand,

---

[1] Pierre Legouis (*André Marvell*, Paris, 1928, reprinted New York, 1965), p. 193, described the *First Anniversary* as an unsuccessful annal; "L'ordre mi-logique, mi-chronologique amène des répétitions"; and contrasted "la beauté formelle de l'*Ode*" with "le poème funéraire, plus long, plus inégal, boursouflé par ici, ensoufflé par là," which "décourage le lecteur ordinaire prêt à en goûter le pathétique" (p. 215). Unordinary readers who were not discouraged included James F. Carens, "Andrew Marvell's Cromwell Poems," *Bucknell Review* 7 (1957), 41-70, who found the *Anniversary* an "intricately patterned" metaphysical poem, and Donald M. Friedman, *Marvell's Pastoral Art* (London, 1970), pp. 275ff., who was able to find in both later Cromwell poems Marvell's "typical lyrical concerns" with time and transcendence. An overview of Marvell criticism since the 1920s, however, shows these critics to be in a tiny minority.

[2] Beginning with J. A. Mazzeo's article, "Cromwell as Davidic King" in *Reason and the Imagination* (New York, 1962), there has been a dispute over the exact nature of the political role Marvell defined for Cromwell. In "Andrew Marvell and Cromwell's Kingship," *ELH* 30 (1963), 209-235, and again in *Destiny his Choice: The Loyalism of Andrew Marvell* (Cambridge, 1968), pp. 106-140, John M. Wallace

*Upon Appleton House* has proved to be full of literary temptations, "Natural Magic" for the subtlest of Marvell's readers,[3] at the level of wit, genre, metaphor, and metapoesis. What seems to have been forgotten in this process is what all the Cromwell and Fairfax poems have in common. Before they are anything else, they are exercises in praise, remarkably original contributions to the epideictic mode; and their likenesses, as well as their dissimilarities, are governed by its assumptions.

The very form of Marvell's *Miscellaneous Poems* might have kept this in view because, in its originally mixed state as printed in 1681, the collection begs to be compared with Ben Jonson's *Forrest* and *Underwoods*, imitations, as Jonson pointed out, of the classical anthology or *sylva*:

> With the same leave, the Ancients call'd that
> kind of body *Sylva*, or Ὕλη, in which there
> were works of divers nature, and matter congested;
> as the multitude call Timber-trees, promiscuously
> growing, a Wood, or Forrest: so am I bold to
> entitle these lesser poems, of later growth,

---

argued that Marvell wrote to persuade Cromwell to accept the crown; but his arguments were countered by Stephen Zwicker, "Models of Governance in Marvell's 'The First Anniversary'," *Criticism* 16 (1974), 1-12, who pointed out the importance in the poem of Gideon and hence of the political model of the uncrowned Hebrew judges. Simultaneously, A.J.N. Wilson, in "Andrew Marvell's 'The First Anniversary . . .': The poem and its frame of reference," *MLR* 69 (1974), 254-273, rejected all biblical analogies for Cromwell's Protectorate, and supplied instead the "color Romanus," which implied Republicanism. Writing primarily as a classicist, but referring all details to the political background, he provided an important bridge between the two approaches. See also the views of Warren Chernaik, "Politics and Literature in Marvell," *RMS* 16 (1972), 25-36; and my own "Against Polarization: Literature and Politics in Marvell's Cromwell Poems," *ELR* 5 (1975), 251-272, an earlier version of some parts of this chapter.

[3] As Kitty Scoular Datta's title aptly records.

by this of Under-wood, out of the Analogie they hold
to the Forrest, in my former booke, and no otherwise.[4]

Although the 1681 arrangement may not have been Marvell's own, a reminder of the *sylva* concept is an appropriate
entry into his poems of praise and compliment, for both in
rhetorical precept and by the example of Statius, the *sylva*
was established as a grouping of occasional poems whose
mode was epideictic. In Statius' *Sylvae*, each book opens
with an epistle to a friend or patron, and the first of these
repeats Quintilian's definition (x, 3, 17) of *sylva* poems as
improvisations struck out in the heat of the occasion. Statian
*sylvae* include political panegyric (*The Seventeenth Con-
sulship of the Emperor Augustus Germanicus*, iv, i); the
celebration of large personal occasions in *genethliaca, epi-
thalamia*, and *epicedia*; of the smaller social occasions, in
*proempticon* (a send-off poem), or *soteria* (congratulations
for escape or recovery); and a variety of praises of buildings,
country estates, statues, pets, or even natural objects like
*The Tree of Atedius Melior* (ii, 3) whose praise implies the
praise of persons. The sense of contrasting scale and seriousness essential to the total effect is marked particularly by the
different kinds of *epicedia*; the long and deeply felt lament
for the poet's father in the fifth book gains stature by contrast with preceding consolations for the deaths of a favorite slave and a pet parrot. The implications of this
precedent were schematized in the *Poetices* of Julius Caesar
Scaliger where, under the heading of *sylva*, these and other
types of praise are listed and described, along with their
appropriate topics.[5]

I am not implying that Marvell thought of himself as
collecting poems for a *sylva*, nor that he was concerned

---

[4] Ben Jonson, *Underwoods*, "To the Reader," in *Works*, eds. C. H.
Herford and P. and E. Simpson (Oxford, 1965), viii, 126.

[5] Julius Caesar Scaliger, *Poetices Libri Septem* (Lyons, 1561), pp.
150-169.

with the philosophical implications of *hule*.[6] But to remember this classical option is to perceive that epideictic crosses genres and other dividing lines, replacing them with a scheme of formal contrasts. The writer is constantly testing his resources, most of which are traditional, against the tendency of events to innovate; and the reader, though permitted to select, is encouraged to admire variety. In such a scheme, the poems on Cromwell's return from Ireland and Dr. Ingelo's departure for Sweden share a common understanding: that journeys have a definitive function in the shape of a man's career. To banish the latter, for its Latinity, to the back of the volume, deprives us of the contrast between rulers and their emissaries, and the different strategies of direct and reflected praise. The elegiac conventions of the *Poem upon the Death of O.C.* should be investigated with the same sensibilities as those employed on *The Nymph complaining for the death of her Faun*, which incorporates as one of its traditions the Statian *epicedion* for the death of pets. The *First Anniversary of the Government under O.C.* gains both point and stature by being read in the same critical context as *The Picture of little T.C. in a Prospect of Flowers*. T.C. and O.C., marked by fate for exceptional heroism in the wars of the heart and the Commonwealth, represent not two exclusive phases of the poet's experience, but two opportunities for the same flexible mind to exercise itself. Any additional information we may have about Marvell's growth of political consciousness only makes this second exercise seem more demanding. Oddly enough, Eliot's famous essay on Marvell in 1921 contained, among its several contradictions, a recognition of interdependent meanings. While limiting the importance of Marvell to only "a very few poems," Eliot nevertheless perceived, in the select few, "signs of contiguity with other kinds of experi-

[6] *Hule* as mixed experience, the forest of life, was discussed by Rosalie Colie in *"My Ecchoing Song": Andrew Marvell's Poetry of Criticism* (Princeton, 1970), pp. 233-234.

ence which are possible."[7] Of many attempts to locate the quality of Marvell's wit, before deciding it was indefinable, Eliot's sense of "that precise taste . . . which finds for him the proper degree of seriousness for every subject he treats" might well have led him toward the miscellany rather than the anthology principle.

What distinguishes Marvell's *Miscellaneous Poems* from Jonson's, however (apart from his politics), are the tensions which underlie the rhetorical act of praise. He inherited, of course, the didactic approach to epideictic which derived ultimately from Plato, an ideal of the Good made concrete in terms of what was good for the State, along with all the educational consequences of praise and blame; but he asserted the sociopolitical context of praise at a time when other seventeenth-century poets were moving or had moved in other directions. While Jonson had developed a newly individualized poetry of compliment, Donne converted secular praise into a medium of spiritual awareness,[8] and Waller tried to endow political leaders with the glamor of myth,[9] Marvell was interested in public standards of conduct, and how they may be influenced by different forms of publication. Praise, as the exemplary mode, deeply interested him. But he also seems to have been unusually concerned with another imperative, an obligation to accuracy, to telling the precise truth, which has always been recognized as running counter to the exemplary function of literature. Unlike Jonson, whose disclaimers of flattery evince concern for his own reputation as a criterion of taste and judgment, Marvell seems constantly to assert an impersonal standard of truthful evaluation; he is continuous-

[7] "Andrew Marvell," first printed in the *Times Literary Supplement*, 31 March 1921, pp. 201-202.

[8] As demonstrated by Barbara Lewalski in *Donne's Anniversaries and the Poetry of Praise: The Creation of a Symbolic Mode* (Princeton, 1973).

[9] See Warren Chernaik, *The Poetry of Limitation* (New Haven, 1968), on Waller's ability "to turn historical fact into symbol" (p. 125).

# "SO WITH MORE MODESTY WE MAY BE TRUE"

ly probing the real, rather than the rhetorical, significance of inexpressibility topoi, validatory stances like modesty or candor on the part of the speaker, and supportive testimony such as "praise even by enemies."[10]

The truth of this assertion can be tested by comparing Jonson's dedication to Selden's *Titles of Honour* (1614) with a minor complimentary poem of Marvell's, the *Epitaph upon——*, an unnamed lady. Jonson's concern is to make the conventional assertion that he flatters not, that *this* dedication is to be taken more seriously than others of its kind, by admitting an autobiographical, even a confessional tone into his poem:

> I confess (as every Muse hath err'd,
> And mine not least) I have too oft preferr'd
> Men past their termes, and prais'd some names too much,
> But 'twas with purpose to have made them such.
> Since, being deceiv'd, I turne a sharper eye
> Upon my selfe, and aske to whom? and why?
> And what I write? and vexe it many dayes
> Before men get a verse: much lesse a Praise;
> So that my Reader is assur'd, I now
> Meane what I speake: and still will keepe that Vow.[11]

The effect is disarming but, when all is said, it remains only a personal guarantee, of value only as long as the guarantor himself survives, and in no way translatable into social, let alone absolute, standards.

By contrast, Marvell's *Epitaph upon——*, which appears at first sight to be a rather undistinguished collection of

[10] For the history of epideictic from Plato to the Renaissance, and a summary of its topoi, see O. B. Hardison, *The Enduring Monument: A Study of the Idea of Praise in Renaissance Literary Theory and Practice* (Chapel Hill, N.C., 1962), pp. 26-42; E. R. Curtius, *European Literature and the Latin Middle Ages*, trans. Willard R. Trask (New York, 1963), pp. 154-164.

[11] Jonson, *Works*, VIII, 158-161. Other examples are *To Sir Horace Vere*, p. 58; *Epistle, To Katherine, Lady Aubigny*, p. 116-120; *To the worthy Author on the Husband*, p. 385.

# "SO WITH MORE MODESTY WE MAY BE TRUE"55

epideictic topoi, develops on closer scrutiny into a subtle study of the problem of credibility, an issue further complicated in funeral poetry by the convention that one must always speak well of the dead. In another, less successful Latin prose epitaph for Edmund Trott (1667), Marvell had attempted to avoid flattery by the rather astonishing method of inverted insult ("Ut verae Laudis invidiam ficto Convitio levemus"), describing the dead boy as treacherous and parricidal in his desertion of his friends and parents (I, 142), "in order to avert, by false accusation, the envy of true praise." But here he creates, with great economy, the image of a life which had been, paradoxically, both exceptionally virtuous and, in its dutiful simplicity, totally unexceptional:

> Enough: and leave the rest to Fame.
> 'Tis to commend her but to name.
> Courtship, which living she declin'd,
> When dead to offer were unkind.
> Where never any could speak ill,
> Who would officious Praises spill?
> Nor can the truest Wit or Friend,
> Without Detracting, her commend.
> To say she liv'd a Virgin chast,
> In this Age loose and all unlac't;
> Nor was, when Vice is so allow'd,
> Of Virtue or asham'd, or proud;
> That her Soul was on Heaven so bent
> No Minute but it came and went;
> That ready her last Debt to pay
> She summ'd her Life up ev'ry day;
> Modest as Morn; as Mid-day bright;
> Gentle as Ev'ning; cool as Night;
> 'Tis true: but all so weakly said;
> 'Twere more Significant, She's Dead.
>                    (I, 58-59)

Starting from the initial conceit, that the mere naming of an unnamed lady is her truest praise, the poem develops a whole series of inexpressibility topoi. The concept that a chaste woman who avoided "courtship" when alive would be offended by compliments paid to her memory is developed into the paradox that neither "truest Wit" nor "Friend" can define her virtues without diminishing them. Marvell's ambiguous use of "Detracting" implies that even true praise of a woman uniquely virtuous constitutes a form of satire. The poem's own plainness and precision is true to the quiet piety it celebrates, which is conventionally enough contrasted to "an Age loose and all unlac't" but which, in the context of Marvell's other epitaphs, all of them to members of Puritan families, may be topical in both the rhetorical and historical senses. This possibility is enhanced by the epitaph for John Trott Sr. (Sir John Trott's father), which Margoliouth discovered in the family church at Laverstoke, and which may well be the immediate source of Marvell's opening conceit: "If the Just are praised when they are onely named how am I surprised with a Panegyricke whilst I am telling the reader that here lyes the body of John Trott of Laverstock . . . Oct: 24. 1658" (1, 339). The whole poem is, in effect, a rhetorical *occupatio* (the figure which proceeds to tell what it promises to omit), since the more the poet insists on the impossibility of making language express a virtuous reticence, the more it succeeds. The constructive modesty which, in his poem to Lovelace, Marvell had required of the demonstrative poet, is here transferred to his subject, who while living "declined" her own praises; but the final inexpressibility topos is the most effective. Given the inadequacy of even "true" praise, the poet is thrown back upon another criterion, that of "significance." What we no longer have we may fully appreciate, and death itself becomes the most accurate demonstration of value.

Throughout his career, Marvell continued to alternate between these two imperatives, the social responsibility of "speaking well" defined in the poem to Lovelace, and the other responsibility of "speaking true" which can also arise out of social or political circumstances. In Marvell's post-Restoration works it seems that "speaking true" predominates. The premise of the Dutch War satires is the brave and unusual candor of the satirist in a world of flattery and propaganda. Later, Marvell's concern with credibility merged with the demands of a well-documented polemic; his only pseudonym, Andreas Rivetus, an anagram of *Res nuda veritas*, extended his identification with truth into the arena of church history and doctrine. Some of his most explicit statements about validation occur in the *Rehearsal Transpros'd*, where his general attack on Samuel Parker's credibility is often expressed at the level of rhetorical criticism. Parker's egregious flattery of Bishop Bramhall, for example, the counterside of his railing against the Dissenters, convicts him equally of prejudice and stupidity. For "these improbable Elogies too are of the greatest disservice to their own design, and do in effect diminish always the Person whom they pretend to magnifie: Any worthy Man may pass through the World unquestion'd and safe with a moderate Recommendation; but when he is thus set off, and bedawb'd with Rhetorick, and embroder'd so thick that you cannot discern the Ground, it awakens naturally (and not altogether unjustly) Interest, Curiosity, and Envy. For all men pretend to share in Reputation, and love not to see it ingross'd and monopolized."[12] Close contact with another man's literary character had added a psychological dimension to Marvell's interest in the accuracy of evaluation.

By the time he came to write the *Second Part* of the *Rehearsal*, however, Marvell had become uneasy about his own satirical stance; in his remarkable apology for it he returned to the attitude expressed in the poem to Lovelace. It is generally better, he asserted, "that evil men should be left in an undisturbed possession of their repute . . . then that the Exchange and Credit of mankind should be universally shaken, wherein the best too will suffer and be involved." So vital

[12] *The Rehearsal Transpros'd* and *The Rehearsal Transpros'd: The Second Part*, ed. D.I.B. Smith (Oxford, 1971), p. 12.

58

is the preservation of credit to society that "Government too must at one time or another be dissolved where mens Reputation cannot be under Security." All writers, therefore, should emphasize the positive, even at the expense of truth; for "how can the Author of an Invective, *though never so truely founded*, expect approbation . . . who, in a world all furnished with subjects of praise, instruction and learned inquiry, shall studiously chuse and set himself apart to comment upon the blemishes and imperfections of some particular person" (pp. 160-161). The proper context of these statements will have to be filled in later, but for the moment they may perhaps stand as evidence of the depth of Marvell's epideictic theory. Far from being a merely rhetorical problem, the choice between speaking well and speaking true is what connects the writer to his society. In a "world all furnished with subjects of praise, instruction and learned inquiry" there is usually no problem in supplying positive demonstrations of idealism. But in the "degenerate" times of civil war or the "age loose and all unlac't" which followed it, the poet who insists on speaking well must either look for exceptions or keep silent. The other alternative is to try and justify the satirist's destructive accuracy. The tension between alternative modes is not then governed by the pull of public needs against personal integrity, but rather by the changing nature of society itself, and the occasions it offers the poet. How far did Cromwell's Protectorate, we may then inquire, offer the right occasion?

## THE CROMWELL POEMS

In all of his poems about Cromwell, Marvell faced a rhetorical problem which was clearly occasioned by political facts. Cromwell's actions were not only unconstitutional, they were also extremely difficult to assimilate into traditional modes of expression. A training in classical rhetoric provided a writer with a range of attitudes which could be taken toward any given political event, the judicial, deliberative, or demonstrative stances, each of which implied a different degree of knowledge of or certainty about the events in question. History, both sacred and profane, provided him with narrative precedents against which his subject could be measured; and a whole range of writings in different disciplines recorded the symbols by which the abstractions of power and authority had previously been understood. For a writer who understood his responsibilities as Marvell defined them in his poem to Lovelace, the imperative heard by the "forward youth" was not absolutely to "forsake the Muses dear," but to see rather what help they could give him in interpreting the present. In each of the three poems about Cromwell he discovered, apparently, that what was available to him in terms of rhetorical theory, historical precedent, and traditional iconography could not be applied to the Protector without significant modification; and in that process he also acquired some very significant insight into the role of language in history, and history in language.

In the *Horatian Ode*, Marvell's primary concern is with attitude, with what can most constructively be said about a figure whose character as so far known resists classification in either positive or negative terms, and whose future actions cannot be predicted. Part of the strategy he developed for expressing this problem has already been recognized by Marvell's critics. It consists in presenting Charles and Cromwell, the rightful but dead ruler and the supremely successful usurper, in a context of classical precedents which are themselves contradictory. The identification of Cromwell, through echoes from Thomas May's translation of the *Pharsalia*, with Lucan's hated Julius Caesar, killer of Pompey, bringer of civil war, is balanced by the fact that the poet identifies himself through the poem's title with Horace's role as counselor to Caesar Augustus, personification of peaceful rule and cooperation between literary and political values. The contrasting allusions offer the audience, and

Cromwell himself, a choice of two Caesarian roles, which is still further complicated by the statement that Cromwell, like Olympian lightning, had blasted "Caesars head" through the very laurel crown that was supposed to protect it.[13] It has also been pointed out that by seeing himself as Horatian counselor to Cromwell, Marvell established historical and literary precedent for the kind of praise which is given only conditionally, subject to withdrawal if his advice be not taken.

The idea of conditional praise, however, had already been established in English political rhetoric, in a place and manner certain to have come to Marvell's attention. Milton's *Areopagitica* (1644) contains an eloquent definition of and justification for a united stance of praise and advice, as the strategy required to persuade Parliament that, in the 1643 Printing Ordinance, it had passed a bad piece of legislation which it should now withdraw. There are, Milton asserted, "three principall things, without which all praising is but Courtship and flattery. First, when that only is prais'd which is solidly worth praise: next when greatest likelihoods are brought that such things are truly and really in those persons to whom they are ascrib'd, the other, when he who praises, by shewing that such his actuall perswasion is of whom he writes, can demonstrate that he flatters not. . . . For he who freely magnifies what hath been nobly done, and fears not to declare as freely what might be done better, gives ye the best cov'nant of his fidelity. . . . His highest praising is not flattery, and his plainest advice is a kinde

---

[13] See H. M. Margoliouth, *The Poems and Letters of Andrew Marvell*, rev. ed., Pierre Legouis (Oxford, 1971), I, 295-298; R. H. Syfret, "Marvell's Horatian Ode," *RES* 12 (1961), 160-172; Wallace, *Destiny his Choice*, pp. 72-103, and John S. Coolidge, "Marvell and Horace," *MP* 63 (1965), 111-120, who defined the conditional nature of Horace's praise. A.J.N. Wilson, however, in "Andrew Marvell: 'An Horatian Ode . . .': the thread of the poem and its use of classical allusion," *CritQ* 2 (1969), 325-341, argued that the "color Romanus" of the poem should be understood much more generally.

of praising."[14] Milton had thus articulated the importance of credible or conditional praise in a context which was doubly relevant to Marvell. He had raised it in connection with the issue of censorship, which Marvell in his poem to Lovelace had seen as undermining the old rhetorical ideals; and he had raised it *theoretically*, as the mode by which a writer might effectively, by persuasion, intervene in the political process.

The genre of the poem, moreover, has another resonance which is simultaneously classical and topical. As the celebration of a return from a significant journey or campaign, it is a Statian *sylva* poem, the obverse of *propempticon*, or congratulatory send-off. It was also a popular Caroline exercise. In late 1640, for example, the minor poets of both universities had risen to the occasion of Charles' return from Scotland, and the superficially happy conclusion of what is sometimes called the First Bishops' War, in which the Scots had risen against the imposition of the Laudian prayer book. Both *Irenodia Cantabrigiensis* and *Eucharistica Oxoniensia*, the congratulatory anthologies produced by Cambridge and Oxford respectively, emphasized that the peace treaty was achieved by negotiation rather than conquest, a conception most agreeable to the pacific Caroline mythology. Typical of both collections was a poem by P. Samwayes of Trinity, Marvell's own college. Its title emphasized that the Scottish campaign had been settled "non vi et armis sed lenitate"; its strophic form is the visual equivalent of Marvell's much discussed stanza; and its opening lines may have considerable bearing on the opening of Marvell's own poem:

> Phoebus volentem praelia me loqui,
> Victas & urbes, & sata languida,
>   Non falce sed stricti resecta
>   Praepropero gladii furore;

[14] Milton, *Complete Prose Works*, ed. D. M. Wolfe *et al.* (New Haven, 1953-), II, 487-488.

Non ante visa commonuit Dea,
Jussitque; molli nectere carmine
    Paci corollas. . .[15]

The opening of Marvell's poem in effect inverts this conceit, delivering a rebuke to the pacifist poet who produces "His Numbers languishing" in the shades of academe.
The "Muses dear" which the "forward Youth" of 1650 is
urged to forsake may include among their meanings both
the universities themselves, and the spirit of retreat from
reality, even of false panegyric, which they encouraged. It
is perhaps worth noticing in passing that Marvell, who was
still a member of Trinity in 1640, did *not* contribute to
*Irenodia Cantabrigiensis*.

The *Horatian Ode*, then, offers itself to the reader as a
congratulatory poem to a military hero who has, in the
most absolute manner possible, negated the Caroline idyll.
It will, genre and title suggest, offer praise without flattery,
and advice as "a kinde of praising." It will function as a
form of political commentary, not only on the actions
which are its own subject, but on previous actions very
differently celebrated by less objective poets. It will, perhaps, face facts, or at least attempt to distinguish between
them and other elements of thought or discourse. The
rhetoric of the poem does indeed, in my reading of it, fulfill these expectations.

To begin with, the possibilities for epideictic are carefully and explicitly limited. If Cromwell is really the instrument of divine justice, then " 'Tis Madness to resist *or
blame*" actions which would normally require our condemnation. Cautious approbation can, however, be given

[15] P. Samwayes, "De rebus in Scotia per Augustissimum Clementissi-
mumque Regem non vi et armis sed lenitate compositis," in *Irenodia
Cantabrigiensis* (Cambridge, 1641), Ir,v: "Phoebus spoke to me as I
was hoping for battles and conquered cities, and crops languishing, cut
down not by the scythe but by the rage of the too-hasty sword; a
goddess not seen before advised and instructed me to weave the garlands of peace in a soft song."

63

to Cromwell's most exemplary act so far, his sacrifice of personal privacy to take on the burdens of leadership:

> And, if *we would speak true*,
> Much to the Man is due.
> Who, from his private Gardens, where
> He liv'd reserved and austere,

subjected himself to public scrutiny. Another strategy is to shift responsibility for evaluating the Irish campaign to the conquered Irish, thereby putting to lively use the "praise even by enemies," and hopefully avoiding any question of the massacres of Wexford and Drogheda:

> They can affirm his Praises best,
> And have, though overcome, confest
> How good he is, how just.

A praise so discreet both validates and is further validated by the "plainest advice" which Marvell can insert into his account of Cromwell's return:

> Nor yet grown stiffer with Command,
> But still in the Republick's hand:
> .  .  .
> He to the Commons Feet presents
> A Kingdome, for his first years rents:
> And, what he may, forbears
> His Fame to make it theirs:

As the crucial "nor yet" warns Cromwell not to exceed his commission, so the qualifying "what he may" draws attention to the problem of fame when the hero is not an individual agent but a public servant.

The effectiveness of these limitations is further assisted by the poem's time scheme, which keeps carefully separate facts, regrets, propositions, and hopes. The first major section of the poem, which describes Cromwell's violent entry into history and has attracted most attention, alternates the incontrovertible past with the immediate problem of assessment. The *res gestae* of Cromwell are aggressively in the past: he "*Did* thorough his own Side/His fiery way divide," and "Caesars head at last/*Did* through his Laurels blast." But these statements are noticeably of a different order from the conclusions the poet draws from these events:

> '*Tis* time to leave the Books in dust
> For '*tis* all one to Courage high
> '*Tis* Madness to resist or blame.

Similarly, the second section, which defines the role of Charles, is all in the past, as befits a figure about whom everything can now be said and who belongs to memory; we discover that the "did's" of this poem are not metrical padding, but epistemological tools:

> He nothing common *did* or mean
> Upon that *memorable* Scene:
>> But with his keener Eye
>> The Axes edge *did* try:
>
> . . .
>
> This was that *memorable* Hour
> Which first assur'd the forced Pow'r.

The third section returns us to the "now" of the poem's occasion, the present tense of Cromwell's return from Ireland, which leads in turn to the imperial and imperative future. Cromwell will "ere long" be recognized as a conquering Caesar by the new "Gaul" whose Catholicism invites attack, and to all other "States not free / *Shall* Clymacterick be."

Marvell's apparent emphasis on this time scheme would not be particularly remarkable were it not for the fact that the relationship between past, present, and future had been established by Aristotle as a key to rhetorical stance. In the *Rhetoric* (I, iii, 9) Aristotle had clearly distinguished the present certainties of demonstrative speech from the questionable past of judicial inquiry and the unknown future of deliberative speculation. Marvell's poem, however, appears to avoid what *is*, in defiance of its generic commitment to the historical moment. Cromwell's past is accessible to praise or regret, but the use of the present tense is restricted to neutral generalizations (" 'Tis time to leave the Books in dust"), polite imperatives about Cromwell's destiny, or logical propositions about his character. It is particularly these last, the enthymemes which Aristotle associated with forensic rhetoric, which reveal Marvell's manipulation of temporal statement. "So much one Man can do, / That does both act and know" and "How fit he is to sway / That can so well obey" subordinate the assertion of Cromwell's virtues to a wisdom and humility not yet certainly demonstrated. It is true that such propositions acquire an appearance of certainty by being presented as classical *sententiae*, with the added assurance of rhyme; but real demonstrative rhetoric closes up the syntactical gap between its subject and those qualities which, if actually possessed, make that subject praiseworthy. As compared to what we would expect from Aristotle's definition (which merely provides an authoritative formula for the obvious), Marvell's poem has a restricted present and a marked shortage of statements. Epideictic confidence has been subverted by forensic and deliberative modes of thought. Like Milton in the *Areopagitica*, Marvell's rhetoric would assure his audience "that such things are truly and really in those persons to whome they are ascrib'd." What he cannot be sure of he will not affirm. The poem remains dominated by the incomplete case of Justice versus Fate, and its temporal and logical structures illustrate finely the limitations of present knowledge.

The *Horatian Ode*, then, responds to political crisis by deft manipulation of appropriate traditions. At the same time as it alerts its audience to the difficulty of evaluating revolutionary events, especially "if we would speak true," it reminds them that such difficulties are not unprecedented. Horace and Lucan faced them and drew their own conclusions; the modes of classical rhetoric provide norms for locating the new experience, and formal strategies for measuring it. But there is no rigid commitment to a one-to-one system of historical analogy or a slavish reproduction of rhetorical structures, either of which would protect the audience from participating in the process of choice. The mixture of classical sources, the rearrangement of rhetorical expectations, provoke a lively, continuous movement between raw political fact and the possibility of categorization, between the strain of empiricism and the relaxation of system.

Recognition of this achievement allows us, in addition, to accept without further controversy both the "affectivist" and the "historicist" response to the *Horatian Ode* as products of Marvell's mediating stance. For all that was said by Douglas Bush,[16] it remains true that for many readers regret for Charles is stronger than the measured weighing of the "antient Rights" against the necessary revolution, the requirement that we temper emotional responses with the generalities of historical experience. In this the poem itself gives formal recognition to what Milton had discovered earlier in *Eikonoklastes*, that even the most powerful arguments are weaker than pathos and sentiment. Like *Eikonoklastes*, the *Horatian Ode* reflects the appeal of *Eikon Basilike*, with its symbolic title page showing the king kneeling in acceptance of the crown of thorns, and treading in rejection upon his earthly crown. Although Marvell excluded any Christological language, and insisted upon his Roman decorum, no reader of *Eikon Basilike* could have read the *Ode* without recognizing what role it was the "Royal Actor" played. Similarly, when the poem moves to the ghastly discovery on the Capitol, which nevertheless foretold the "happy Fate" of the Roman Commonwealth, an affectivist

---

[16] The argument between "affectivist" and "historicist" readings of the *Ode* was initiated by Cleanth Brooks in "Criticism and Literary History: Marvell's 'Horatian Ode'," *SR* 55 (1947), 199-222, and continued in "A Note on the Limits of 'History' and the Limits of 'Criticism'," *SR* 61 (1953), 129-135, as a rejoinder to Douglas Bush's critique of his methods in "Marvell's 'Horatian Ode'," *SR* 60 (1952), 362-376.

response of shock is explicitly countered by a historicist recognition, however reluctant, that the analogy is appropriate, that it seems to work. It is this tension between different kinds of responses in which, I think, Marvell was interested, as it had been developed by earlier commentaries on the king's death. In taking a position somewhere between *Eikon Basilike* and *Eikonoklastes*, the *Horatian Ode* mediates not between two political camps but between two interdependent theories (which rhetoric has always recognized as pathos and ethos) of how language works upon the human mind.

At first sight the *First Anniversary* suggests a simple development from choice in progress to choice complete, from a mixed rhetorical stance supported by the classics to Christian determinism supported by biblical typology. However, any attempt to develop a straightforward reading of the poem as an alternative to the *Ode*, a "committed" Puritan poem which knows where it stands, is quickly defeated. Cromwell may resemble Elijah or Gideon, but he is also an Amphion of classical harmony, particularly as that figure had been interpreted by Horace's *Ars Poetica*. The poem seems extraordinarily digressive and, while invoking the temporal structures both of classical *encomium* and Christian prophecy, it also seems to subvert them in ways which can scarcely be accidental. Considered as an *encomium*, we find that praise of Cromwell's achievements at home and abroad precedes mention of his parentage and birth (*genesis*) and that a lament for his death (which turns out to be hypothetical) precedes his education (*anatrophe*) and choice of destiny (*epitedeumata*).[17]

Considered as Christian prophecy, the poem is even more subversive, indeed explicitly so. The poet's hopes for a millennium in his own time under Cromwell's leadership are

[17] Compare the formula for *encomium* in the *Rhetorica ad Herennium*, III, vii, 13-15: "We shall recount the events, observing their precise sequence and chronology" (Loeb). See also Hardison, *The Enduring Monument*, p. 205, n. 8.

presented not as a conclusion, but toward the middle of the poem, and they are presented in the most hypothetical terms:

> Hence oft I *think*, *if* in some happy Hour
> High Grace *should* meet in one with highest Pow'r,
> And then a seasonable People still
> *Should* bend to his, as he to Heavens will,
> *What we might hope*, what wonderful Effect
> From such a *wish'd* Conjuncture *might* reflect.
> Sure, the mysterious Work, where none withstand,
> Would forthwith finish under such a Hand:
> Fore-shortned Time its useless Course would stay,
> And soon precipitate the latest Day.
> But a thick Cloud about that Morning lyes,
> And intercepts the Beams of Mortal eyes,
> That 'tis the most which we determine can,
> *If* these the Times, then this must be the Man.
>
> (ll. 131-144)

This language is all conditional, in the grammatical sense; but as compared to the conditional praise of the *Ode*, which was merely dependent on Cromwell's fulfilling certain political responsibilities, the *Anniversary* indicates the limitations of vision. Thinking, wishing, and hoping are all very well, but a "thick Cloud" comes between the would-be prophet and his glimpses of the Apocalypse, as he considers exactly how unseasonable the people are at present:

> Men alas, as if they nothing car'd,
> Look on, all unconcern'd, or unprepar'd;
> . . .
>
> Hence that blest Day still counterpoysed wastes,
> The Ill delaying, what th'Elected hastes;
>
> (ll. 149ff.)

As the poem continues, then, "the most which we determine can" is that its subject is indeed exceptional. Deprived of structural guidance, its readers "hollow far behind / Angelique Cromwell," whose legendary speed of action makes him as hard to catch as the shape of the uncertain future.

In fact, the more one investigates, the more the *First Anniversary* reveals itself to be an exercise in how to *avoid* conventional definitions and postures. The theoretical question with which the poem deals is not the conflicting claims of two different types of hero, two different views of what is "right," but how to express Cromwell's uniqueness, the unprecedented position he holds in England, in Europe, in God's providential plans and, above all, in the literary imagination. Marvell is here less concerned with what attitudes toward Cromwell were available to the writer than with the larger question of what, indeed, Cromwell was. His whole poem is a complex political version of the inexpressibility topos he had developed in the *Epitaph* for an unnamed lady; but in this context the problem of definition was one in which the whole country shared, the problem of what title could best express the nature of Cromwell's government and its sanctions. Rather than an argument that Cromwell ought to accept the crown of England, and so assimilate himself to traditional definitions of single rule by divine sanction, Marvell, I believe, decided in the *First Anniversary* that no conventional category, and certainly not that of kingship, was adequate to delimit the "One Man" whose like had never been seen before. Every analogy we are offered for Cromwell's career proves not, on inspection, to be exact. The act of hypothesizing is underlined at every turn. Fictions proclaim themselves as fictions, and in the critical awareness which such discoveries promote Marvell distinguishes a "true" political poetry from the automatic responses encouraged by propaganda. One might add that it is this quality particularly which distinguishes the *First Anniversary* from the poem *On the Victory obtained by Blake over the Spaniards*, a piece of unquestioning (and uninteresting) propaganda which does appear to argue for Cromwell's kingship. If Marvell was indeed responsible for this poem, which I doubt (since it was actually removed from the printed portion of the Popple manuscript), he must by 1657 have changed his mind considerably, not only on the kingship issue, but on the nature of political commentary.

The immediate occasion of Marvell's poem was not Cromwell's refusal of the crown, which had occurred in 1652 and was to be repeated in 1657. It was, rather, the first anniversary of the Instrument of Government, and also the session of the first Protectorate Parliament, which symbolized a return to some kind of constitutional government but which, between 3 September 1654 and 22 January 1655, when Cromwell dissolved it, fought to amend the terms of the Instrument and to limit Cromwell's powers, particularly with regard to control of the army. Written late in 1654, Marvell's poem was not designed to provide symbolic sanction for the kind of rule Cromwell apparently wanted, although that inference has been drawn from his magnificent musical and architectural metaphors for the "ruling Instrument." Rather he is concerned to investigate the historical significance, the internal paradoxes, and indeed even the disadvantages of that rule, subjecting the topoi normally associated with rulers to the scrupulous pressure of his own intelligence.

The central paradox of the Protectorate was, of course, implicit in the title of the Protector, a title with no constitutional precedent whose beneficent significance, some clearly felt, was merely a cover for despotism. Why, in any case, if Cromwell was only the servant of his country, did he need a title at all? In Milton's *Second Defence of the English People*, published earlier in 1654, there is an elaborate rationalization of the title in terms of a republican ethos: "Your deeds surpass all degrees, not only of admiration, but surely of titles too. . . . But since it is, not indeed worthy, but expedient for even the greatest capacities to be bounded and confined by some sort of human dignity . . . you assumed a certain title very like that of Father of your country. You suffered and allowed yourself, not indeed to be borne aloft, but to come down so many degrees from the heights and be forced into a definite rank, so to speak, for the public good." The name of Protector, Milton asserts, though an inadequate expression or devaluation of Cromwell's natural superiority, is nevertheless better than the title he has recently refused: "The name of king you spurned from your greater eminence, and rightly so. For if when you became so great a figure, you were captivated by the title which as a private citizen you were able to send under the yoke and reduce to nothing, you would be doing almost the same thing as if, when you had subjugated some tribe of idolaters with the help of the true God, you were to worship the gods that you had conquered."[18]

In June of 1654 Milton had entrusted Marvell with the delivery of a complimentary copy of the *Second Defence* to John Bradshaw, and Marvell reported in a letter how the gift had been received, adding his own accolade. "I shall now studie it," he wrote, "even to the getting of it by Heart: esteeming it according to my poor Judgement . . . as the most compendious Scale, for so much, to the Height of the Roman eloquence" (II, 306). It looks as though Marvell had so far succeeded in getting the *Second Defence* by heart that he incorporated this central paradox of the Protectorate into his own poem. Commenting, as in the *Ode*, on the great man's sacrifice of privacy to the demands of public life, he wrote:

> For all delight of Life thou then didst lose,
> When to Command, thou didst thy self Depose;
> Resigning up thy Privacy so dear,
> To turn the headstrong Peoples Charioteer;
> For to be Cromwell was a greater thing,
> Then ought below, or yet above a King:

[18] Milton, *Complete Prose Works*, IV, i, 672. Compare also Cromwell's account of his position as a limitation rather than a promotion, in his speech to the Protectorate Parliament, 12 September 1654, in W. C. Abbott, *The Speeches and Writings of Oliver Cromwell*, III, 452.

Therefore thou rather didst thy Self depress,
Yielding to Rule, because it made thee Less.

(ll. 221-228)

The similarity is palpable; but the differences are, if anything, more interesting. By avoiding all mention of Cromwell's actual title, Marvell's version of the paradox shifts
slightly toward the idea of an indefinable selfhood. The idea
of what it is "to be Cromwell" appears for a moment on a
confusing vertical scale, only to disappear as soon as one
probes it. Nothing could be more unlike the propagandist
tactics of George Wither, whose poem *The Protector . . .
Briefly illustrating the Supereminency of that Dignity; and
Rationally demonstrating, that the Title of Protector . . .
is the most Honorable of all Titles* (1655) allows, to say the
least, no possibility of misunderstanding. In all likelihood
following the *First Anniversary*, which was advertised in
*Mercurius Politicus* for the week beginning 11 January 1655,
Wither reduces the constitutional paradox to bluntly expedient terms:

Why by the name of King, should we now call him,
Which is below the Honours, that befall him;
And makes him to be rather less than great,
(As in himself) and rather worse then better
As to his People . . .
It will deprive him ev'n of that Defence
Which seems intended; and, will him expose
To all the purposed Cavils of his Foes.

(p. 31)

The difference is not just that Marvell's obliqueness allows
for a more high-minded interpretation of Cromwell's motives, though that may be relevant. It is rather that the problem of what it is "to be Cromwell," in a constitutional sense,
is more significant than any available verbal formulation.
It recalls, in fact, the opening conceit of his anonymous
*Epitaph upon——*, which proposed that the naming of an
unnamed lady constituted her truest praise.

This functional indeterminacy also helps to explain those features of the *First Anniversary* which have caused Marvell's critics, taken as a group, to divide among themselves. On the one hand, it is clear that Marvell associates with Cromwell a range of images and topoi which have or had traditional associations with kingship, and which in some cases had acquired a new topicality in the poetry of Stuart panegyrists. On the other hand, Cromwell is also presented in terms of biblical types and metaphors more appropriate to a Puritan warrior saint. Not only do these two frames of reference conflict with each other, producing diametrically opposed readings of the poem, but the comparisons so invoked are themselves not simple. Neither "royalist" nor "biblical" types will apply to Cromwell without some adjustment, some diversion from their normal referential function; the effect is to make us look more closely, both at Cromwell's uniqueness and at the iconography itself. If the function of political symbolism is to endow sanctions on particular regimes, then it behooves the political poet to treat those symbols with a respectful exactness, in order that what is of permanent power and relevance may be preserved.

We can test this proposition by considering the best-known of Marvell's allusions to Stuart panegyric, the comparison between Cromwell, as creator of the Instrument of Government, and the harper Amphion, by whose musical skill the city of Thebes was magically built. It is generally accepted that in making this analogy Marvell was distinctly echoing not only Horace's *Ars Poetica* but also Edmund Waller's poem, *Upon his Majesties repairing of Paul's*. In Ruth Nevo's important study of Stuart and Commonwealth poetry of state, this echo exemplifies a tendency she sees in Marvell; he is reanimating, "with a kind of poetic justice," the language of Cavalier poets to celebrate the new regime.[19] But Marvell's use of Waller is more specific than this suggests, and extends over a larger area of the poem. The aim

[19] Ruth Nevo, *The Dial of Virtue: A Study of Poems on Affairs of State in the Seventeenth Century* (Princeton, 1963), pp. 20-27, 74-118.

of Waller's poem was to justify the repairs to St. Paul's Cathedral, undertaken by Charles and Laud in the 1630's, against the attacks of the Puritans, who interpreted the project as a consolidation of Anglican polity.[20] Its rhetorical method was to praise the modesty of Charles in merely improving a structure begun by James:

> Ambition rather would effect the fame
> Of some new structure; to have borne her name.
> Two distant vertues in one act we finde,
> The modesty, and greatnesse of his minde;
> Which not content to be above the rage
> And injury of all impairing age,
> In its own worth secure, doth higher clime,
> And things half swallow'd from the jaws of time
> Reduce; an earnest of his grand designe,
> To frame no new Church, but the old refine:[21]

It was these lines which inspired not only Marvell's superb version of the Amphion passage but also his opening *comparatio* between Cromwell and the "heavie Monarchs" of a hereditary succession, who never complete even a limited project in one generation:

> Their earthy Projects under ground they lay,
> More slow and brittle then the China clay:
> Well may they strive to leave them to their Son,
> For one Thing never was by one King don.

(ll. 19-22)

The point is not merely the speed and vigor of Cromwell's escape from the slow cycles of classical time, but the difference in scale between Charles's achievement and Cromwell's. Waller invoked the Amphion image to describe a set of renovations to one end of an existing building. No note struck by Cromwell as Amphion "but *a new Story* lay'd"

---

[20] Chernaik, *The Poetry of Limitation*, p. 41, n. 23.

[21] Edmund Waller, *Workes* (London, for Thomas Walkley, 1645), p. 4.

(with a pun on the making of history); and his "great Work" is no mere tinkering, but a harmonious construct of military, civil, and religious order:

> Now through the Strings a Martial rage he throws,
> And joyning streight the Theban Tow'r arose;
> Then as he strokes them with a Touch more sweet,
> The flocking Marbles in a Palace meet;
> But, for he most the graver Notes did try,
> Therefore the Temples rear'd their Columns high:
>
> (ll. 59-64)

The building of the Temple was, of course, a favorite Puritan metaphor for reform of the English church, particularly during the Civil War. In 1642 Thomas Goodwin inspired his party with *Zerubbabels Encouragement to Finish the Temple*. In 1643 Edmund Calamy reproached the House of Lords for slackness in reform by comparing the situation of the Westminster divines with that of "Nehemiah when he undertooke the great worke of rebuilding the Temple, he was opposed by great men especially."[22] In 1644 Milton had incorporated into the *Areopagitica* an appeal against those who resisted, by censorship, diversity of opinion: "as if, while the Temple of the Lord was building, some cutting, some squaring the marble, others hewing the cedars, there should be a sort of irrationall men who could not consider there must be many schisms and many dissections made in the quarry and in the timber, ere the house of God can be built."[23] Marvell's reproach of kings who "neither build the Temple in their dayes, / Nor Matter for succeeding Founders raise" (ll. 33-34) is therefore a direct response to Waller's praise of those conservative rulers who, like Charles, do not move forward the Protestant Reformation, who "frame no new Church, but the old refine." Politically, Marvell's adjustment is precise, locating his opinions on the

[22] Edmund Calamy, *The Noble-Mans Patterne of True and Reall Thankfulnesse* (1643), p. 50.
[23] Milton, *Complete Prose Works*, II, 555.

Puritan side. In terms of literary theory he is equally exact for, by making his ideological correction of Waller within the same symbolic construct, he asserts the permanence and accepts the sanctions of the great architectural and musical metaphor.

One of the most interesting problems for the panegyrist, and one that had become topical in the 1640s, was the narrow boundary between symbolic sanction and actual sacrilege. It has been observed that, as the crisis of the Civil War approached, the classical tone of Caroline panegyric gave way to religious language and Christic imagery, and poets escaped from anxiety into idolatry.[24] Even when fear was not the motive, in a period when the Divine Right of kingship was being most fully articulated the borderline was easily crossed. This problem was raised (and dismissed) by Ben Jonson, in his *Epigram to the Queene, then lying in* (1630):

> Haile Mary, full of grace, it once was said,
> And by an Angell, to the blessed'st Maid,
> The Mother of our Lord: why may not I
> (Without prophanenesse) yet a Poet, cry,
> Haile Mary, full of honours, to my Queene,
> The Mother of our Prince?[25]

It was a matter of some importance, however, to writers on the other side of the political spectrum. In *Anti-Cavalierisme* (1642) John Goodwin maintained that those who sought to deify their mortal rulers by sacrilegious language and unquestioning obedience in effect only revealed their mortality: "they that will devest the great God of heaven and earth, to cloath Kings and Princes, or whomsoever, with the spoils of his Name, as all those doe, who obey them with disobedience unto God, as in one sense they make them Gods, so in another . . . they make them indeed more men then they were, more obnoxious to his displeasure, who hath

---

[24] Nevo, *The Dial of Virtue*, pp. 24, 26.
[25] Jonson, *Works*, VIII, 238.

the command of their life and breath."[26] In the light of after-knowledge, the passage seems to contain a threat. Milton was later to return to the same theme in his efforts to justify the regicides: "the People, exorbitant and excessive in all thir motions, are prone oft times not to a religious onely, but to a civil kinde of Idolatry, in idolizing their Kings."[27] No more extreme an expression of this folly could have been found than in Robert Herrick's *To the King, to Cure the Evill*, which mixes Ben Jonson's notion that the "Poets Evill" is poverty[28] with the biblical story of the miracle at Bethesda:

> To find Bethesda, and an Angell there,
> Stirring the waters I am come; and here
> . . .
>
> I kneele for help; O! lay that hand on me,
> Adored Cesar! and my Faith is such,
> I shall be heal'd, if that my King but touch.
> The Evill is not Yours: my sorrow sings,
> Mine is the Evill, but the Cure, the Kings.[29]

Marvell's adaptation of this conceit for the last lines of the *First Anniversary* is a condensed refutation of all of Herrick's premises. Rejecting the identification between his subject and Christ, who alone has the power to subvert natural process, Cromwell comes merely as the Angel of the pool, whose mysterious but regular "Troubling the Waters" manifested the workings of Providence in a less than miraculous form. The spirit of reform embodied in Cromwell, reactivating stagnant institutions, heals through their agency, not his own. But, most importantly, the power of healing is

[26] John Goodwin, *Anti-Cavalierisme* in *Tracts on Liberty in the Puritan Revolution: 1638-1647*, ed. William Haller (New York, 1965), II, 239-240.

[27] Milton, *Eikonoklastes* (1649) in *Complete Prose Works*, III, 343.

[28] Jonson, *Works*, VIII, 325.

[29] Herrick, *Poetical Works*, ed. L. C. Martin (Oxford, 1956), pp. 61-62.

directed, through rhyme, to the good of the nation as a whole; and in the full significance of "Commonweal" the poem finally rests. If one knew Herrick's version, Marvell's must have made terrible irony in the 1650s, when the King's Evil had been cured indeed.

It is in the context of echoes like these that we may set the description of Cromwell's coaching accident, an event which occupies the center of Marvell's poem. Like George Wither's *Vaticinium Causuale*,[30] this passage is a response to various hostile responses to the incident, a conversion of material potentially open to satiric interpretation. The six runaway horses, which had been a gift from the Duke of Holstein, were all too convenient a metaphor for the three kingdoms Cromwell was trying to manage; and *A Jolt on Michaelmas Day*, which drew the obvious analogy with Phaeton but suggested that Cromwell had been saved for the hangman's cart, represented the direction of contemporary lampoons. Wither's response was to congratulate the Protector upon his escape, to replace Phaeton with Hippolytus, and to interpret Cromwell's lucky escape as a sign of his special relationship with Providence, which had nevertheless given him due warning of his mortality. His poem draws the obvious constructions in a tone of pompous didacticism. Marvell's response is to replace ambitious Phaeton with Elijah, "the headstrong Peoples Charioteer" (l. 224), itself a neat inversion, and by concentrating not on the escape but the danger, he produces a radical innovation in poetic strategy.

Preservation from danger (or recovery from sickness) of a public figure was in itself a recognized subject for poetry, producing *soteria*, as in Statius' congratulation to Rutilius Gallicus (*Sylvae*, I, iv), and all too many imitations by Caroline poets. Apart from the university anthologies, Marvell would probably have been aware of Waller's *Of the danger*

[30] George Wither, *Vaticinium Causuale. A Rapture Occasioned By the late Miraculous Deliverance of His Highnesse The Lord Protector, From a Desperate Danger* (London, 1654).

79

*his Majesty (being Prince) escaped in the rode at St. An-dere*, or *To my Lord Admirall of his late sicknesse and Recovery*, both of which appeared in the 1645 editions. The latter, particularly, provides a close analogy for Mar-vell's pathetic fallacies, which have sometimes disconcerted his modern readers. The purpose of *soteria*, to define value by exploring its near loss, requires or at least justifies the use of hyperbole. Nature's lament for the death of Orpheus, which is imported from Ovid into both Waller's and Mar-vell's poems, is only excessive because it is not needed, be-cause a death of equal significance has in fact been averted. It indicates the extravagance of *relief*. There is, however, a peculiar development in Marvell's poem, which goes far beyond anything similar in Waller or Jonson. The poet becomes trapped in his own fiction, and begins to describe Cromwell's death as if it had actually occurred. It only "seem'd" that "Earth did from the Center tear," but the effects on human institutions were less retractable:

> Justice obstructed lay, and Reason fool'd;
> Courage disheartned, and Religion cool'd.

In the analogy with Elijah the sense of deliverance disap-pears entirely from view, to be imaginatively replaced by another kind of escape altogether:

> But thee triumphant hence the firy Carr,
> And firy Steeds had born out of the Warr,
> From the low World, and thankless Men above,
> Unto the Kingdom blest of Peace and Love:
> We only mourn'd our selves, in thine Ascent,
> Whom thou hadst left beneath with Mantle rent.
>
> (ll. 215-220)

Fiction has taken over, but only, paradoxically, to insist on another kind of truth. The "elegy" enforces dramatic recognition of Cromwell's human status. It cuts through literary and political illusions to assert his "Mortal cares" and "silver Hairs," his part in the Fall, the fragility of his regime, the problem of the succession. Its realism, Marvell tells us, is essential to the validity of the whole poem:

> Let this one Sorrow interweave among
> The other Glories of our yearly Song.
> Like skilful Looms which through the costly thred
> Of purling Ore, a shining wave do shed:
> So shall the Tears we on past Grief employ,
> Still as they trickle, glitter in our Joy.
> *So with more Modesty we may be True,*
> *And speak as of the Dead the Praises due.*
>
> (ll. 181-188)

The conclusion of Marvell's anonymous epitaph, that " 'Twere more Significant, [S]he's Dead," is deepened in this political context. In the *Horatian Ode* Marvell had perceived that "if we would speak true" it must be by looking to the past, to Cromwell's inarguable sacrifices and the dead king's intelligible dignity. In the *Anniversary* he controls his praise of Cromwell's life by imagining him dead. From that perspective, flattery has no object, and other forms of false perspective vanish in the precise knowledge of what we would miss.

This provocative use of "royalist" panegyric serves both in the particular and in general to distinguish Cromwell from previous rulers. Without invalidating the conventions he uses, Marvell has applied them with scrupulous attention to meaning, with an innovative seriousness which rebukes the frivolity of less careful poets, the inadequacy of less worthy subjects of praise. But because the materials so scrutinized have, so to speak, been set up for him by the political opposition, it does not follow that he accepts without question the conventions of his own side. The Old Testament types and millennial images, so appropriate to a Puritan definition of the rule of the saints, do not, in Marvell's poem, attach to Cromwell as clichés. There is no exact equivalence between the new Protector and Noah, Gideon, Elijah, and the hero of the Apocalypse; and if the use of royalist topoi had had the effect of making Cromwell seem infinitely better than a king, the adjustment of biblical topoi seems, conversely, to make him seem less than perfect as patriarch, judge, prophet, or millennial hero.

To begin (where Marvell does not) with Noah, the point of connection chosen seems almost perverse. The survival of the race, the fresh start under Noah's governance, are not expressed in the Ark and the rainbow, but rather through the discreditable tale of Noah's drunkenness, which has to be twisted back to positive statements:

> Thou, and thine House, like Noah's Eight did rest,
> Left by the Wars Flood on the Mountains crest:
> And the large Vale lay subject to thy Will,
> Which thou but as an Husbandman wouldst Till:
> And only didst for others plant the Vine
> Of Liberty, not drunken with its Wine.
> That sober Liberty which men may have,
> That they enjoy, but more they vainly crave:
> And such as to their Parents Tents do press,
> May shew their own, not see his Nakedness.
>
> (ll. 283-292)

It is characteristic of Marvell's intelligence that his discussion of dictatorship should raise the question of human inadequacy even while denying it. The episode he had chosen was recognized in scriptural commentary as symbolizing the perpetually unregenerate nature of man. "Who would look," asked Bishop Joseph Hall, "after all this, to have found righteous Noah, the father of the new world, lying drunk in his tent! . . . that he, who could not be tainted with the sinful examples of the former world, should begin the example of a new sin of his own!"[31] But, as if announcing that his subject is controversial, Marvell converts the tale to an allegory of benevolent and peaceful government, which is threatened but not dishonored by the activities of Levellers

[31] Bishop Joseph Hall, *Contemplations On The Historical Passages of the Old and New Testaments* (Edinburgh, 1770), I, 20.

and Fifth Monarchy men. It is true, of course, that the Noah passage follows, with at least some semblance of progress, Marvell's account of how Cromwell as the "lusty mate" had seized from its incompetent steersman the tiller of the ship of state,[32] which, during the Revolution, was often assimilated to the Ark; and it is also possible that Marvell had been attracted to the episode of Noah's drunkenness by the satirical rumor that Cromwell was a brewer's son.[33] However, such explanations cannot account for the deliberate challenge of the passage, which in a nonpolitical poem would have been readily understood as wit. It does, in fact, quite directly recall the syntax of the inverted myths of *The Garden*: "Apollo hunted Daphne so, / *Only* that She might Laurel grow"; Cromwell "*only* didst for others plant the Vine / Of Liberty, *not* drunken with its Wine." And, as the impropriety of Cromwell's "Chammish issue" may only reveal "their own, *not* see his Nakedness," so the Pan of Marvell's metamorphosis pursues his Syrinx "*Not* as a Nymph, but for a Reed."

Gideon and Elijah, as metaphors for other aspects of Cromwell, are no less problematic. Both sets of analogies are highly condensed and ambiguous, and their particular points of emphasis both depend on, and diverge from, contemporary interpretations of these figures. Marvell's choice of Elijah depends on a common view of the prophet as solitary and courageous proponent of reformation, opposing his

---

[32] J. M. Wallace, in "Marvell's 'lusty Mate' and the Ship of the Commonwealth," *MLN* 76 (1961), 106-110, described the political history of this metaphor in the Puritan Revolution. He has subsequently supplied me with the following information: In Cicero's *Letters to Atticus* (ii, vii) he writes: "I had grown weary of piloting the state even while I was allowed to do so. Now, though, that I have been turned out of the boat, and have not abandoned the tiller but had it snatched out of my hands, my desire is to watch the shipwreck from the shore." Quoted in another context by J. B. Leishman, *Milton's Minor Poems* (London, 1969), pp. 147-148.

[33] See "The Protecting Brewer," in *Political Ballads of the Seventeenth and Eighteenth Centuries*, ed. W. W. Wilkins (London, 1860), I, 132-134.

moral authority to the tyranny of Ahab. The often-repeated statement that Elijah achieved more for Israel by his prayers than any military force could have done did not confine the prophet to a contemplative role. In 1643 John Lightfoot preached before the House of Commons on the theme of "Elias Redivivus," identifying Parliament with the spirit of the prophet, for whom millennial prophecy foretold a second coming, and asserting that "Elias is a proper and pregnant pattern for Reformers."[34] Milton, in the antimonarchical pamphlets, frequently identified Ahab with Charles I and, by implication, the regicides with Elijah.[35] Elisha's ambiguous lament, "My father, my father, the chariot of Israel, and the horsemen thereof," was glossed by Bishop Joseph Hall as referring simultaneously to the visionary mode of Elijah's departure and, metaphorically, to his political role: "Certainly the view of this heavenly chariot and horses, that came for Elijah, put Elisha in mind of that chariot and horsemen which Elijah was to Israel."[36] It is this context which explains Marvell's unstated transitions between Elijah's apotheosis, his role as the "Peoples charioteer" and his responsibility for the rainstorm that, in 1 Kings 18, finally "o'rtook and wet the King." In the mood of his hypothetical elegy for Cromwell Marvell adjusts the account of Elisha's response to produce a far less positive conclusion. Elisha's grief, which causes him to tear his own clothes, should be followed by his triumphant assumption of Elijah's mantle, symbol of his inheritance of a "double portion" of the prophet's spirit. Cromwell's survivors have no such inheritance:

> *We only mourn'd our selves*, in thine Ascent,
> Whom thou hadst left beneath *with Mantle rent.*
> (ll. 219-220)

[34] John Lightfoot, *Elias Redivivus: A Sermon Preached Before the Honorable House of Commons, March 29, 1643*, p. 30.

[35] Milton, *Complete Prose Works*, III, 216, 234, 353, 365, 394, 551, 554.

[36] Hall, *Contemplations*, II, 259.

In a state where the sole ruler governs only by virtue of his unique fitness for the role, logic itself dictates that there can be no natural succession. Since Cromwell had (properly) refused the crown and its consequence, the right to found a dynasty, one hardly needed to be a prophet to foresee what would follow the Protectorate.

Like Noah's, the role of Gideon as a type was largely predetermined by a consensus of ethical and political commentary, in which he was identified as the best of the Hebrew judges, modest, moderate, without personal ambition. Arthur Jackson's *Annotations* (1646) stress his humility in threshing his own corn, and the significance of the altar building which preceded the Midian campaign: "ere Gideon might go to fight against the Midianites the enemies of God and his people, he was enjoyned to set on foot the reformation of Religion, and the extirpation of superstition and idolatry."[37] The most important evidence of Gideon's character was his rejection of the crown of Israel, later to be acquired by his illegitimate descendant Abimelech, his political opposite in every way. For Bishop Hall, there was "no greater example of modesty" than Gideon's refusal of kingship,[38] and Jackson's commentary draws out the religious significance of the judges' rule: "he judged Israel unto his dying day, but it was . . . the regall power, which they proffered, and he now refused . . . because the accepting of this would have been in a manner of taking of the government out of God's hand."[39] After the deposition of Charles I, the virtues of Gideon had taken on a new relevance for Commonwealth theorists. In Milton's *First Defence* of the regicides, Gideon exemplified the superiority of the Jewish commonwealth under the Judges to the later monarchy, and his refusal of the crown taught "that it was not fit for any man, but for God alone, to rule over men."[40] John Cook applied the epi-

[37] Arthur Jackson, *Annotations upon the remaining Historical Part of the Old Testament* (London, 1643-1646), II, 127.

[38] Hall, *Contemplations*, II, 313.    [39] Jackson, *Annotations*, II, 137.

[40] Milton, *Complete Prose Works*, IV, i, 370.

85

sode to his thesis that "hereditary Kingdomes have no foot-step in Scripture," and appealed to his "miserably deluded and discontented Countrey-men" to apply to themselves the parable of Jotham: "undoubtedly whoever shall by plots and conspiracies endeavour to introduce any of Abimelech's race or conditions to be King of England, Ireland or Scotland, or act anything against the late statute for the abolishing of kingly power shall perish by the sword of Justice. . . . The Lord grant . . . that the Parliament may give us every day more and more of the fatnes of the Olive, the peace bringing Olive quicke, cheape, and sure Justice, which can onely make peace and harmony in a Commonwealth."[41] It is clear that Marvell accepted the general direction of this tradition in his reminder that Cromwell, like Gideon, "would not be Lord, nor yet his Son" and, like his namesake, the "Olive" of Jotham's parable, had refused the crown in 1652. At the same time he exploited both the ambivalence of biblical heroism and the ambiguity of fable. As with Noah, he fastened on the one episode in Gideon's career which seemed to require apology, his revenge on the elders of Succoth and Penuel for refusing his army provisions; this stands in the poem for the dissolution by force of the Long Parliament. Bishop Hall, who found Gideon's revenge extremely painful to contemplate, justified it in terms which bring out its relevance to an army leader faced with a recalcitrant group of legislators: "Well might he challenge bread, where he gave liberty and life. It is hard, if those which fight the wars of God, may not have necessary relief."[42] But Marvell, declining apology, presents the problem nakedly. Cromwell "on the Peace extends a Warlike power" because that is his solution to the conflict of authority. Marvell likewise adjusts the parable of Jotham to create a more assertive Olive, one which itself puts down "Th' ambitious Shrubs" of the Leveller party. Between the old tyranny of kingship and the new tyranny of mindless egali-

[41] John Cook, *Monarchy No creature of God's making* (Waterford, Ireland, 1651), pp. 20-21.
[42] Hall, *Contemplations*, ii, 308.

tarianism lies the problematic realm of Christian justice and, if the duties of the Christian magistrate include the solidification of authority, it is implicit in Marvell's allusion to Succoth and Penuel that he wished it could have been otherwise.

Perhaps the most interesting piece of scriptural rewriting, however, occurs in Marvell's treatment of the "holy oracles" of Revelations 17 and 19, with their supporting texts from Daniel and the second Psalm. These prophecies had come in handy for Milton in *Eikonoklastes*, where with little adjustment they had authorized his attack on monarchy in general: " 'To bind thir Kings in Chaines, and thir Nobles with links of Iron,' is an honour belonging to his Saints; . . . and first to overcome those European Kings, which receive thir power, not from God, but from the Beast; and are counted no better than his ten hornes. 'These shall hate the great Whore,' and yet 'shall give their Kingdoms to the Beast that carries her.' . . . Thus shall they be . . . doubtfull and ambiguous in all thir doings, untill at last, 'joyning thir Armies with the Beast' . . . they shall perish with him by the 'King of Kings.' . . . This is thir doom writt'n, . . . and the utmost that we find concerning them in these latter days."[43] However, the small contradiction in Revelations 17:16, which Milton disposes of as "doubtfull and ambiguous . . . doings," becomes for Marvell the basis of an appeal for reformation, the possibility that Cromwell may change the shape of the future without the necessity for force. The "Unhappy Princes" of Europe are urged to "Kiss the approaching, *nor yet angry Son*," and to follow Cromwell's lead toward a peaceful European Reformation. With the threats of the Apocalypse thus modified by the counsel of Psalm 2, the poet anticipates a personal role in this less destructive millennium:

> If gracious Heaven to my Life give length,
> Leisure to Time, and to my Weakness Strength,

---

[43] Milton, *Complete Prose Works*, III, 598-599.

> Then shall I once with graver Accents shake
> Your Regal sloth, and your long Slumbers wake:
>
> (ll. 119-122)

Within the temporal boundaries of the *Anniversary*, however, the ultimate Christian epic remains a hypothesis only.
Between "the latter Dayes" and the moment lies the cloud
of human imperception, which restricts the poet to Cromwell's actual but solitary heroism. Even the committed must
operate on trust, rather than knowledge ("And well he
therefore does, and well has *guest*, / Who in his Age has
always forward prest"), but the majority are not committed
at all:

> . . . Men alas, as if they nothing car'd,
> Look on, all unconcern'd, or unprepar'd;
> And Stars still fall, and still the Dragons Tail
> Swinges the Volumes of its horrid Flail.
>
> (ll. 149-152)

The echo of Milton's *Nativity Ode* is not an accident, for
it serves as a footnote, acknowledging a strategic debt. The
hypothesis of an immediate millennium which is immediately withdrawn is central to Milton's conception of the
birth of Christ, which only initiates, not subverts, the course
of Christian history. In both poems the canceled fictions
underline the problem of wishful thinking, and serve to
distinguish prophecy from fantasy.

The "Unhappy Princes" of seventeenth-century Europe
were, in fact, to make a final appearance in the *First Anniversary*, in a speech which reveals how far they were from
any immediate hopes of reformation. This much expanded
version of the "praise even by enemies" provides a hostile
validation of all the poem's major themes:

> That one Man still, although but nam'd, alarms
> More then all Men, all Navies, and all Arms.
> . . .
> He Secrecy with Number hath inchas'd,

88

Courage with Age, Maturity with Hast:
The Valiants Terror, Riddle of the Wise;
And still his Fauchion all our Knots unties.
Where did he learn those Arts that cost us dear?
Where below Earth, or where above the Sphere?
He seems a King by long Succession born,
And yet the same to be a King does scorn.
Abroad a King he seems, and something more,
At Home a Subject on the equal Floor.
O could I once him with our Title see,
So should I hope yet he might Dye as wee.
But let them write his Praise that love him best,
It grieves me sore to have thus much confest.

(ll. 375-393)

Their recognition that Cromwell, "although but nam'd, alarms" more than all ordinary military threats is the enemy version of inexpressible admiration: "'Tis to commend . . . but to name." Their half-endorsed proposal that he possesses supernatural powers is the foreign equivalent of idolatrous royalist panegyric. Their attempt to define the contradiction between his domestic humility, as "Subject on the equal Floor" and his unquestioned superiority to themselves recalls the earlier paradox of what it means to be "greater . . . Then ought below, or yet above a King," and they vainly hope to see him accept their own title which, by implying mortality, would relieve their superstitious fears. The "Praise . . . best/confest" structure, which directly connects them to the conquered Irish of the *Horatian Ode*, serves also to underline the limitations of this later inverted praise. The Irish could, against their own interest, provide a simple affirmation of Cromwell's goodness and justice; but the kings of Europe can only offer inadequate standards of measurement, questions, and paradoxes. Cromwell's enemies may have provided a more objective evaluation of their great opponent than Cromwell's poet has been able to achieve; but neither, finally, has succeeded in controlling the subject:

Pardon, great Prince, if thus their Fear or Spight
More then our Love and Duty do thee Right.
I yield, nor further will the Prize contend;
So that we both alike may miss our End:
Whilst thou thy venerable Head dost raise
As far above their Malice as my Praise.

The poem can only end by reminding the audience of its title and, therefore, that other anniversaries will present new opportunities for evaluation.

If the first (and only) *Anniversary* for Cromwell questions its success in defining the unique, *A Poem upon the Death of O. C.* seems to sound a deliberate retreat. Far from adjusting or arguing with conventions, Marvell seems to have fallen back into one of the best defined and most luxurious, the classical *epicedion* with its well-marked topoi. A simple chronology presents the prior circumstances and causes of Cromwell's death (his grief for his daughter), the natural and supernatural portents, the date (coincidentally that of the battle of Dunbar), and the response of his survivors. To them is given the task of enumerating his cardinal virtues (ll. 179-226) as modified by a Christian–Stoical tradition; and giving the lament of what is "no more" (ll. 228-246) in language imitative both of Virgil's description of the heroic underworld[44] and Milton's pastoral elegy for Lycidas/King.[45] The poem concludes with three different but equally conventional passages of *consolatio*: Cromwell's immortality in the imagination and "martiall Verse" of "th' English Souldier"; a Christian heaven for Cromwell himself, where he can meet face to face the biblical types (Moses, Joshua, and David) he now resembles; and a political rein-

[44] Compare the lament of Cromwell's "survivors" that "All, all is gone of ours or his delight / In horses fierce, wild deer, or armour bright" (ll. 243-244) with *Aeneid* vi, 653-655: "Quae gratia currum / Armorumque fuit vivis, quae cura nitentes / Pascere equos, eadem sequitur tellitur repartos."

[45] Compare the repetition of "thou art gone" in the *Elegy*, ll. 299-304, with that in *Lycidas*, ll. 37-38.

carnation in his successor, for "Richard yet, where his great parent led,/Beats on the rugged track" (ll. 305-306). Our after-knowledge of Richard's inadequacies as a solution to the constitutional problem perhaps distorts our view of the last lines and makes them seem unduly fatuous; but Marvell has made no effort here to distinguish himself from conventional idiom at its most obvious.

What are we to make of this apparent collapse of critical intelligence into the swaddling bands of convention? The poem has been largely dismissed by both schools of criticism on the grounds of the same assumption, that Marvell's devotion to Cromwell had by this time become the dominant motive. The literary critic, as represented by Legouis, compares the *Elegy* unfavorably to the hard formalism of the *Ode*, and discovers to its credit only pathos;[46] the political analyst is likely to grant it only a personal status, which does not justify a major evaluation.[47] But there is no need to assume that Marvell was unable to write a public poem on Cromwell's death because a political force had become a friend, nor that feeling is incompatible with speculation. There is evidence in the *Elegy* that Marvell found Cromwell's death as *significant* as his rule, and that the conventionality of his response was a deliberate response to his understanding of it. A remarkable series of echoes link the *Horatian Ode*, the *Anniversary*, and the *Elegy* in a sequence of argument which prevents a merely sentimental reading of the latter.

In all the attention given to Marvell's use of Lucan in the *Ode*, nobody seems to have noticed that the famous passage describing Caesar as lightning is preceded by a description of Pompey as a majestic but decayed oak. In Thomas May's translation, firmly established as the source of many phrases and attitudes in the *Ode*, the passage reads:

[46] Legouis, *André Marvell*, p. 215.
[47] Wallace, *Destiny his Choice*, p. 143. An exception to these generalizations is Friedman's sensitive and judicious reading (*Marvell's Pastoral Art*, pp. 285-290).

> one in yeares was growne,
> And long accustomde to a peacefull gowne
> Had now forgot the Souldier: . . .
> . . . new strength he sought not out,
> Relying on his ancient fortunes fame,
> And stood the shadow of a glorious name.
> As an old lofty Oake, that heretofore
> Great Conquerours spoiles, and sacred Trophyes bore,
> Stands firme by his owne weight, his roote now dead,
> And through the Aire his naked boughes does spread,
> And with his trunke, not leaves, a shadow makes:
> Hee though each blast of Easterne winde him shakes,
> And round about well rooted Trees doe grow,
> Is onely honour'd;[48]

It seems clear that Marvell had this passage close at hand when, after an opening which emphasizes the peacefulness of Cromwell's last years, he describes his appearance in death:

> Yet dwelt that greatnesse in his shape decay'd,
> That still though dead, greater than death he lay'd;
> . . .
>
> Not much unlike the sacred oak, which shoots
> To Heav'n its branches, and through earth its roots:
> Whose spacious boughs are hung with trophies round,
> And honour'd wreaths have oft the victour crown'd.
> When angry Jove darts lightning through the aire,
> At mortalls sins, nor his own plant will spare;
> (It groanes, and bruises all below that stood
> So many yeares the shelter of the wood.)
>
> (ll. 257-268)

Marvell has here combined the Pompeian oak, honored but decayed, with the Caesarian lightning to give a double resonance to Cromwell's death. Once the lightning himself,

---

[48] Thomas May, *Lucan's Pharsalia . . . The whole ten Bookes* (London, 1627), A3.

blasting Caesar's head through his laurels, Cromwell has now become subject to the natural cycles of change and vulnerable to Jove's bolt. Even the phrase "nor his own plant will spare" derives from Lucan's subsequent description of the Caesarian lightning ("Not Joves own Temple spares it"), which not only helps to substantiate the source but emphasizes the deliberate synthesis which Marvell's allusions achieve.

The *Elegy*, then, returns via Lucan to a concept of time and history essentially repetitive, a view denied by the *Anniversary* in its attempt to grapple with the man of the moment. While it corrects the perspective of the *Anniversary*, this passage also uses the fallen oak to expand and support one of the *Anniversary*'s major theoretical positions:

> The tree ere while foreshortned to our view,
> When fall'n shews taller yet than as it grew:
> So shall his praise to after times encrease,
> When truth shall be allow'd, and faction cease,
> And his own shadows with him fall; the eye
> Detracts from objects than itself more high:
> But when death takes them from that envy'd seate,
> Seeing how little, we confess how greate.[49]
>
> (ll. 269-276)

The point of the hypothetical elegy in the *Anniversary* is that epideictic cannot function properly in the view of the moment; truth and modesty of evaluation depend on the perspective of death and, by extension, the only poem which can be both occasional and a true "praise" is the funeral elegy. In the real *Elegy*, Marvell's image of the tree provides graphic expansion of this previously elliptical statement. The fallen tree and the finished career can be accurately measured; the foreshortening produced during a great man's life by irrelevant emotions of envy and political prejudice disappears when he is leveled by the common fate

[49] I have taken the liberty of altering Margoliouth's punctuation in the last line, since his version obscured the paradox.

93

of humanity; and the traditional generosity of statements about the dead is revealed, paradoxically, as truly historical objectivity.

Cromwell's submission to natural law, the end of his unique trajectory, the final speed trap, allows him, in the *Elegy*, to appear as a figure no longer antipathetic to Charles. His "last Act" recalls the "Royal Actor" of the "Tragick Scaffold." Action gives way to "gentle Passions." His military victories are expressed as the victories of prayer. Awkward questions likely to be raised with respect to the cardinal virtues are resolved by the substitution of Friendship for Justice; while the fusion of military and spiritual values permits Cromwell to find a place, however preeminent, in the structure of Christian legend. A simple out-doing topos defines an intelligibly active/passive hero:

> Whose greater Truths obscure the Fables old,
> Whether of British Saints or Worthy's told;
> And in a valour less'ning Arthur's deeds,
> For Holyness the Confessor exceeds.
>
> (ll. 175-178)

None of this makes the return to convention intrinsically better, of course. The *Elegy* competes effectively neither with the strenuous mental activity of the earlier Cromwell poems nor with the voluptuous emotional activity of an elegy, like *Lycidas*, written to explore the meaning of grief. But the return to conservatism in form is at least strategic, the result of a decision to reabsorb Cromwell into the known patterns of human experience. It looks forward to the constructive conservatism of the *Rehearsal Transpros'd*, where Marvell could celebrate, as the next cycle, "his present Majesties happy Restauration." Nor did that later conviction that "all things happen in their best and proper time, without any need of our officiousness" (p. 135) imply the rejection of Cromwell's phenomenal activity, since that had already been absorbed into a formal pattern of interdependent modes of experience.

94

## THE FAIRFAX POEMS

If the last phase of Cromwell's career allowed Marvell to admit the contemplative virtues, and so soften the edges of his occasionally brutal profile, the retirement of the Lord General Fairfax at the height of his career offered, it would seem, a better occasion. Despite general recognition that a few stanzas of *Upon Appleton House* politely rebuked Fairfax for his desertion of England's garden for his own flowerbeds, the praiseworthiness of the retired life *per se* has not been questioned; and even the discovery of suspicious behavior at Nunappleton (by the nuns and the poet) has not reflected badly on Fairfax himself. Marvell's obvious interest in the dialectical interplay of doing and knowing, valor and holiness, books and weapons, would seem to guarantee Fairfax as great, if not greater, honor than Cromwell.

Even at the dialectical level, though, a shadow of doubt appears. The famous interlocking couplets from the *Horatian Ode* and *Upon Appleton House* require the two types of praise to be considered together:

> So restless Cromwel could not cease
> In the inglorious Arts of Peace

points to the matching description of Fairfax:

> Who, when retired here to Peace,
> His warlike Studies could not cease;

and the movement from "private Gardens" to public service, from public service to private gardens, completes the chiasmus. The mental configuration is marginally weighted in Cromwell's favor: "inglorious" is never canceled; and in the context of Fairfax's flowery playground, it never can be. We, if not Marvell's audience, are uncomfortably aware of the resemblance between the Lord General's "warlike Studies" and those of Uncle Toby.

Beyond this, contemporary documents betray the possibility that Fairfax's retirement, as much as Cromwell's government, was open to interpretation in a distinctly unfavorable light. Rumors that Lady Fairfax made all her husband's decisions (off the battlefield) centered on the fact that his refusal to participate in the king's trial at Westminster was announced in his absence, from the gallery, by herself.[50] His apparent inaction between Charles's trial and execution gave rise to another discreditable legend, that he had been kept foolishly praying with Colonel Harrison, on Cromwell's instructions, until the execution was over, thereby losing his chance for a last-minute rescue.[51] These rumors point in caricature to an interpretation of Fairfax as politically indecisive and not exactly acute. Clarendon remarked, in his definitive manner, upon "the drowsy, dull Presbyterian humour of Fairfax; who wished nothing that Cromwell did, and yet contributed to bring it all to pass."[52] Richard Baxter's portrait is the more revealing for being intended as praise. Chosen to command the army, "because they supposed to find him a Man of no quickness of Parts, of no Elocution, of no suspicious plotting Wit, and therefore One that Cromwell could make use of at his pleasure," Fairfax was "acceptable to sober men, because he was Religious, Faithful, Valiant, and of a grave, sober resolved Disposition; very fit for Execution, and neither too great nor too Cunning to be Commanded by the Parliament."[53] Whoever wrote the royalist elegy for Francis Villiers (sometimes attributed to Marvell) shared this view, and maliciously looked forward in 1648 to the death of "long-deceived Fairfax." Mildmay Fane, Earl of Westmoreland, regarded

[50] C. R. Markham, *A Life of the Great Lord Fairfax* (London, 1870), p. 349.

[51] As recorded in Richard Perinchieffe's *Life and Death of Charles-the First* (London, 1693), pp. 219-220. Markham (p. 351) rejected this story partly on the grounds that it represented Fairfax as a "born idiot."

[52] Edward Hyde, Earl of Clarendon, *The History of the Rebellion and Civil Wars in England* (Oxford, 1702-1704), II, 66.

[53] Richard Baxter, *Reliquiae Baxterianae* (London, 1696), I, 48.

his brother-in-law's resignation as a quarrel between thieves, a selfish exchange of positions between those "whose Fayths amount / Unto an Exchequer account / Where figures their owne places fill / And Cifers remain Cifers still."[54]

Perhaps the most revealing testimony of all is contained in Fairfax's own commonplace book, which contains a poetical comment on the regicide:

> Oh Lett that Day from time be blotted quitt
> And lett beleefe of't in next Age be waved
> In deeper silence th'Act Concealed might
> Soe that the King-doms Credit might be save'd
> But if the Power devine permited this
> His Will's the Law and we must acquiesse.[55]

Beside such dreary religious passivity, Marvell's *Horatian Ode*, for all its strategic compromises, appears a model of resolution and, worse still, Fairfax's lack of control over the political situation was clearly accompanied by total helplessness in the face of English syntax. It was the author of this poem, and the owner of this ambiguous reputation, whom Marvell set out to praise; and many of the peculiarities of the Fairfax poems become, on inspection, less peculiar when related to epideictic strategy, necessary maneuvers in the art of speaking well without stretching the truth.

The three estate poems, *Epigramma in Duos montes*, *Upon the Hill and Grove at Bill-borow*, and *Upon Appleton House* represent three apparently successive attempts to exploit a *sylva* technique, to praise a person indirectly through

---

[54] "Upon the Generall the Lord Fairfax resigning up his commission to Oliver Crumwell," in "Fugitive Poetry," Harvard MS, Eng. 645, fo. 89. See the article by Eleanor Withington, who discovered the manuscript of "Fugitive Poetry" in the Houghton Library at Harvard, "Mildmay Fane's Political Satire," *Harvard Library Bulletin* 11 (1957), 60-61: "To Fane . . . Fairfax in retirement was a cold, niggardly opportunist unwilling to settle the state by joining or routing the regicides but trying by his very aloofness to reserve through his one child the real balance of power."

[55] Bodleian MS, Fairfax 40, p. 600.

the praise of something which belongs to him, which reflects his own personality. From all three poems Fairfax himself is absent, as he had absented himself from the political process; and at the same time Marvell explores the rhetorical notion of modesty, until it becomes the center of his method, the key to Fairfax's nature. As a larger embodiment of the temperament of the anonymous lady who declined courtship, Fairfax has shown the kind of "Courage" which "its own Praises flies," as the poet explains to the trees in Bilborough Grove; and the development of this topos justifies, ultimately, all kinds of silences. If the man of conscience, letters, and wisdom does not appear in these poems, the modesty topos protects us from the inference that he does not exist; and by this happy notion Marvell himself is protected from affirming qualities of which, perhaps, he might have had some doubt.

The *Epigramma in Duos montes* is, it must be admitted, an unsuccessful experiment. Marvell had apparently decided to draw attention to the surprising aspect of Fairfax's resignation, which is presented as the result of a split personality, the diversity of Nature joined under one master: "Dissimilis Domino coiit Natura sub uno." A harsh military and a mild, retired Fairfax are to be understood in terms of Amos Cliff and Bilborough Hill, a Gothic and an Augustan landscape, both of which imply stature. The two sets of classical allusions and contrasting adjectives do not, however, produce a logical opposition, still less *discordia concors*. Fairfax's cliffside may reasonably be compared to public-spirited Atlas or even the ambitious Titans piling Pelion on Ossa, but his hillside invokes images of nymphs along with Herculean shoulders, and a rather inappropriate string of feminine characteristics: "Acclivis, placidus, mollis, amoenus hic est." ("This is sloping, gentle, soft, and pleasing.") These errors of tact and procedure were noticeably corrected in the English version, *Upon the Hill and Grove at Bill-borow*, which in no way could be described as a translation. Not only do the overt classical allusions disappear, and with them their inappropriateness; but the feminine component of mildness has been carefully rescued and put in a happier form. Explained and domesticated, it appears as the influence on Fairfax of "Vera the Nymph that him inspir'd," a neat defense of both lord and lady against the charge of henpecking. Most importantly, the Gothic cliff is discarded for a single landscape which can represent both halves of Fairfax's personality without discontinuity:

> See how the arched Earth does here
> Rise in a perfect Hemisphere!
> The stiffest Compass could not strike
> A Line more circular and like;
> Nor softest Pensel draw a Brow
> So equal as this Hill does bow.
> It seems as for a Model laid,
> And that the World by it was made.

Since a smoothly rounded hill imitates the upper curve of Fortune's Wheel, Marvell is able to present the shape of Fairfax's career to the imagination as a "perfect Hemisphere"; while masculine and feminine types of draughtsmanship, "stiffest Compass" and "softest Pensel," mathematics and portraiture, signify the joint control which husband and wife exercise over that career, in imitation of the Great Draughtsman. The precise gradient of this modest curve is further defined by moral paradox; the hill ascends courteously, and "all the way it rises bends." Even on the way up the career is governed by unselfish aspiration for others.

The cliff, of course, is not discarded completely from the English poem, but appears now as the image of other, less modest men:

> Here learn ye Mountains more unjust,
> Which to abrupter greatness thrust,
> That do with your hook-shoulder'd height
> The Earth deform and Heaven fright,

For whose excrescence ill design'd,
Nature must a new Center find,
Learn here those humble steps to tread,
Which to securer Glory lead.

With considerable daring Marvell here recalls the opening definition of Cromwell in the *Horatian Ode*, to which
this stanza is a partial answer. There, also, verbs of violent
action required massive adjustment in the scheme of things,
and the criticism here of the "unjust" mountain is also a
criticism of Cromwell's "climbe/To ruine the great Work
of Time." But lest we too readily assume that the hill's
"securer Glory" refutes the earlier reference to the "inglorious Arts of Peace," the Bilborough landscape also recalls Cromwell's achievements in the service of the Commonwealth. At the completion of the Irish campaign, Victory allegorically "plumes" Cromwell's "crest"; Fairfax's
victories may now be represented only by anthropomor-
phic substitution:

Upon its crest this Mountain grave
A Plume[56] of aged Trees does wave.

Cromwell's praise, though withheld by the poet, was af-
firmed by the conquered Irish: Fairfax's can only be spoken
by the living oak trees which must now replace "all the
Civick Garlands due" to his military greatness.

The ambivalence of Fairfax's resignation, which had been
smoothed away in the opening stanzas, and reactivated in
the implied dialogue with the *Horatian Ode*, is finally countered by a new hypothesis. Fairfax does not wish to be reminded of his glorious past. Even the "modest Whispers"
of his own trees, and their strategy of presenting military
achievements in pastoral language ("Through Groves of
Pikes he thunder'd then, / And Mountains rais'd of dying
Men") are an offense to the absolute modesty of his retirement. The bold definition of a "Courage [which] its own

[56] In view of the anthropomorphism of this poem, "Plume" seems
more appropriate an emendation than Margoliouth's conjectural
"Plump."

100

Praises flies" defeats the charge of cowardice by trapping
it in paradox; and the syntactical control which Fairfax himself so sadly lacked compels us to experience the form, if
not the substance, of reconciliation:

> Nor he the Hills without the Groves,
> Nor Height but with Retirement loves.

In *Upon Appleton House* Marvell's concern is not to im-
pose symmetry on Fairfax's career, but rather to locate its
downward curve among traditionally sanctioned forms of
retreat. It has long been recognized that in its stress on the
"sober Frame" and unpretentious architecture of Appleton
House the poem belongs among modest estate poems de-
riving from Martial and Horace, as opposed to the Statian
celebration of conspicuous consumption.[57] In its classical
and neoclassical forms this genre has been succinctly described as depending, both for its images and its sanction, on
"the wholesome moderation of rural living, the possibility
of contentment with a small, choice acquaintance, and on
the continuation of familial and cultural traditions in a place
and manner untouched by the shifting fads of the city."[58]
This neoclassical context of Appleton House is further re-
inforced by allusions to Aeneas' stooping to enter Evander's
world, and to Romulus' "bee-like cell." But Casimire Sarbiewski and his translators had already gone beyond neoclassi-
cism to supply an explicitly Christianized version of *otium*,
replacing the "beatus ille" of Horace's second epode with
the "beatior ille" of contemporary Christian Stoicism.[59]
Marvell, whose patron had cited his conscience as the

[57] By M-S. Røstvig, *The Happy Man: Studies in the Metamorphoses of a classical ideal. 1600–1708* (Oslo, 1954), p. 90; G. R. Hib-
bard, "The Country House Poem of the Seventeenth Century,"
*JWCI* 19 (1956), 159-174; J. B. Leishman, *The Art of Marvell's Poetry* (London, 1966), pp. 253-260; Wallace, *Destiny his Choice*, pp.
239-242; and Friedman, *Marvell's Pastoral Art*, pp. 210-214.

[58] Friedman, *Marvell's Pastoral Art*, p. 213.

[59] Røstvig, *The Happy Man*, pp. 126-139; and see also her introduction to George Hill's translation, *The Odes of Casimire* (1646),
*Augustan Reprints* 44 (Los Angeles, 1953), i-iv.

ground for his resignation, clearly required a religious context for his praise; but only a few readers have found *Upon
Appleton House* to behave as a religious poem should.

Marvell's reference to Fairfax's act of conscience actually
occurs at the structural center of the poem, but it does not
seem to be the center of attention. It is, perhaps, a Christian
version of a modesty topos, quietly asserting a sanction we
might have assumed. Instead of the "Courage [which] its
own Praises flies," *Upon Appleton House* celebrates the
"prickling leaf" of Conscience, which by definition cannot
be celebrated, "which shrinks at ev'ry touch" of human inquiry. For the solution of paradox Marvell now substitutes
transcendence, the mortal leaf merely signifying the existence of "Flowrs eternal, and divine, / That in the Crowns
of Saints do shine" (ll. 355-360). As in all acts of transcendence, something must be left below; in the approach to
the abstract and the absolute Fairfax has abandoned the political garden he might have cultivated. The formulaic division of responsibility, "had it pleased him and God,"
matches Marvell's earlier statement in the *Horatian Ode*
that one does not "blame" a Providential force; but his note
of regret in this passage is considerably stronger than anything in the *Ode* ("Unhappy! shall we never more . . .") and
overpowers the sense of sanction. Although it may seem
perverse to argue from negative evidence, one wonders why
there is no positive paradigm of spiritual fortitude or self-
sacrifice; and why there is not even any mention of Fairfax's stated motives for resigning, his unwillingness to fight
an "unjust" war against the Scots.

On either side of this undemonstrative center are two
vast blocks of material from which the value of Fairfax's
state may be inferred only indirectly; the 25-stanza "digression" on the convent that once occupied the estate and
threatened the genealogy of the Fairfax family; and the 35
stanzas during which the poet-tutor usurps his patron's
function as the contemplative man. Marvell's anticonventual

satire is, of course, an easily recognizable example of praise by contraries. The rhetoric, the sensuality, the self-indulgence of the "Suttle Nunns" who practice idolatry and goodness knows what else must invite both categorization and destruction. For all its absurd fiction, we welcome William Fairfax's rescue of Isabella Thwaites because it romanticizes the dissolution of the monasteries, and the building of Nunappleton, like dozens of other Elizabethan and Stuart mansions, from historically venerable stones. The conclusion, when it comes ("Twas no Religious House till now") is almost pat. At the same time the nun's speech identifies itself as a type of poetry, the "sucreries dévotes" of a highly affective and feminized devotion which had developed under the influence of the Pléiade in France.[60] The nun's definition of their "doux-coulant" style of contemplation is expressed, significantly, in terms of jam making:

> Here Pleasure Piety doth meet;
> One perfecting the other Sweet.
> So through the mortal fruit we boyl
> The Sugars uncorrupting Oyl:
>                          (ll. 171-174)

On the other side of Fairfax lies another Continental attitude to contemplation: the equally self-indulgent, if not actually *libertin*, "solitude" poems of Théophile and St. Amant, defined by the undirected play of ideas over a natural environment. Even in *Le Contemplateur*, which ends in a religious vision of the end of the world, St. Amant *s'amuse*. Like the subject of *Le Contemplateur*, but more ostentatiously, the poet-tutor conjures out of the landscape an irresponsible mixture of analogues, and refuses to limit himself to images proper to the meditative state. Like Fairfax, he plays at making mental warfare, perceiving the mowing as a "Massacre" of grass, the accidental death of

[60] See Terence C. Cave, *Devotional Poetry in France, c. 1570–1613* (Cambridge, 1969), pp. 244-266.

the rail as an argument *against* the pastoral ethos, since "Lowness is unsafe as Hight," the call of the other frightened birds as "Death-Trumpets" at a military funeral, and the hayfield itself "A Camp of Battail newly fought . . . quilted ore with Bodies slain." This frivolity of the imagination is the exact echo of Fairfax's, who "when retired here to Peace,/His warlike Studies could not cease," and therefore laid his "Gardens out *in sport*" as a military fortress. Biblical images, a more appropriate component of contemplative process, are forced to compete with "Alexander's sweat," "Roman camps," and "bloody Thestylis," whose name may derive from Virgil's second Eclogue, but whose role has been distorted by the tutor's militant classicism. Ironically, it is the brutal literalism of Thestylis which first alerts us to this overly casual use of scripture. Snatching up the injured rail, she cries:

> he call'd us Israelites;
> But now, *to make his saying true*,
> Rails rain for Quails, for Manna Dew.
> (ll. 406-408)

In the woods, the idea of the Ark has no more authority for the poet than that of a pagan temple, whose "Corinthean Porticoes" grow in as "loose an order" as his mental images; and the misuse of Noah, first Carpenter, type of the active and regenerative life, contrasts with the *First Anniversary*, where even the patriarch's errors serve as metaphors for Cromwell's statesmanship. In the undiscriminating intellect, "What Rome, Greece, Palestine, ere said" is reduced to a single "light Mosaick." Similarly, St. Amant's emphasis on the pleasures of solitude is caricatured as a fully libertine sensuality and laziness. "Languishing with ease," "On Pallets swoln of Velvet Moss," the "easie Philosopher" merely thinks he is thinking. His claims to universal knowledge and penetration of "Natures mystick Book," sometimes taken so gravely, exaggerate to the point of folly St. Amant's already dubious claims:

> Tantost faisant agir mes sens
> Sur des sujets de moindre estoffe,
> De marche en autre je descens
> Dans les termes du Philosofe:
> Nature n'a point de secret
> Que d'un soin libre, mais discret,
> Ma curiosité ne sonde,
> Ses cabinets me sont ouvers,
> Et dans ma recherche profonde
> Ie loge en moy tout l'Univers.[61]

The solipsism of this condition is further admitted in the stanza which contains Marvell's best-known echo of St. Amant. The river which has, like the tutor's serpentine mind, wound its "wanton harmless folds" throughout the estate, turns again and becomes a "Chrystal Mirrour slick":

> Where all things gaze themselves, and doubt
> If they be in it or without.
> And for his shade which therein shines,
> Narcissus like, the Sun too pines.
>
> (ll. 637-640)

Marvell has *added* the reminder of Narcissus, and so transformed St. Amant's conceit[62] into another admission of

[61] St. Amant, *Le Contemplateur*, in *Oeuvres* (Rouen, 1638), pp. 18-19: "Meanwhile, agitating my senses on subjects of lesser substance I descend progressively into philosophical terms; Nature has no secret which, with generous but careful attention, my curiosity cannot fathom. Her cabinets are open to me, and in my profound research I contain within myself the entire Universe."

[62] St. Amant, *La Solitude*, p. 12:

> Le Soleil s'y fait si bien voir,
> Y contemplant son beau visage.
> Qu'on est quelque temps a scavoir
> Si c'est luy mesme, ou son image.

("The sun can there so well be seen, contemplating his fair face, that it takes some time to be sure whether it is himself or his image [in the water].") By contrast, Fairfax's translation (Bodleian MS, Fairfax 40, pp. 562-563) is entirely literal.

error. Both the poet-tutor and his model have "mistook" the purpose of solitude, and degraded genuine contemplation of Nature into imaginative self-regard.[63]

If Fairfax's retreat is to be understood in contrast to these false contemplatives, the responsibility for defining it is left entirely with the reader, who was presumably Fairfax himself. What is strikingly missing from *Upon Appleton House* is the sober figure of Protestant contemplation, free from any Pre- or Counter-Reformation excesses, whose character had already been established in English devotional theory and poetry. Richard Baxter's *Saint's Everlasting Rest*, appearing in January 1650, a few months prior to Fairfax's resignation, had provided Puritan authorization for a new religious solitude:

> Though I would not perswade thee to Pythagoras his Cave, nor to the Hermets Wilderness, nor to the Monks Cell; yet I would advise thee to frequent solitariness, that thou mayest sometimes confer with Christ and with thy self, as well as with others. We are fled so far from the solitude of superstition, that we have cast off the solitude of contemplative devotion.

(p. 713)

Still more relevant to Fairfax's new role was the young but highly respectable tradition of Christian Stoicism grafted upon Horace, which had reached England through the translators and followers of Casimire Sarbiewski. Closest of these to Fairfax and Marvell was probably Mildmay Fane, whose *Otia Sacra* (1648) must surely have found its way

---

[63] This view of the poet-tutor is supported by M.J.K. O'Loughlin's reading of *Upon Appleton House*, "This Sober Frame," in *Andrew Marvell: A Collection of Critical Essays*, ed. G. de F. Lord (Englewood Cliffs, 1968). For O'Loughlin, the poem's "I" is "the *homo ludens* whose poetic game enacts in miniature the recreation of his patron" (p. 122), and his frivolity is particularly revealed in his wish to stand on his head, reversing the proper direction of the Platonic *arbor inversa* (p. 135).

into his brother-in-law's library despite the signs of friction in their relationship. *Otia Sacra*, previously seen as a source for parts of *Upon Appleton House*,[64] contains a perfect definition of the Protestant man of letters and conscience whom we do *not* find in Marvell's poem.

In *Otia Sacra*, the relationship between Grace and Nature is carefully articulated in pastoral terms. Book I presents an initial emblematic pillar of Faith with an appropriate Latin motto ("Deus nobis haec Otia fecit") and contains only religious verse. Book II, a secular miscellany, replaces Faith's pillar with a pastoral scene, a new semi-Virgilian epigraph ("tutus in Umbra/Silvestram tenui Musam meditatus avena")[65] and an opening proposition that "Humane Science [is] Handmaid to Divine." Both books contain poems on the art and end of contemplating Nature aright. In Book I a paraphrase of Psalm 19 (*Coeli enarrant Gloriam Dei*) offers the heavenly bodies as the primary objects of contemplation, drawing the mind upward and providing a "Lecture in Divinity"; and *Contemplatio Diurna* extends this method to other natural phenomena. In Book II Fane christens Horace's second Epode in *My happy life, to a Friend*; and *To Retiredness* sets out a complete program for the proper use of solitude:

> Here I can sit, and sitting under
> Some portions of His works of wonder,
> Whose all are such, observe by reason,

[64] See especially M. Bradbrook, "Marvell and the Poetry of Rural Solitude," *RES* 17 (1941), 37-46; her presentation of "parallels," however, points rather to the difference between Marvell's poem and Fane's.

[65] Derived from the opening lines of Virgil's first eclogue:

> Tityre, tu patulae recubans sub tegmine fagi
> Silvestrem tenui musam meditaris avena:
> . . . tu, Tityre, lentus in umbra
> formosam resonare doces Amaryllida silvas.

The Christian pastoral poet, safe under the shadow of the cross, is preserved from both the laziness and eroticism of the original.

Why every Plant obeys its season

. . .

For so my Thoughts by this retreat
Grow stronger, like contracted heat.
Whether on Nature's Book I muse
Or else some other writes on't, use
To spend the time in, every line,
Is not excentrick, but Divine;
And though all others downward tend,
These look to heaven, and ascend
From whence they came; where pointed hie,
They ravish into Mysterie,
To see the footsteps here are trod
Of mercy by a Gracious God.

(pp. 173-174)

The absence of this "beatior ille" from Marvell's poem is surely strategic. In the inferential space between the nuns and the tutor he exists as a possibility only, a possibility indicated in the crucial and warning lines:

Thrice happy he who, *not mistook*,
Hath read in Natures mystick Book.

His audience is there obliquely directed, *not* to the pursuit of "thrice-great Hermes," but to the three-fold happiness (beatus, beatior, beatissimus) which results when Stoicism, mysticism and Christianity are properly blended. Fairfax, who had himself laboriously translated St. Amant's *La Solitude*, and who had explored hermeticism, could draw his own conclusions.

There remains, of course, the last phase of the poem, where the praise of Fairfax is fulfilled in (as his estate is entailed on) his daughter. Praise of a man by his descendants is the obverse of praise by his ancestry, enlarged by the knowledge that the family virtues have been preserved by his paternal care. Mary Fairfax not only exemplifies Fairfax's "Discipline severe" but in her modesty, both natural and philosophical, must surely demonstrate his. When Nature offers her the river as a looking-glass, it immediately repents of its error, and the "Wood about her draws a Skreen" in acknowledgment that she is no Narcissus:

> For She, to higher Beauties rais'd,
> Disdains to be for lesser prais'd.
> She counts her Beauty to converse
> In all the Languages as hers;
> Nor yet in those her self imployes
> But for the Wisdome, not the Noyse;
> Nor yet that Wisdome would affect,
> But as 'tis Heavens Dialect.
>
> (ll. 705-712)

We are given in this stanza another Fairfax who flies her own praise, but in so doing begs none of the questions attached to her father's modesty. As her use of solitude is unambiguously devotional, so the force of her personality ensures that no one will ever suspect her of escapism. Shaming the poet-tutor out of his self-indulgent laziness, she acts like a military commander reviewing her slack troops. "Loose Nature, in respect/ To her, it self doth recollect." Dialectically, she belongs with Cromwell, as a figure who will leave her private gardens to fulfill her dynastic obligations; what actually happened to Mary after her reckless marriage to the Duke of Buckingham only underlines the problem of validation, the temporal and cognitive limitations of true praise in the human perspective. A consideration of "laus" in its spiritual sense is outside the present terms of reference; but it should not be forgotten that in *Musicks Empire*, also addressed to a patron who "flies the Musick of his praise," Marvell identified the alternatives to secular epideictic. In turning from evaluating "Mens Triumphs" to the unquestionable validity of "Heavens Hallelujahs," he turned, in *Bermudas*, *The Coronet*, and *On a Drop of Dew*, from the problems of classical epideictic to the problems of Protestant poetics. Cromwell himself, in Marvell's *Elegy*, was equally significant "In warre, in counsell, or in pray'r, and praise" (l. 240); and in the context of the Puritan Revolution, the two sets of problems could never be clearly separated.

## "The Painter and the Poet dare":
## Experiments in Satire

Simultaneously the most controversial and the least appreciated of his poems, Marvell's satires have been treated with various combinations of wariness and distaste. Between the continued doubt as to which satires are indisputably Marvell's, and the suppressed wish that none of them were, few critics have wasted good analysis on poems at once unauthenticated and unrewarding. Not even the *Last Instructions*, which has received most attention, and of which Margoliouth remarked that "of all the satires attributed to Marvell there is none of which one can feel less doubt" (I, 346), had its authenticity confirmed by appearance in the *Miscellaneous Poems*; even the *Last Instructions* has damaged its author's reputation for delicacy of mind and sureness of touch. Still, there have been several attempts to show that at least that poem's effects are justified by a theory of satiric decorum, and therefore witness rather to Marvell's flexibility as a writer than to the collapse of his art in political disillusionment.[1]

[1] George de F. Lord included in his invaluable edition of *Poems on Affairs of State, 1660-1678* (New Haven, 1963), I, xliv-xlvii, some suggestive remarks on the relationship between satire and panegyric, as also did Warren Chernaik, *The Poetry of Limitation* (New Haven, 1968), pp. 172-202, and Ruth Nevo, *The Dial of Virtue: A Study of Poems on Affairs of State in the Seventeenth Century* (Princeton, 1963), pp. 164-187; John M. Wallace's chapter on the *Last Instructions* in *Destiny his Choice: The Loyalism of Andrew Marvell* (Cambridge, 1968), pp. 148-183, initiated discussion of the poem's Horatian background; Earl Miner, in "The 'Poetic Picture, Painted Poetry' of *The Last Instructions to a Painter*," *MP* 63 (1966), 288-294, and Michael Gearin-Tosh, "The Structure of Marvell's *Last Instructions to a Painter*," *EIC* 22 (1972), 48-57, explored in different directions the

This chapter is a continuation of those arguments toward the inclusion and acceptance of Marvell's satirical activity in our view of his poetics. The concern with public standards which led him, in the 1649 poem to Lovelace, to reject satire as socially destructive, led him also, in the crisis of the Second Dutch War, to regard it as socially necessary. The rhetorical training which allowed him, in the 1650s, to explore the problems of political panegyric in relation to Cromwell's Protectorate, forced him, in the years following the Restoration, to parody the propagandists of Charles's government, and to shift from qualified praise to various forms of qualified blame. At the heart of both activities lie the same theoretical issues, the same questions about public iconography, the relationship between partisanship and objectivity, and the interdependence of aesthetic and political values. Though Marvell's major satires have a still more direct relationship with events than do the Protectorate poems, being apparently connected with Opposition strategy to control the Cabal and Charles himself in fiscal and foreign policy, their pragmatic focus is not their most noticeable feature. What is most striking about them is the invention of a new, highly topical medium for satire, the pictorialism which was everywhere current in the early seventeenth century, and was normally used as a vehicle for the expression of high ideals. It will be apparent from this description that this chapter has nothing to say about *Fleckno*, Marvell's first and last attempt to write Roman cultural satire in the manner of Donne, nor about the handful of ballads and squibs on which his editors agree. Its focus will be, rather, on the *Last Instructions to a Paint-*

---

relationship between satire and contemporary analogies in the visual arts (political cartoons and state paintings); Alan S. Fisher, in "The Augustan Marvell," *ELH* 38 (1971), 223-238, asserted the continuity between Marvell's lyric and satiric "states of mind"; and David Farley-Hills included a chapter on the deliberately chaotic structure of *Last Instructions* in *The Benevolence of Laughter* (London, 1974), pp. 72-98.

*er*, as a major foray into heroic satire, and on the generic program which connects to the *Last Instructions* the *Second and Third Advices to the Painter*; the result will be, inevitably, a reopening of the whole canonical question.

## THE "PAINTER" POEMS

The possibility that Marvell wrote at least some of the satirical *Advices*, under the obviously fictional name of Denham,[2] has been in the air for a long time. Aubrey's brief sketch of Marvell included the statement that "The verses called *The Advice to the Painter* were of his making," and Anthony à Wood, presumably on Aubrey's authority, described the volume entitled *Directions to a Painter*, remarking that, despite the ascription to Denham, "yet they were then thought by many to have been written by Andrew Marvell, Esq."[3] James Yonge the physician, who was in London in 1678 "in company with several parliament men," mentioned Marvell as the "author of some poems, Advice to the Paynter, Miscellany, Rehersal transposed," and showed knowledge also of *Mr. Smirke* and the *Remarks* in defense of John Howe.[4] He seemed, in other words, to be rather well informed. And Marvell's enemy Roger L'Estrange implied in his attack on the *Growth of Popery* in 1678 that at least one of the "Painter" poems could be laid at his door: "By his Vein of improving the Invective Humour, it looks in some places as if he were Transprosing the First Painter."[5]

Most important of all, as we increasingly recognize, was the testimony of Edward Thompson who, in the preface

[2] For a summary of the arguments against Denham's authorship, see Margoliouth, *The Poems and Letters of Andrew Marvell*, rev. ed., Legouis (Oxford, 1971), I, 348.

[3] Anthony à Wood, *Athenae Oxonienses* (London, 1691), II, 303.

[4] *The Journal of James Yonge*, ed. F.N.L. Poynter (London, 1963), pp. 23, 155.

[5] Sir Roger L'Estrange, *An Account of the Growth of Knavery* (London, 1678), p. 6.

to his 1776 edition of Marvell's works described how, when his three volumes were already complete, he "was politely complimented by Mr. Mathias (Marvell's grandnephew) with a manuscript volume of poems" belonging to William Popple, "being a collection of his uncle Andrew Marvell's compositions after his decease." "By this manuscript," Thompson added, "I also find, that those two excellent satires, entitled *A Direction to a Painter concerning the Dutch War in 1667*, and published in the State Poems, . . . as Sir John Denham's, are both of them compositions of Mr. Marvell; but as the work is already so largely swelled out, I shall beg leave to omit them." The acquisition by the Bodleian Library in 1945 of what is almost certainly the "Popple manuscript" (Ms. Eng. Poet. d. 49) revealed "those two excellent satires" to be the *Second* and *Third Advices*.

Margoliouth's original decision not to include any of the *Advices* in his edition, despite the comments of Aubrey, Wood, and Thompson, was based primarily on cautionary and qualitative grounds: Marvell's satirical canon was quite doubtful enough already; the *Second* and *Third Advices*, which deal with the Dutch War directly, "would be more naturally assigned to some writer who took part in the naval actions"; and he thought that a "generally consistent level of style and intelligence" linked the *Second* and *Third Advices* with the *Fourth* and *Fifth*, which Marvell certainly did not write, rather than with the *Last Instructions*, which was "more the work of a learned man" (I, 349). The discovery of the Popple manuscript did not materially alter this opinion. But it did impress George de F. Lord, who in the late 1950s argued for the inclusion of the *Second* and *Third Advices* on the grounds of provenance, and supported his case with a certain amount of internal evidence: the two *Advices* shared with the *Last Instructions* attitudes and techniques which implied a common author—consistent hostility toward the same political and court figures; a stance of deferential advice toward the king, expressed in a

separate envoy; and a similar use of mock-heroic and classical allusion, particularly to Ovid's *Metamorphoses*.[6] His suggestion, put forward tentatively enough, was rejected
acrimoniously by E. G. Fogel, again largely on qualitative
grounds, including the assertion that the authors of the *Advices* were incompetent in their handling of the "Painter"
convention, because they allowed painted figures to speak.[7]
(In anticipation of later arguments, it must be observed here
that this objection rather flies in the face of a central proposition of *ut pictura poesis*, the governing conceit of the
"Painter" poems; for incorporated into the theory of *ut
pictura poesis* was the motto of Simonides, that if painting
is mute poetry, poetry is a speaking picture, an oxymoron
which, as we shall see, was deliberately built into the structure of the *Third Advice*.)

Subsequently, an attempt was made by Brendan O Hehir
to restore to Denham authorship of the *Second Advice*, an
attempt which required a frontal attack on Lord's arguments.[8] He applied himself almost exclusively to the question
of consistency, assuming that, for all three poems to have
been written by one poet, the same persons would have had
to be mentioned in all three, and to have been subjected to
the same criticisms. This approach, while a logical response
to some of Lord's claims, seems somewhat odd in view of
the fact that the poems have clearly demarked functions,
the *Second Advice* addressing itself to the Battle of Lowestoft in June 1665, the *Third Advice* to the disastrous Four

[6] George de F. Lord, "Two New Poems by Marvell," *Bulletin of
the New York Public Library* 62 (1958), 551-570; and "Comments on
the Canonical Caveat," ibid., 63 (1959), 355-366.

[7] E. G. Fogel, "Salmons in Both, or Some Caveats for Canonical
Scholars," *Bulletin of the New York Public Library* 63 (1959), 223-
236. The Lord–Fogel controversy was reprinted in *Evidence for
Authorship: Essays on Problems of Attribution*, eds. D. V. Erdman
and E. G. Fogel (Ithaca, 1966).

[8] Brendan O Hehir, *Harmony from Discords: A Life of Sir John
Denham* (Berkeley and Los Angeles, 1968), pp. 210-229.

Days battle in June of the following year, and the *Last Instructions* to the English naval disaster at Chatham in June 1667. Further, O Hehir assumed (I think incorrectly) that the chief butts of the *Third Advice* were General George Monck and his wife, and that this would have been inconceivable to a poet as sympathetic to Monck as was Marvell in the *Last Instructions*. O Hehir made no mention of the structural feature, the separate "advice" to the king, shared by all three poems (but not by the *Fourth* and *Fifth Advices*); nor did he mention the presence of all three poems (and the absence of the *Fourth* and *Fifth Advices*) in the Popple manuscript. Finally, he put some stress on the fact that the *Second* and *Third Advices* were published together with the *Fourth* and *Fifth*, but not with the *Last Instructions*, in the volume entitled *Directions to a Painter for Describing our Naval Business* . . . and deduced from this that Marvell had no hand in the publication of this volume. He was apparently unaware of an important copy of the *Directions* volume in the Bodleian Library (Gough Ms. London 14), which is closely related to the Popple manuscript. Not only does it contain many manuscript corrections which match the Popple text but on the title page has been written the same quotation from Persius, Satire 3, that precedes the *Second Advice* in the Popple manuscript, but in no other early edition or manuscript. Beneath it, the same hand has inscribed: "London written for the Company of Poets. Anno. Dom. 1666."[9]

Finally, when Pierre Legouis published his revised version of Margoliouth's edition, he supported the original decision to exclude the *Second* and *Third Advices*, remaining unconvinced by Lord's arguments. Despite his acceptance of the

[9] The textual relationships between the Popple and Gough manuscripts and the other 1667 editions of the *Advices* are examined in detail in my bibliographical article, *The Second and Third Advices to a Painter, Publications of the Bibliographical Society of America* 71, No. 4 (1977), 473-486.

Popple manuscript as unquestionably the one described by Thompson, Legouis's edition does not reflect its textual and canonical importance. The fact that Margoliouth knew of its existence in 1952, when he himself reissued the *Poems and Letters*, is given as a precedent for the 1971 decision not to alter the canon; we should also remember that in 1952 Margoliouth *could* not have materially altered it, since without being offered a reset edition he was confined to minor revision and whatever additional material could be inserted on "spare pages" (I, vii). He had suffered, in other words, from the same spatial discouragement as had Thompson.

It would be strange indeed if the accidents of printing history were the determining factors in establishing Marvell's satirical achievement. In my own view the question is not yet settled. Those who reject Marvell's authorship of the *Second* and *Third Advices* are in disagreement or at a loss as to whose name should be supplied in his stead. Their arguments, moreover, are almost entirely from internal evidence. That being the case, it is odd that so little attention has been paid to the satiric program of *ut pictura poesis* which is the most distinctive feature of these poems. In the following pages I shall argue, *pace* Fogel, that what most noticeably connects the *Second* and *Third Advices* to the *Last Instructions*, and distinguishes all three from the other "Painter" poems, is their rather sophisticated application of *ut pictura poesis* and Renaissance aesthetic theory. In this respect, with all due deference to Margoliouth, all three poems may be seen as the work of a "learned" man or men. All three poems, moreover, manipulate the device of the Advice-to-the-Painter so as to make it peculiarly relevant to the contemporary political situation and the satirist's task. The very theme of these poems, it appears, is *advice*. The satirist's purpose is to replace the king's present advisers with other, more honest counsel, which includes his own. The final "advices" to the king present the world of ideals which *ut pictura poesis* normally conjured up, the positive conduct on Charles's part which is implied and required by the previous attacks on members of his court and privy council. This same strategy is also employed at the end of Marvell's last political statement, the *Account of the Growth of Popery and Arbitrary Government*, and in that pamphlet it is consciously related to political theory. It enacts, in fact, the constitutional fiction expressed earlier in the *Account*, that the king's person is "most sacred and inviolable," and that whatever criticism can be leveled against his regime, "nothing of them all is imputed to him . . . but his ministers only are accountable for all."[10]

This is only one of many connections between Marvell and the *Second* and *Third Advices* which result from directing one's attention to the "Painter" device. Marvell's interest in pictures and pictorial theory is, of course, well in evidence in the *Miscellaneous Poems*, in the ecphrases of *The Gallery* and the *Picture of Little T. C. in a Prospect of Flowers*, and in the lines which Marvell chose to extract from George de Brebeuf's translation of Lucan, published in 1655:

> C'est de luy que nous vient cet Art ingenieux
> De peindre la Parole, et de parler aux Yeus;
> Et, par les traits divers de figures tracées,
> Donner de la couleur et du corps aux pensées.
>
> (I, 57-58)

These lines celebrate the discovery of the alphabet, visual hieroglyphs for the expression of thought; what probably attracted Marvell to them, and inspired his own Latin re-translation, was the flavor of *ut pictura poesis* (*pingere voces*) introduced by Brebeuf. A different interest appears in the two epigrams on a portrait of Cromwell sent to Queen Christina of Sweden (I, 108), and in a related passage in the

[10] *Complete Works*, ed. A. B. Grosart (New York, 1875; reprinted 1966), IV, 249.

verse-letter to Dr. Ingelo, which records the reception by Cromwell and his associates of a reciprocal portrait:

Vidimus Effigiem, mistasque Coloribus Umbras:
Sic quoque Sceptripotens, sic quoque visa Dea.
. . .

Et, simulet falsa ni Pictor imagine Vultus,
Delia tam similis nec fuit ipsa sibi.[11]

In each of these Protectorate ecphrases there is a hint of subtle inquiry into political image making as that has become relevant to diplomatic exchange. All three poems feature the word *umbra*, which in the *Letter to Ingelo* is used technically to describe shading, but in the two epigrams on Cromwell's portrait seems rather to carry its classical meaning of imperfect copy or shadow in the Platonic sense.[12] Both epigrams stress the ambiguity of portraiture, the first describing "an image which put all his enemies to flight, / But under which citizens spend leisurely hours," the second making a similar distinction between the face Cromwell shows to most of the kings of Europe, and the more respectful "shadow" he presents to Queen Christina. The *Letter to Ingelo* takes these hints a stage further by implying the possibility of a flattering portraiture: *if* the painter has not created a false image, Christina resembles the classical goddess of chastity.

It is slightly surprising, then, to recognize in *The Character of Holland*, which may be Marvell's first political satire,[13]

[11] "We have seen her picture, shadows mixed with colours: She seemed both Queen and Goddess . . . And, unless the painter represented her features with a false image, Delia herself was not so similar to her," trans. from *The Latin Poetry of Andrew Marvell*, eds. W. A. McQueen and K. A. Rockwell (Chapel Hill, 1964), pp. 55, 57.

[12] Compare Cicero, *De Officiis* (III, xvii, 69): "veri juris germanaeque justitiae solidam et expressam effigiem nullam tenemus, umbra et imaginibus utimur."

[13] If we exclude the troublesome *Tom May's Death*, on the grounds that it was excluded from the Popple manuscript.

a poem which is based on that cheapest of jokes, the abuse of national character, particularly as that can be represented in cartoons. Marvell's poem is, in fact, an educated ecphrasis of the anti-Dutch pictorial broadsides which circulated in England during the three wars of 1652-1653, 1665-1667 and 1672-1674. Written at a time when Marvell had not yet established personal connections with Holland, the poem was probably a response to the English naval victory off Portland Bill in February 1653, and the solemn public thanksgiving ordered by Parliament on 12 April. In that context it surpasses in quality but not in taste a broadside of 1665 which carried this message above its engraved cartoon: "The Dutch Boare Dissected, or a Description of 'Hogg-Land. A Dutch man is a Lusty, Fat, two Legged Cheese-worm: A Creature that is so addicted to Eating Butter, Drinking fat Drink, and Sliding, that all the World knows him for a slippery Fellow. An Hollander is not a High-lander, but a Low-lander; for he loves to be down in the Dirt, and Boar-like to wallow therein." (See Plate 2.) Mar-vell's poem contains a similarly ungenerous interpretation of the Lowlanders' battle against the sea, the same demeaning references to cheese, butter, pickled herring, and drunken-ness, the same bad puns on "boer" and "Hoog," and the same unwarranted accusation that the Dutch could not be trusted diplomatically.

For all that, it is possible to feel the pressure of a critical intelligence struggling to emerge from this stereotypical shell. The witty poet of *Upon Appleton House*, who was only too delighted to "imbark" himself in the "yet growing Ark" of Fairfax's forest, is now prepared to reproach the Dutch for *their* loose catholicity:

> Sure when Religion did it self imbark,
> And from the East would Westward steer its Ark,
> It struck, and splitting on this unknown ground,
> Each one thence pillag'd the first piece he found:
> Hence Amsterdam, Turk-Christian-Pagan-Jew,

Staple of Sects and Mint of Schisme grew;

. . .

In vain for Catholicks our selves we bear;
The universal Church is onely there.

(ll. 67-76)

### The Dutch Boare Dissected, or a Description of HOGG-LAND.

A *Dutch* man is a Lusty, Fat, two Legged Cheese-Worm : A Creature, that is so addicted to Eating Butter, Drinking fat Drink, and Sliding, that all the VVorld knows him for a slippery Fellow. An *Hollander* is not an *High-lander*, but a *Low-lander*; for he loves to be down in the Dirt, and *Boar*-like, to wallow therein.

THe *Dutch* at first,
When at the worst,
e *English* did relieve them :
They now for thanks,
Have play'd base Pranks
'ith *Englishmen* to grieve them,
Those Spider-Imps,
As big as Shrimps,
e lively Reprefent,
How that the States
Spin out their Fates
t of their Bowels vent.
The *Indian* Ratt
That runs in at
e Mouth of Crocodile,
Eates his way through,
And shews well how
Nations they beguile.
The Monstrous Pig,
With Vipers Big,
at Seven-headed Beast,
Shews how they still,
Pay good with ill
th' *English* and the Rest.
The Vipers come
Forth of the Wombe,
ith death of their own Mother:
Such are that Nation,
A Generation,
t rise by fall of Other.
One of the Rout
Was Whipt about
e Streets for telling lyes :
More of that Nation
Serv'd in such Fashion
ght be for Forgeries.
Their Compass is
An *Holland* Cheese,
ticer a Cup of Ale-by :
The Knife points forth
Unto the North
Needle these Worms sail-by.

F   Their Quagmire Isle
    ('Iwould make one smile)
In Form lyes like a Custard :
    A Land of Bogs
    To breed up Hogs
Good Pork with *English* Mustard.
G   If any asks,
    What mean the Casks?
'Tis Brandy, that is here :
    And Pickle-Herring,
    (Without all Erring :)
'Tis neither Ale nor Beere.
H   Those Two you see,
    That yonder bee
Upon the Bog-Land Walking ;
    Are Man and Wife,
    At woful Strife
About last Night's work talking,
    He Drinks too long ;
    Shee gives him Tongue,
In Sharp hot-scolding Pickle,
    With Oyle so glib
    The same for Tib,
Her tipling man to Tickle.
    I Spin all Day,
    You Drink away
More then I get by Wheeling:
    I doesly part,
    Sayes he, Sweet Heart,
For I doe come home Reeling,
I   The *Holland* Boare,
    Hath Stock-Fish store,
As good as can be eaten :
    And such they are,
    As is their Fare,
Scarce good till soundly beaten,
K   Their State-House such is,
    It stands on Crutches,
Or Stilts, like some old Creeple:
L   Frogs in great Number
    Their Land doth Cumber,
And such-like Croaking People,

2. *The Dutch Boare Dissected*, a broadside of 1665.

The neoclassical poet appears momentarily in his allusion to what "their Carthage . . . / Would render fain unto our better Rome," and his assurance that they have never heard of the civic virtues, despite the name of their ancient hero,

Civilis, who opposed the Romans in the first century A.D. Most recognizably, too, the voice of political conscience is heard, both in the allusion to Hugo Grotius, whose *De jure belli et pacis* (1625) was itself an argument against any crudely stereotypical view of what was "Dutch," and in the conclusion of the poem. There Marvell turns, in effect, from describing the Dutch "character" to recommending, however obliquely, the direction in which he hoped the English national character would develop. The war is recognized as something like that wholesome "troubling" of the waters soon to be celebrated at the end of the *First Anniversary*:

> The Common wealth doth by its losses grow;
> And, like its own Seas, only Ebbs to flow.
> Besides that very Agitation laves,
> And purges out the corruptible waves.
>
> (ll. 131-134)

This allusion to the parliamentary inquiry which, during the winter of 1652-1653, resulted in the arrest and discharge of some of Blake's officers, is connected by its ethical pressure to the lines that urge "our Senate" not to refuse the peace terms offered by the Dutch, and to look forward *conditionally* to a healthy peace:

> For now of nothing may our State despair,
> Darling of Heaven, and of Men the Care;
> Provided that they be what they have been,
> Watchful abroad, and honest still within.

It is one of the historical ironies which have since attached themselves to this poem that the "Senate" to whom these lines were addressed was itself, in just over a week following the national celebration, purged out of existence. On 20 April 1653 Cromwell dissolved the "Rump" of the Long Parliament by force, and the following year concluded with the Dutch the peace to which that recalcitrant Parliament had refused to agree.

The other historical irony which has accrued to *The Character of Holland* is the fact that it was republished, presumably without Marvell's consent, to serve the purposes of government propagandists in both the Second and Third Dutch Wars.[14] For by the autumn of 1666 Marvell had become sufficiently disillusioned with the causes and conduct of another campaign against the United Provinces that he returned to satire, now directed against the English side. The simple-minded jingoism of *The Character of Holland*, only mildly qualified by a position akin to Cromwell's own, was replaced in the satires of the Second Dutch War by a much more complicated scheme of approval and disapproval. At the same time, the public iconography with which his first satire had had affiliations became a subject of profound scrutiny; and a coincidental appearance of "pictures" and pictorialism in the political arena provided the occasion for a major breakthrough in satiric theory and practice.

There were several elements to this coincidence, and for Marvell to have perceived their conceptual connection is powerful testimony to his sense of the moment. On the one hand, the hostilities between England and Holland continued to be expressed in part through the medium of visual propaganda. There is some evidence that this procedure had, under Cromwell, been somewhat controlled. In *Graphice*, a painter's instructional handbook published in 1658, Sir William Sanderson illustrated his remarks on the emotive force of "Picture" by recalling how it was used "to enforce a more horrid reception of the Dutch cruelty upon our English at Amboyna in the East Indies." So "monstrous" was the printed cartoon, he added, that it seemed "prudentiall" to those in power to suppress it, "lest, had it come forth in common, [it] might have incited us then (1653), to a rationall quarrell and revenge."[15] The English, however,

---

[14] Margoliouth, *Poems and Letters*, I, 309, discovered evidence of publication in 1665 and 1672.

[15] Sir William Sanderson, *Graphice: The Use of the Pen and Pencil* (London, 1658), p. 14.

returned to cartooning in the Second and Third Dutch Wars, while protesting in lofty terms the insolence of the Dutch equivalents. On 28 November 1663 Pepys recorded in his diary that "in Holland publickly they have pictured our King with reproach. One way is with his pockets turned the wrong side outward, hanging out empty; another with two courtiers picking of his pockets; and a third leading of two ladies, while others abuse him, which amounts to great contempt." In 1672 the circulation of Dutch "pictures" was cited as one of the official causes of England's declaration of war and examples of the offending cartoons were republished in Henry Stubbe's militant *Justification of the Present War Against The United Netherlands*. (See Plate 3.) Marvell was eventually to take mocking cognizance of this political absurdity, in his *Account of the Growth of Popery and Arbitrary Government*. Invoking *ut pictura poesis* with heavy irony, he observed that "a poet indeed, by a dash of his pen [had] once been the cause of a war against Poland; but this was certainly the first time that ever a painter could by a stroke of his pencil occasion the breach of a treaty."[16]

During the Second Dutch War, however, Marvell had occasion to take *ut pictura poesis* more seriously as a medium of political influence. Returning from his diplomatic mission under Lord Carlisle in Russia and Sweden, he shortly found himself in a situation in which his own view of the war differed radically from that being expressed by the public poetry of the day. At the heart of Marvell's objections to the war was the Opposition view that it was neither a "just war" in the legal sense defined by Grotius nor an expedient trade war that would enrich the country. Rather, it appeared to the majority in the Commons to be an excuse for extracting from them as the country's elected representatives an exorbitantly large Supply, most of which quickly vanished with very little to show for it. Charles's

---

[16] *Complete Works*, ed. Grosart, IV, 283.

3. "Dutch Pictures," from Henry Stubbe: *A Justification of the Present War Against the United Netherlands*, 1672.

own speech of 24 November 1664, in which he announced his military intentions, took pains to counter "a vile jealousy, which some ill men scatter abroad":

that, when you have given me a noble and proportionable Supply for the support of a war, I may be induced by some evil counsellors (For they will be thought to think very respectfully of my own person) to make a sudden peace, and get all that money for my own private occasions . . . let me tell you, and you may be most confident of it, that when I am compelled to enter into a war, for the protection, honour, and benefit of my subjects, I will (God willing) not make a peace but upon the obtaining of those ends for which the war is entered into.[17]

Clarendon himself gives an account of the Cabal maneuver by which the first unprecedented Supply of £2,500,000 had been moved by Sir Robert Paston, a previously respected member of the Country party, as a way of lulling these suspicions; he also describes the rage of the Commons when they learned that all the money, including the additional £1,250,000 voted at the Oxford session of 1655, had been spent with no tangible results.[18] In October 1665 the Commons appointed the first of several committees to investigate the conduct of the war, in this case to inquire into the embezzlement of prize goods taken from the Dutch. Marvell became a member of this committee on 25 October 1665 (*JHC* VIII, 621). In early June 1666, largely as a result of the imprudent division of naval command between Prince Rupert and General George Monck, the Duke of Albemarle, Monck was defeated at sea, thereby canceling the effect of the Duke of York's victory in the Battle of Lowestoft exactly a year earlier. Within a few months it became clear that the English navy was in bad shape administratively; and on 3 December Marvell wrote to Mayor Franke in Hull that the House of Commons had been busy creating commissioners "to inspect and examine thorowly the former expense of the 2500000[li], of the 1250000[li], of the Militia mony, of the Prize goods &c" by a new Act which he hoped would be "of very good service to the publick" (II, 47). It was in this atmosphere of tension and distrust that there had appeared, in the spring of 1666, Edmund Waller's *Instructions to a Painter, For the Drawing of the Posture and Prog-*

[17] William Cobbett, *Parliamentary History of England* (London, 1806-1812), IV, 297.
[18] Ibid., 303-306.

*ress of his Majesties Forces at Sea,*[19] which presented the Duke of York's victory of 3 June 1655 as a symbol of the heroic conduct and high motives of the war in general. How far it was actually intended to operate as defensive propaganda is hard to know but, in adapting to political panegyric the venerable concept of *ut pictura poesis,* it clearly offered an intellectual challenge. By December, while the Commons were debating the new Act for inspecting public accounts, there appeared the first of a series of satirical *Advices to the Painter,* which parodied Waller's *Instructions,* and presented the war not as a British triumph but as a debacle of mismanagement, cowardice, and venality.

The significance of this satirical response cannot be fully understood without some grasp of the special status held by *ut pictura poesis* in cultural and rhetorical tradition, a tradition whose details and topoi had particular currency in seventeenth-century England. Its origins, of course, were classical. The familiar phrase from Horace's *Ars Poetica,* the *ut pictura poesis* motto itself, was taken out of context as early as the fourth century, and interpreted as a prescription that poetry and painting *should* imitate each other's methods. To this was assimilated the motto of Simonides, that painting is mute poetry, poetry a speaking picture, which tied the arts firmly together in what Lessing called "the dazzling antithesis of the Greek Voltaire."[20] The original motive for the development of the analogy in the Quattrocento was a desire to give painting the social status of literature, to elevate it to the ranks of the liberal arts.

[19] Waller, *Instructions To A Painter, For the Drawing of the Posture and Progress of his Majesties Forces at Sea, Under the command of His Highness Royal. Together with the Battel and Victory obtained over the Dutch, June, 3, 1655.* The Stationer's Register for 10 March 1665 also records an earlier version of the poem: "a paper intituled 'Instructions to a Painter for drawing of a picture of the state and posture of the English Forces at sea under the Command of his highese royall in the conclusion of the yeare 1664,' by Edmund Waller, Esq."

[20] Gotthold Lessing, *Laocoön* (London, 1914), p. 4.

127

However, by the middle of the sixteenth century there had been developed for painting a theory involving both the aims and techniques of rhetoric and poetics, and from this point on the relationship became one of cross-fertilization.[21] The embryonic shape of what was to become doctrine could be seen in Leon Battista Alberti's *Della Pittura* (1436), despite its essentially practical nature; but it was given full and clear expression in Ludovico Dolce's dialogue, *L'Aretino*, of 1557. In place of Alberti's three divisions—drawing, composition, and manipulation of light—Dolce applied to painting the three first parts of rhetoric: Invention, Disposition, and Ornament. Where Alberti merely spoke of what is seemly or appropriate in the representation of figures, Dolce, who had earlier published a translation of the *Ars Poetica* (Venice, 1535), developed a fully fledged theory of Horatian decorum. In discussing Invention, or the choice of an appropriate subject for a picture, Dolce gave as an example of what is unacceptable ("una sconvenevolissima invenzione") the grotesque figure described by Horace in the opening lines of the *Ars Poetica*: "Humano capiti cervicem pictor equinam / Jungere si velit." "Who would not laugh at a picture in which a human head appears on the neck of a horse, or the tail of a fish below the bust of a beautiful woman." He also undermined Horace's provision for a certain imaginative license—"Pictoribus atque poetis / Quidlibet audendi semper fuit aequa potestas"—by removing the implications of *quidlibet* and insisting that the freedom of

21 For Italian pictorial theory, see W. G. Howard, "*Ut Pictura Poesis*," *PMLA* 24 (1909), 40-123; W. Rensselaer Lee, "*Ut Pictura Poesis*: The Humanistic Theory of Painting," *Art Bulletin* 22 (1940), 197-269, republished as a separate monograph in 1967; Jean Hagstrum, in *The Sister Arts: The Tradition of Literary Pictorialism and English Poetry from Dryden to Gray* (Chicago, 1958), dealt extensively with *ut pictura poesis* as a literary phenomenon, but frequently overemphasized the elements of naturalism or realism in the tradition. For the development of *ut pictura poesis* into emblem literature, see R. J. Clements, *Picta Poesis: Literary and Humanistic Theory in Renaissance Emblem Books* (Rome, 1960), esp. pp. 173-174.

genius be not abused.[22] This was perhaps the most often repeated topos of *ut pictura poesis*, which remained at all times Horatian in its general tone. In 1637, for example, the *De Pictura* of Francis Du Jon, translated into English the following year as *The Painting of the Ancients*, reminded the cultured audience of the early seventeenth century that Horace had prohibited the grotesque in either art:

> Now as the Artificer may not abuse the libertie of his Imaginations, by turning it unto a licentious boldnesse of fancying things abhorring from Nature; so must also a right lover of Art preferre a plaine and honest worke agreeing with Nature before any other phantastically capricious devices . . . It is then a very grosse errour to deeme with the vulgar sort that Painters as well as Poets have an unlimited libertie of devising; for if we doe but marke what Horace telleth us in the first entrance of his booke written about the Poeticall Art, wee shall confesse that neither Poets nor Painters may take such a libertie as to stuffe up their workes with all kinds of frivolous and lying conceits.
>
> (p. 43)

And similar strictures were repeated by Henry Peacham in his *Graphice: or the Most Auncient and Excellent Art of Drawing and Limming* (1612) where he warns his "young Scholler" neither to waste his time nor to lose "his eares for a libeller," by accepting the original meaning of Horace's *quidlibet audere*, "for there be many things which as well Nature or Religion would have freed from the pencill" (p. 9).

Decorum blends easily with idealism. Alberti had qualified his advice about the use of models and precise anatomical observation by recommending a certain selectivity, an aesthetic tact which emphasizes the beautiful and suppresses unattractive features as, according to Pliny, Apelles had

---

[22] *Dolce's "Aretino" and Venetian Art Theory of the Cinquecento*, ed. and trans. Mark W. Roskill (New York, 1968), pp. 119-127.

done in his portrait of Antigonus. But art theorists of the sixteenth and early seventeenth centuries calmly invested this notion with a confused blend of Aristotelian and Platonic theory. *Ut pictura poesis* became associated with an ideal of perfection, whether physical or moral, which it was the duty of both arts to express, and which in fact contradicted the mimetic theory to which these same critics gave lip service. Dolce said that it was the painter's duty "not only to imitate but to surpass nature": and that where nature failed to supply models of adequate perfection he could either (1) look to classical sculpture; (2) adjust the actual proportions of his model to some ideal scheme, as Apelles did for his famous Venus Anadyomene; or (3) abstract the best features from a number of less than perfect models, as Zeuxis of Croton did for his Venus (pp. 131-139). At the same time Alberti's claim that "painting has contributed considerably to the piety which binds us to the gods" became expanded into a defense of its religious usefulness by Counter-Reformation theorists; and his claim for its use as historical record, because "it represents the dead to the living many centuries later," became the basis for an analogy between historical painting and epic poetry. Other stories about ancient painters found in Pliny's *Natural History* were forced into the service of this preceptive idealism. Alexander's gift to Apelles of his favorite courtesan Campaspe—he had painted her in the nude and become enamored in the process (Loeb ed., xxxv, xxxvi, 86)—became evidence of the great esteem in which monarchs held their painters; and even the competitions in skill between Zeuxis and Parrhasius, Apelles and Protogenes, shifted from illustrations of extreme realism—Zeuxis painted grapes so like the real thing that birds flew down and pecked them; Parrhasius painted a curtain over the picture so real that it deceived Zeuxis himself (Loeb ed., xxxv, xxxvi, 64-65)— to metaphors for perfectionism. One Plinean story which caused Dolce some embarrassment told how Protogenes became enraged at his failure to represent the slaver on a dog's mouth, and how by throwing a sponge at the picture in his annoyance he accidentally achieved the desired result (xxxv, xxxvi, 102-103). This classical anticipation of action painting did not fit easily into a doctrine which stressed high skills and high ideals.

There were other things also which did not fit. According to Francisco de Hollanda, Michelangelo's scorn of Flemish painters was based on their undiscriminating naturalism.[23] But when Michelangelo turned from the Neoplatonic beauties of the Sistine Chapel ceiling to the *terribilitas* of the Last Judgment, he himself became the great example of pictorial indecorum. Dolce pointed in displeasure to the indecencies of embracing saints, a beardless Christ, the general nakedness, and a devil clutching the testicles of one anguished sinner (p. 190). His arguments were echoed, though from a different standpoint, by Counter-Reformation theorists who eventually got the picture draped in the appropriate places; and Dolce's contrast between Raphael and Michelangelo was still current in 1662, when Roland Fréart de Chambray published his *Idée de la perfection de la peinture*. As de Chambray put it (and I cite from John Evelyn's translation of 1668), "we may observe in most of Raphael's Compositions a generous and free Invention, noble and Poetick; So in those of his Antagonist, a dull and rusticall heaviness; so as he never seems to have made use but of some Porter or sturdy Booby for his Modell." Raphael is praised for his decision "never to paint anything of Licentious, . . . whilst the other, on the contrary, made it his glory, publickly, to be ashamed of nothing, no, not to prophane either the most holy Places or Histories by the infamous Freedome which he assumed."[24] The summative statement of *ut pictura poesis* as a vehicle of idealism is, however, to be found in Charles Du Fresnoy's *De Arte*

[23] de Hollanda, *Four Dialogues of Painting*, trans. A.F.G. Bell (London, 1928), p. 15.

[24] John Evelyn, trans., *An Idea of Painting* (London, 1668), pp. 67-68.

*Graphica*, written in obvious imitation of Horace, and published in 1668 with a French translation and commentary by Roger de Piles; and Dryden's translation in 1695 indicates that this remained theoretical orthodoxy throughout the seventeenth century:

> Painting and Poesy are two sisters, which are so alike in all things, that they mutually lend to each other both their Name and Office. One is call'd a dumb Poesy, and the other a speaking Picture. The Poets have never said anything but what they believed wou'd please the Ears. And it has been the constant endeavour of the Painters to give pleasure to the Eyes . . . For both of them, that they might contribute all within their power to the sacred Honours of Religion, have rais'd themselves to Heaven, and, having found a free admission into the Palace of Jove himself, have enjoy'd the sight and conversation of the Gods . . . They dive . . . into all past Ages; and search their Histories, for subjects which are proper for their use: with care avoiding to treat of any but those which, by their nobleness . . . have deserved to be consecrated to Eternity.[25]

The only real exception to this tradition had been Leonardo da Vinci, whose *Trattato della Pittura* rigorously rejected idealism for naturalism, as it also rejected the equal sisterhood of the arts for a *paragone* or formal comparison in which painting was defined as a superior medium—superior in directness, power, and truthfulness. One feature of the *paragone*, which was to have particular influence on political poetry, was Leonardo's insistence that only painting can properly represent a battle:

> If you, poet, describe a bloody battle, will it be with the air dark and murky, in the midst of frightful and

[25] Dryden, *The Art of Painting, by C. A. Du Fresnoy. With Remarks Translated into English, Together with an Original Preface containing A Parallel betwixt Painting and Poetry . . . Ut Pictura Poesis erit—Hor. de Arte Poetica* (London, 1695), pp. 3-4.

death-dealing arms, mixed with thick dust that defiles the atmosphere and the frightened flight of miserable men afraid of a horrible death? In this case, the painter will surpass you because your pen will be worn out before you describe fully what the painter with his medium can represent at once—Your tongue will be paralysed with thirst and your body with sleep and hunger, before you depict with words what the painter will show you in a moment.[26]

With this we have moved from questions of mimesis to problems of expressivism, and indeed Leonardo's later admission that neither the noise of battle nor the souls of his painters could be represented on canvas became part of a discussion of even greater importance for poetry. Leonardo's position connected and contrasted with another Renaissance position, that painting was to poetry as body is to mind;[27] this in turn connected with Pliny's statements that before Aristides Greek painting had not attempted psychological analysis, while Apelles was unique in his ability to paint things such as thunder and lightning that cannot normally be represented pictorially (xxxv, xxxvi, 96, 98). Although Leonardo's text was not published in any form until the Paris edition of 1651 by De Fresne and then appeared without the *paragone*, versions of his notes were reported circulating in manuscript;[28] and the *paragone* as a topos had clearly entered literary tradition by the end of the sixteenth century. In the opening scene of Shakespeare's *Timon of Athens*, for example, a poet and a painter discuss the problems of representing Fortune, and the painter claims superiority:

[26] Leonardo, *Treatise on Painting*, trans. and ed. A. P. McMahon (Princeton, 1956), I, 24.

[27] Benedetto Varchi, "In che siano simili et in che differenti i poeti et i pittori," in *Lezzioni* (Florence, 1590), available in *Trattati d'Arte Del Cinquecento*, ed. P. Barocchi (Bari, 1960), I, 55.

[28] See *Treatise on Painting*, trans. and ed. McMahon, I, xxi-xxiii.

A thousand moral paintings I can show
That shall demonstrate these quick blows of Fortune's
More pregnantly than words.

(1, i, 91-93)

In contrast to this Ben Jonson observed in *Timber, or Discoveries* that "the Pen is more noble, than the Pencill. For that can speake to the Understanding; the other, but to the Sense"; and in *Underwoods* (1616) he included two poems occasioned by an actual portrait of Lady Venetia Digby, "The Picture of the Body" being followed by "The Mind," in which the painter is dismissed from a subject beyond his range:

> to express a Mind to sense
> Would aske a Heavens Intelligence;
> Since nothing can report that flame,
> But what's of kinne to whence it came.[29]

There is abundant evidence that all of these topoi were known in seventeenth-century England, and that they had acquired some kind of official currency, as a result of the interest in painting of the Stuart courts. Although this interest survived and was to some extent democratized by the Puritan Revolution,[30] it is fair to say that the doctrines of *ut pictura poesis* remained in close association with the court, and were turned by royalist writers to the service of royalist ideals. Sir William Sanderson's *Graphice*, for example, which was published in 1658, was preceded by a portrait of Charles I and a commemorative verse. Although strictly speaking not a work of theory but a textbook on the "Use of the Pen and Pencil," *Graphice* occasionally reveals an idealizing bias. Repeating the story of Zeuxis of Croton, Sanderson advises the portrait painter to gather

[29] Jonson, *Works*, ed. C. H. Herford and Percy and Evelyn Simpson (Oxford, 1947), VIII, 609-610, 277-278.

[30] H.V.S. and M. S. Ogden, "A Bibliography of Seventeenth-Century Writings on the Pictorial Arts in English," *Art Bulletin* 29 (1947), p. 63.

"from several beauties . . . a conceived Idea . . . of accomplished Pulchritude, grace or comlinesse, according to the true rule of Symmetry. So like the Life, (if done by Lilly) that by the Lines and Colour, a skilfull Physiognomer (another Lilly) may by the Picture tell her fortune" (p. 46). This double allusion to the court portraitist Sir Peter Lely and his partial namesake the astrologer William Lilly brings the old orthodoxy rather confusingly up to date. Richard Lovelace included in *Lucasta* (1649) a significant comment on one of Lely's earliest royal portraits, the picture of Charles I and the Duke of York (Plate 4), which has unmistakably a psychological depth nor found in Lely's Restoration work. "The amazed world," wrote Lovelace, recalling the mind–body distinction of the *paragone*, "shall henceforth find / None but my Lilly ever drew a Minde."[31] Lovelace himself was complimented, in one of the dedicatory poems to *Lucasta*, by a related distinction, the elegance of Cavalier verse being praised in terms of Plinean anecdote:

Poets and Painters have some near relation,
Compar'd with Fancy and Imagination;
The one paints shadowed persons (in pure kind,)
The other points the Pictures of the Mind
In purer Verse. And as rare Zeuxes fame
Shin'd till Apelles Art eclipsed the same
By a more exquisite and curious line
In Zeuxeses (with pensill far more fine,)
So have our modern Poets, late done well
Till thine appear'd (which scarce have paralel.)
They like to Zeuxes Grapes beguile the sense,
But thine do ravish the Intelligence;
Like the rare banquet of Apelles, drawn,
And covered over with most curious Lawn.

(Ar)

Edmund Waller's poems of 1645 contained, among half a dozen ecphrastic poems, one "To the Queen, occasioned

[31] Lovelace, *Lucasta* (London, 1649), pp. 57-58.

4. Charles I and the Duke of York, by Sir Peter Lely, 1647 (Syon House).

upon sight of her Majesties Picture," and one in praise of Sir Anthony Van Dyck, whom Robert Herrick had called "the glory of the World,"[32] and who had painted the famous "Charles I in Three Positions." When Abraham Cowley, in his *Poems* of 1656, celebrated the death of Van Dyck, he not only referred obliquely to that great tragic triptych, but also condensed into a single epitaph the major propositions

[32] Edmund Waller, *Workes* (London, for Thomas Walkley, 1645), pp. 11-13, 19.

of *ut pictura poesis*—Horatian decorum, Simonidean interchange, and the expressive arguments of the *paragone*:

> Vandike is Dead; but what Bold Muse shall dare
> (Though Poets in that word with Painters share)
> T'expresse her sadness. Poesie must become
> An Art, like Painting here, an Art that's Dumbe.
> Let's all our solemn grief in silence keep,
> Like some sad Picture which he made to weep,
> Or those who saw't, for none his works could view
> Unmov'd with the same Passions which he drew.
>
> (p. 9)

Such personal or elegiac expressions of royalist feeling were, however, a very different matter from Waller's *Instructions to a Painter*, which knowingly combined the topoi of the tradition, including its essential idealism, with a politically provocative message. Waller was, of course, adapting to English political purposes the poem by Giovanni Francesco Busenello which had celebrated a Venetian naval victory over the Turks in 1655,[33] and had been translated into English by Thomas Higgons in 1658.[34] In all three poems the device (derived ultimately from the Greek Anthology) of giving advice to a portrait painter had become an organizing principle for a description of historical events, and in all three, of course, historical events had been raised to heroic and mythic proportions. Waller, in particular, abandoned any pretense of historical realism, and his painter was actually instructed to replace image with concept ("With his Extraction, and his Glorious Mind / Make the proud Sails swell, more than with the Wind," p. 4); while in defiance of Leonardo's position he had asserted the superiority of poetry over painting when it comes to representing a com-

[33] Giovanni Francesco Busenello, *Prospettiva del Navale Trionfo Riportato Dalla Republica Serenissima Contro il Turco* (Venice, 1656).

[34] *A Prospective of the Naval Triumph of the Venetians over the Turk*, trans. Thomas Higgons (London, 1658).

plex military action. Painting, being static, cannot, he claimed, interpret or select. Only poetry can "Light and Honour to Brave Actions Yield, / Hid in the Smoak and Tumult of the Field" (p. 16). Indeed, the argument of his poem could be summarized as a mythic celebration of the courage showed by the English in the Battle of Lowestoft, and a justification of the war in terms of national prestige ("Happy! To whom this glorious Death arrives . . . / For such a Cause").

The *Second Advice to the Painter* was seen by Pepys shortly before Christmas 1666, and the first surviving printed text is dated 1667. It may, however, have been circulating earlier in the year, for the Popple manuscript of Marvell's poetry specifies that it was written in April 1666, the month following the appearance of Waller's poem, which appeared on the Stationers' Register for 1 March. The *Second Advice* has been criticized for uninventive imitation of the structure of Waller's poem. In fact, its scope is much wider, but where it hews most closely to its offending model it does so in order to exploit the pictorialist tradition. Waller, for example, had thought to dignify his account of the Duchess of York's farewell visit to the Duke at Harwich by alluding to the Birth of Venus. Recalling that scene as conceived in antiquity by Apelles and in the Renaissance by Botticelli, the *Advice* contrasts classical beauty and economy with Restoration tastelessness and extravagance:

> One thrifty Ferry-boat of Mother-Pearl,
> Suffic'd of old the Cytherean Girle.
> Yet Navys are but Properties when here,
> A small Sea-masque, and built to court you, Dear;
>
> (ll. 61-64)

This is followed by an insinuation that the duchess was indulging in an insincere display of marital affection. Her farewell celebrations with the duke are given a sinister ethical and historical counterpart: "Never did Roman Mark, within the Nyle, / So feast the fair Egyptian Crocodile";

and the painter is advised to "spare [his] weaker art, forbear / To draw her parting Passions and each Tear." Any
reasonably alert reader would appreciate the significance of
crocodile tears; but the *paragone* topos, that painting is weak
on emotional representation, demanded a more educated
sense of irony.

When the satirist turns to the battle itself, his intentions
are further clarified by allusions to pictorial theory. The
painter is asked to "draw the Battell terribler to show /
Than the Last Judgement was of Angelo." The allusion to
Michelangelo's "Last Judgement" in this context is both an
invocation of *terribilitas* and a statement of the poet's
audacity, since that painting, itself motivated by political disillusionment following the Fall of Rome, was the most celebrated Renaissance example of stylistic irreverence and impropriety. The *Advice* also responds to the challenge of
Leonardo, who had declared the poet incapable of representing "a bloody battle . . . with the air dark and murky
. . . mixed with thick dust that defiles the atmosphere and
the frightened flight of miserable men afraid of a horrible
death." Waller's response has been to declare the poet superior to the painter in scenes of battle because he could
discover "Light and Honour" where the painter would
show merely "Smoak and Tumult." The *Second Advice*
asserts instead that the real nature of battle is not, in the
end, accessible to any form of artful expression:

> The Noise, the Smoak, the Sweat, the Fire, the Blood
> Is not to be exprest nor understood.
>
> (ll. 203-204)

Neither painting nor poetry can accurately convey the
*terribilitas* of war to those who have not experienced it
directly.

It is in this context, firstly, that we are to understand the
satirist's undermining of Waller's theme of heroism. That
assumption of omnipresent, patriotic courage is challenged,
in the *Second Advice*, by the representative English "Gal-

lant" who speaks his fear and rage at being dragged into a war to satisfy Clarendon's personal ambitions. This input from the common man begins with what looks, at first sight, to be an absurd attack on the father of navigation:

> Noah be damn'd, and all his Race accurst,
> That in Sea brine did pickle Timber first.
> What though he planted Vines! he Pines cut down,
> He taught us how to drink, and how to drown.
> He first built ships, and in the Wooden Wall
> Saving but Eight, ere since indangers all.
>
> (ll. 131-136)

The connection between this and his attack on Clarendon as the war's chief architect is, however, more precise than it seems; for if we look back at the *First Anniversary*, we find the same ambivalent typology of Noah as originator of shipbuilding and viniculture put to deft and positive use as a metaphor for a great head of state:

> Thou, and thine House, like Noahs Eight did rest,
> Left by the Warrs Flood on the Mountains crest:
> And the large Vale lay subject to thy Will,
> Which thou but as an Husbandman wouldst Till:
> And only didst for others plant the Vine
> Of Liberty, not drunken with its Wine.
>
> (ll. 283-288)

Where Cromwell as Noah had brought the war-tossed ship of the Commonwealth safely to rest, and had used the opportunities of peacetime to develop a more fruitful constitution, the Restoration regime for which Clarendon is held responsible calls for an inverted typology; and the emphasis on Cromwell's "House," which he had, in refusing the crown, resolutely refused to convert to a dynasty, puts into shameful contrast "Our Seventh Edward and his House and Line," whose aspirations have been revealed by his attempts to marry Anne Hyde to the Duke of York.

The satirist shows far less sympathy to those leaders of

the fleet whose cowardice had resulted in an indecisive victory, who, like William Berkeley or the "halcyon Sandwich," had "judg'd it safe and decent . . . to lose the Day"
(ll. 189-190). In contrast to them, however, are a few brave
men who did not let the prevailing cynicism interfere with
their duty, men like James Ley, Earl of Marlborough, who
"knew and dared too more than all" (l. 211). In a situation
where the alternatives are a self-serving decency or a self-
sacrificing daring, Marlborough's death drives home the
unhopeful message that "Death picks the Valiant out, the
Cow'rds survive" (l. 216) and so provides one intelligible
motive for the qualified pacificism of the poem.

The other motive, and the second major indecorum of
the *Advice*, is to question the justice of the war. In response
to Waller's provocative remarks about self-sacrifice
("Happy! To whom this glorious Death arrives . . . / For
such a Cause") the *Second Advice* provides an ironic summary of the "Cause" and its practical results:

> Thus having fought we know not why, as yet,
> We've done we know not what, nor what we get.
> If to espouse the Ocean all this paines,
> Princes unite and will forbid the Baines;
> If to discharge Fanaticks, this makes more,
> For all Fanatick turn when sick or poore,
> Or if the House of Commons to repay,
> Their Prize Commissions are transfer'd away;
> But for triumphant Checkstones, if, and Shell
> For Dutchesse Closet, 't has succeeded well.
> If to make Parliaments all odious passe,
> If to reserve a Standing Force, alas,
> Or if, *as just*, Orange to reinstate,
> Instead of that, he is regenerate;
> And with four Millions vainly givn, as spent,
> And with five Millions more of detriment,
> Our Summe amounts yet only to have won
> A Bastard Orange for Pimp Arlington.
> (ll. 313-330)

This cynical analysis of the political motives and consequences of the war is central to the satirist's attack on
Waller's ethos. It is only in a just war that military courage
and hence heroic language are validated. The financial
emphasis of the passage and its parliamentary focus are directly connected to the satirist's most daring adaptation of
the pictorial tradition. Perceiving that Waller, under the
device of giving advice to the painter, had in effect been
advising the king on the war's acceptability, the *Second
Advice to the Painter* concludes with its own passage of
formal advice "To the King" and a counter-recommenda-
tion. Preserving the fictional distinction to which Charles
himself had drawn attention in his speech of 24 November
1664, between his "own person," of which his critics would
"be thought to think very respectfully," and the responsibility of his "evil counsellors," the *Second Advice* urges
Charles to get rid of his chief troublemaker Clarendon, as
well as the other "Swarms of Insects" which, by interfer-
ing between the king and his people, "intercept our Sunn."
Parodying Waller's allusion to Charles as Minos, king of
Crete, the *Advice* identifies Clarendon as the State Dedalus,
at whose door may be laid all of the cynicism identified
earlier in the satire, and who is therefore responsible for the
failure of *ut pictura poesis* as a medium of idealism. The
king is urged to look upwards, to "those Kingdomes calm
of Joy and Light / Where's universall Triumphs but no
Fight" for his "pattern," to "let Justice only draw" and the
war come to an end. The poem's final advice is a return to
the simple moral absolutes that have disappeared in the
labyrinthine structures of policy.[35]

[35] In the third printed edition of the *Second Advice* (*Directions
to a Painter. For Describing our Naval Business. In Imitation of Mr.
Waller. Being The Last Works Of Sir John Denham. Whereunto is
annexed, Clarindon's House-Warming. By an Unknown Author.
Printed in the Year 1667*), the "just war" passage is not included in
the envoy to the king, as it had been in the two earlier editions, but
transferred to the conclusion of the main satire, the position it also

It is extremely significant that when the *Second Advice* was reprinted in 1667, along with a satirical *Third Advice to the Painter*, the new edition contained a feature which underlined its purpose and conceptual context. The title page of the *Second Advice* now carried a familiar, but also unfamiliar Latin motto: "Pictoribus atque Poetis, / Quidlibet Audendi semper fuit potestas. / Humano Capiti cervicem pictor equinam, / Jungere si velit." The two statements from Horace's *Ars Poetica*, which in the pictorialist tradition had always been used to support a theory of poetic or artistic decorum, were now yoked by violence together as if to authorize poets and painters who dared to portray unnatural monsters. The alternatives of daring and self-serving decency, then, which the *Second Advice* had explored in a naval context, are revealed as being also the dialectic of the political commentator; and the satirist of the *Second* and *Third Advice* which, we are told, was "written by the same Hand as the former was" identifies himself as a courageous iconoclast or, in Henry Peacham's terms, a "libeller" who puts himself in danger of losing his ears.

The *Third Advice* was to develop with some subtlety the idea of what it means to portray monsters but, before following that up, it is necessary to investigate two more public poems which contributed their share to this political argument, and may have affected the shape of the *Third Advice*. The less well known of these was Christopher Wase's *Divination*, which no longer survives in printed form, but whose appearance in manuscript between the *Second* and *Third Advice*[36] accurately represents its place in the sequence. *Divination*, as its title suggests, substituted for the unnamed painter of the "advice" the figure of William Lilly the astrologer, whom Wase instructed to reveal the

---

takes in the Popple manuscript. The effect of this change is to remove all cynicism from the envoy, leaving it to express only advice and conditional enthusiasm.

[36] In Bodleian Ms. Eng. Poet. E4, dated about 1680, "a collection of 79 pieces, almost all English poems, copied out by an Oxford Man."

face of the anonymous satirist who had so ungenerously betrayed his country:

> I would know what hand,
> Envious of royal honor, late hath stain'd
> Valor and beauty with lamp-black defac'd,
> And what he ought to worship hath disgrac'd.
> . . .
>
> Who draws the landscape of our woes, our wracks,
> Disasters, errors, aggravates our tax;
> What every faithful subject ought to hide
> (His country's shame) makes his delight and pride.[37]

In trying to identify this new demonic "Angelo," who fetches his charcoal from Hell rather than from an appropriate level of political idealism, Wase is an important witness to the contemporary reception of the *Second Advice*, which he described as "polish'd," "well contrived and high," the work of a "master-builder" and, carefully rejecting a number of possibilities, including Sir John Denham, he supplied a "face," an interesting ecphrasis, perhaps, of some portrait known to him, whose dark features matched the "sober malice" he found in the poem.

The second provocation was given, it seems, by Dryden's *Annus Mirabilis*, a piece of royalist propaganda which directed its attention to the two most distressing events of 1666: the division of the fleet under Monck and Prince Rupert, with its disastrous consequences in the Four Days' Battle, 3-6 June; and the Great Fire of London, 2-6 September. Dryden's poem, even more than Waller's, offered an intellectual challenge of irresistible proportions; for it appeared with a theoretical preface addressed to Sir Robert Howard, in which his political motives were presented in an elaborate dress of generic and rhetorical theory. "I have chosen," wrote Dryden, "the most heroick Subject which any Poet could desire: I have taken upon me to describe the

---

[37] Cited from Lord, *Poems on Affairs of State*, I, 55, 63.

motives, the beginning, progress, and successes of a most just and necessary War; in it the care, management, and prudence of our King; the conduct and valour of a Royal Admiral and of two incomparable Generals; the invincible courage of our Captains and Seamen, and three glorious Victories, the result of all."[38] This high-minded refusal to look at the facts was, however, justified by a general discussion of epic theory which in the last paragraph of the preface, was identified with an ideal pictorialism. The Virgilian images incorporated into his own poem are, Dryden asserts, the main source of the pleasure derived from heroic poetry: "for they beget admiration, which is its proper object; as the images of the Burlesque, which is contrary to this, by the same reason beget laughter; for the one shows Nature beautified, as in the picture of a fair Woman, which we all admire; the other shows her deformed, as in that of a Lazar, or of a fool with distorted face and antique gestures, at which we cannot forbear to laugh, because it is a deviation from Nature" (p. 46). In this context of "Nature beautified," Dryden proceeds, in the poem itself, to offer a neoclassical panegyric to Charles for his wisdom in dividing the fleet, to interpret Monck's narrow escape, which had included having his breeches shot off, as "naked Valour," and to make the whole account of the fire subservient to a praise of Charles's grief for, and munificence to, his devastated London, and a prophecy of its rising anew like the phoenix from its flames. In response to the widespread rumors that the fire had been started by Roman Catholic saboteurs, he imagined that "Ghost of Traitors from the Bridge descend, / With bold Fanatick Spectres to rejoyce" (st. 223), implying that responsibility for arson lay rather with the Nonconformists; nor could he resist the temptation to suggest that St. Paul's had not been spared from the flames because it had been "prophan'd by Civil War" (st. 276). The nature of the poem's royalism is best defined,

[38] Dryden, *Works*, eds. E. N. Hooker and H. T. Swedenberg, Jr. (Berkeley and Los Angeles, 1961), I, 50.

however, in his brief apostrophe to the Royal Society, which carries an unmistakable flavor of Platonic idealism:

> O truly Royal! who behold the law
> And rule of beings in your Maker's mind:
> And thence, like limbecs, rich Ideas draw,
> To fit the level'd use of humankind.
>
> (st. 166)

Dryden's *Account* to Sir Robert Howard of his poem's intentions was dated 10 November 1666. The poem was licensed for publication by Sir Roger L'Estrange on 22 November, and entered in the Stationers' Register for 21 January 1666/7. This sequence makes it virtually certain that the poem was inspired in part by the parliamentary committee to investigate the causes of the fire, to which Marvell was appointed on 2 October (*JHC*, VIII, 629, 654). If the *Second Advice* had indeed, as the Popple manuscript suggests, been written in April and circulating in manuscript since then, *Annus Mirabilis* could also be seen as a counter-proposition to the satirist's assertion that the war was neither just, necessary, nor successful. And contrariwise, if *Annus Mirabilis* had been circulating since November, it would help to explain why the *Third Advice*, reported by Pepys to be in circulation by 20 January 1666/7, divides *its* focus between the Four Days' Battle and the Fire of London, while choosing as a spokesman for Nonconformist integrity General Monck's own wife, the Duchess of Albemarle. It is not without significance, too, that the reported appearances of *Annus Mirabilis* and the *Third Advice* closely coincide with the parliamentary debates on naval administration and the causes of the fire. On 21 January the Commons, in an unprecedented act of intervention in financial policy, set aside £380,000 of the new Supply specifically for seamen's wages; and on 22 January the committee appointed to investigate the fire made its first report to the House, "full of manifest testimonys," as Marvell reported to Hull, "that it was by a wicked designe" (II, 53).

In this now greatly complicated situation of specific political repartee, the *Third Advice* appeared and with considerable dexterity achieved, it seems, a response simultaneously to Wase's strictures and Dryden's lofty insistence that all was for the best under "the best of Kings." The opening invokes a particular painter, Richard Gibson, who is required to "expresse . . . in little, how we yet do lesse," a clear warning of deflationary tactics. While the choice of Gibson, who happened to be a dwarf as well as a miniaturist (Plate 5), may be seen as rather a tasteless joke, it illustrates the precision with which pictorial and political knowledge is interlocked; for Gibson had begun his career as a page under Charles I, had then become Cromwell's portraitist, and was now, as official miniaturist to Charles II, assimilated into the atmosphere of the Restoration court.

Along with the invocation of Gibson goes a rejection of Sir Peter Lely as a possible artist for this project, on the grounds that "Lilly's a Dutchman, danger in his Art: / His Pencills may intelligence impart." At one level this is a simple warning against making secrets of state accessible to the enemy; at another it implies the traditional association between Dutch painting and excessive realism, which, as a mode of representation, could also impart "intelligence" to the poem's audience; and at a third, it is a punning response to Wase's appeal to Lilly the astrologer to show him the face of this new dangerous writer. If we recall the comment in Sir William Sanderson's *Graphice*, that a portrait "(if done by Lilly)" may be so "like the Life" that "a skilfull Physiognomer (another Lilly)" might prognosticate from the picture alone, we can recognize the same pun here; it is not without significance that Marvell was one of the few authors reported or known to have had their portraits painted by Lely. George Vertue recorded in one of his notebooks that a portrait of Marvell by Lely was in the

5. Richard Gibson, miniaturist, by Sir Peter Lely? (National Portrait Gallery, London).

possession of the Ashley family;[39] and in *Upon Appleton House* Marvell summons an image of Lely's studio, with its "Clothes" or canvases "strecht to stain" (l. 444). It may just be possible that the finest portrait we have of Marvell (book jacket) is not "by an unknown artist," but a good example of Lely's Commonwealth style, in which the figures

[39] George Vertue, *Notebooks* (Oxford, 1930-1947), II, 22. See the note by E. E. Duncan-Jones, *Poems and Letters*, I, 286.

often appear painted simply in ovals, without elaborate pose or background, and the severity of dress and expression is relieved only by the characteristic Lely eyes—fine, long, and mildly challenging.[40] Vertue also noted that Thomas May and Thomas Carew were "both painted in Ovals by S^r Peter Lilly."[41] May died in 1652; and it is more than likely that his portrait and Marvell's were painted at about the same time, in 1650 or 1651.

The use, or rather the rejection, of Lely as the painter for the *Third Advice* has, however, still another dimension. As a "Dutchman," his native tendency to realism required adjustment to the exigencies of court painting. In contrast to Van Dyck, who became, of course, the greatest of the Caroline iconographers, Lely responded to the climate of Civil War and the Puritan ethos. By 1651 he had painted a portrait of Cromwell, for which Cromwell had reportedly issued his own "instructions," insisting that it be fully realistic, without flattery, even to the inclusion of "roughnesses, pimples, warts." And he was also associated with Sir Balthazar Gerbier in a proposal, never fulfilled, to decorate Whitehall with pictures celebrating the military achievements of the Revolution. By the 1660s, however, he was principal painter for the Restoration court, and of great topical interest in 1666 was his series of naval portraits commissioned by the Duke of York to commemorate the Battle of Lowestoft.[42] This great series of portraits, though far superior in realism to the more famous "Hampton Court beauties" or other portraits of courtly compliment, is nevertheless far from the satirist's point of view; for the terms of his commission required Lely to make no distinction between William Berkeley, who had "judgd it safe and decent . . . / To Lose the Day" and the unequivocal heroism of Christopher Myngs or Jeremy Smith. It is with a most

[40] For Lely's Commonwealth style, see C. H. Collins Baker, *Lely & the Stuart Portrait Painters* (London, 1912), I, 143, 160-162.

[41] Vertue, *Notebooks*, I, 88.

[42] See R. B. Beckett, *Lely* (London, 1951), pp. 11, 17-18.

complicated and knowing irony, then, that the *Third Advice* deploys Lely, and many of its evaluative comments on the naval commanders in the Four Days' Battle acquire a new meaning in the light of Lely's portraits. Sir John Harman, for example, is recognized as "the great Harman chark'd almost to coale" (l. 116); but William Berkeley, "as he long deserv'd, was shot" (l. 110). (Plates 6 and 7.)

6. Sir William Berkeley, by Sir Peter Lely, 1666 (National Maritime Museum, Greenwich).

Equally ironic is the hypothesis the satirist now develops, that concealment, rather than realism, is necessary to save the nation's honor: "Ah, rather than transmit our scorn to Fame / Draw Curtains, gentle Artist, o'er this Shame / . . . And, if the thing were true, yet paint it not" (ll. 105-107). In obvious parody of Wase's position (and of the draping to which Michelangelo's "Last Judgement" was submitted)

7. Sir John Harman, by Sir Peter Lely, 1666 (National Maritime Museum, Greenwich).

the painter is asked "in a dark cloud" to "cover" the defection of Sir George Ayscue (one of Lely's subjects) and, in the episode of General Monck's wound in the buttock, to "Conceale, as honour would, his Grace's Bum." The theme of protective secrecy is supported by the historical, if mock-heroic, fog which had shielded the English fleet from de Ruyter: "Old Homer yet did never introduce, / To save his Heroes, Mist of better use" (ll. 159-160). When Richard Leigh joined the Anglican outcry against Marvell in 1673, he included in his *Transproser Rehears'd* a scurrilous allusion both to Marvell's authorship of the *Advices*, and to this strategy of ironic "draping" of the indecent. "I shall only advise his Painter," wrote Leigh, "if ever he draws him below the Wast, to follow [in reverse] the example of that Artist, who having compleated the Picture of a Woman, could at any time . . . change her in an instant into a man." Rather deftly, Leigh then proceeds to justify his use of innuendo (about homosexuality) in terms of the pictorial tradition, where "Fig-leaves, or White Linnen" are conventionally used to *suggest* "what ought to be conceal'd in Shadow" (p. 134).

About one-third through the poem, this pose of decorous concealment and mock-heroic tone are suddenly dropped. Commenting upon the bonfires and rejoicings at home after this "empty Triumph," the satirist speaks in a new intonation of vehemence and foreboding:

> Alas: the time draws near, when overturn'd
> The lying Bells shall through the tongue be burn'd;
> Papers shall want to print that Lye of State,
> And our false Fires true Fires shall expiate.
>
> (ll. 163-166)

In order to present this new, truthful view of events, as distinct from official propaganda and flattering royalist panegyric, the satirist abandons his own role as director of his painter's procedures. Introducing the Duchess of Albemarle, "Paint thou but her," he says, "and she will paint the rest." This new persona is herself presented as one of the grotesques that the satirist's inverted Horatianism allows; "the Monky Dutchesse," with a "Trunk cartaliginous," a bouncing "Udder," and in a most indecorous position, nailing up hangings on a horizontal ladder carried by her servants, and therefore "In posture just of a four-footed Beast" (ll. 171-200). Yet despite this unpropitious portrait, which has led both seventeenth- and twentieth-century readers to misinterpret her role,[43] the duchess's very coarseness has a special appropriateness to her task. Originally a common seamstress, and still a "Presbyterian Sibyll," she is doubly an outsider whose exclusion from Cavalier and Anglican circles gives her a necessary distance, while her connection with Monck gives her credibility. She wears metaphorically "a foule Smock, when [she] might have clean" (l. 236) because it matches her view of society. Herself a grotesque, she is at liberty to apply the "Humano capiti cervicem" perspective of satire to her husband's colleagues at court: "What, say I Men? nay rather Monsters: Men / Only in Bed, nor (to my knowledge) then" (l. 230).

Consequently, it is given to the duchess to express the graver part of the satirist's message. She distinguishes, for example, between the "egregious Loyalty" of the Cavaliers who escorted Charles into a comfortable exile, and the "true Royalists" struggling to make government work at home. In this she identifies herself with the Presbyterian divine Edmund Calamy ("I told George first, as Calamy did me, / If the King these brought over, how 'twould be," ll. 217-218) and thus with the Nonconformist "martyrs"

---

[43] Pepys (20 January 1667) thought it "a bitter satire upon the service of the Duke of Albemarle last year"; and Francis "Elephant" Smith, the underground printer who tried to negotiate a July printing of the *Second* and *Third Advices* (*CSPD* 26 July 1667), thought it "reflected" upon the Duchess of Albemarle. Wallace, one of the few modern critics to see the importance of the duchess, nevertheless felt that she "is presented as so lewd and ignorant a woman that her hostile narrative about the government might appear to be discredited before it began" (*Destiny his Choice*, p. 154).

expelled from their pulpits on St. Bartholomew's Day, 1662, the "ejection" which, as the duchess also points out (ll. 243-244), claimed equality with the original massacre. And she wittily applies the silencing, truth-concealing topos of the earlier sections of the *Advice* to the restoration of the bishops to the House of Lords:

> The Lords House drains the Houses of the Lord,
> For Bishops voices silencing the Word.
> (ll. 241-242)

In this she incidentally recalls a sermon by Calamy, who had during the Long Parliament used the same pun in rebuking the Lords for their slackness in church reform.[44]

The duchess also provides, in her "advice" to her husband, the positive norms of practical and moral conduct required of an honest naval administrator which, we are finally reminded, have a religious base:

> Fall to thy worke there, George, as I do here:
> Cherish the valiant up, the cow'rd cashiere.
> See that the Men have Pay and Beef and Beere;
> Find out the cheats of the foure-millioneer.
> . . .
> Looke that good Chaplains on each Ship do wait,
> Nor the Sea-Diocesse be impropriate.[45]
> (ll. 325-328, 341-342)

Her language reminds us of Marvell's appeal in the Convention Parliament on behalf of university livings, and his request that the king should instruct "the Colleges in the

---

[44] Edmund Calamy, *The Noble-Mans Patterne of True and Reall Thankfulnesse*, a sermon to the House of Lords, ordered printed 16 June 1643: "the best way for the House of Lords to prosper, is to indeavour earnestly and faithfully to reforme the Lords House" (A4r).

[45] The last two lines were added in the *Directions* edition (and the Popple manuscript) indicating later revision in favor of the duchess's religious sincerity.

Universities, that they would take into Consideration their respective Impropriations."

It is also worth noting that, in her analysis of Monck's earlier disaster, the duchess focuses accurately on the incompetence of Arlington in discovering the location of the Dutch fleet:

> The Secretary that had never yet
> Intelligence but from his own gazett,
> Discovers a great secret, fit to sell,
> And pays himself for't ere he would it tell.
> He'll see the Fleet devided like his Face,
>
> . . .
>
> And through that cranny in his gristly part,
> To the Dutch chink intelligence may start.
> (ll. 283-286, 298-300)

This passage connects with the opening rejection of Sir Peter Lely as a Dutchman, whose "Pencills may intelligence impart." It is also oddly linked to the occasion when, on 15 February 1667/8, the committee appointed to inquire into the miscarriages of the late war brought in its first report on the "want of intelligence" and Marvell, who was himself a member of that committee (*JHC* IX, 4), spoke "somewhat transportedly" on the issue, accusing Arlington of incompetence and financial corruption.[46] Both Milward and Pepys alluded to this speech in their diaries, and Arlington himself mentioned it in a letter to Sir William Temple two days later, as the most significant event of the debate from his point of view.[47] The Duchess of Albemarle's angry candor provides a striking anticipation of Marvell's own considerable impropriety in the House in the speech that attracted so much attention.

By the end of the satire the duchess has been transformed,

[46] Anchitell Grey, *Debates of the House of Commons from the year 1667 to the year 1694* (London, 1769), I, 70-71.

[47] *The Earl of Arlington's Letters to Sir W. Temple*, ed. Thomas Bebington (London, 1701), I, 226.

by her own performance, from a grotesque figure with animal connotations to a prophetess, mourning with complete conviction her vision of the fire as the Fall of Troynovant which, in defiance of Dryden's easy optimism, is presented as an end, not as a new beginning:

> Alas the Fate
> I see of England, and its utmost date.
> Those flames of theirs, at which we fondly smile,
> Kindled, like Torches, our Sepulchrall Pile.
> Warre, Fire, and Plague against us all conspire:
> We the Warre, God the Plague, who rais'd the Fire?
> . . .
>
> So of first Troy, the angry Gods unpaid,
> Ras'd the foundations which themselves had lay'd.
>
> (ll. 413-428)

Moreover, the change in point of view has been effected by antipictorial means. The very feature of the poem to which the most hostile criticism has been directed—the duchess's long speech—has, by revealing her basically admirable feelings and standards, canceled the original portrait, based on externals only, of her introduction; or, perhaps more accurately, the positive side of a mixed personality, "Half Witch, half Prophet," has become one medium by which true advice may reach the king.

The final "advice-to-the-king" both capitalizes on this shift in the duchess's role and clarifies its connection with the Horatian motto on the title page. "Pictoribus atque Poetis, Quidlibet Audendi" becomes explicitly relevant to the problems of veracious and courageous counsel: "What Servants will conceale, and Couns'lours spare / To tell, the Painter and the Poet dare." The king is warned to avert the destruction of his own Troy by his "own Navy's wooden horse," and the Duchess of Albemarle is defined as a new Cassandra, who must not be ignored; while, in a final simile, her role is compared to the mythic truth teller Philomela, whose tale has the same conceptual structure as *ut pictura poesis* itself:

> So Philomel her sad embroyd'ry strung,
> And vocall silks tun'd with her Needle's tongue.
> (The Picture dumbe, in colours lowd, reveal'd
> The tragedy's of Court, so long conceal'd.)
> But, when restor'd to voice, increas'd with Wings,
> To Woods and Groves what once she painted sings.

It is difficult to do justice to the puns, paradoxes, reversals, and condensations of this passage. The story of the enforced muteness of Philomela, whose tongue was cut out but who nevertheless revealed the facts of her rape in tapestry, is a most elegant illustration of the Simonides motto that poetry is a speaking picture, painting a dumb poetry. It also echoes the poet's earlier prophecy of a time when the "lying Bells" of political propaganda "shall through the tongue be burn'd," while alluding to the Duchess of Albemarle's earlier profession as a seamstress. Finally, Philomela's metamorphosis into the nightingale, long established as a symbol of the poet, replaces painting with poetry as the revelatory medium, and thus strengthens the impression given in the duchess's own character development that poetry, which can see beyond externals, has a closer relationship with the truth. A final postscript to this dark conclusion may be found in Marvell's letter to William Popple, dated 21 March 1670, in which he describes how three months after his death the Duke of Albemarle's body "yet lys in the Dark unburyed" and unhonored by his countrymen. The duchess, true to her wifely character, died twenty days after him (II, 315-316).

The *Last Instructions to the Painter*, which has always been accepted as Marvell's, continues and confirms the generic and strategic procedures of the *Second* and *Third Advices*. Politically, its relationship to events is equally direct and, although no printed text earlier than 1689 survives, its function is clearly to support an Opposition campaign, in which Marvell himself took part, to place the blame for the war's failure on the shoulders of those actually responsible, the notable exception being, of course, Charles himself. The major event with which the *Last Instructions* was concerned was the unmitigated naval disaster of 10-12 June 1667, when (symmetrically completing the pattern set by the June battles of the two previous years) the Dutch sailed up both the Thames and Medway, and burned the English fleet at Chatham. On 19 June Peter Pett, superintendent of the dockyard at Chatham, was brought before the Privy Council to answer charges of negligence. On 17 October Marvell was appointed to a new parliamentary committee charged with investigating the "miscarriages" of the war (*JHC* IX, 4), and on 31 October he spoke in the House in defense of Peter Pett, who gave evidence before his committee two weeks later. At the same time, however, impeachment proceedings had been started against Clarendon, who fled the country on 29 November, before the hearings were concluded, and in December another parliamentary committee, of which Marvell was also a member, was appointed to arrange for his statutory banishment.

In this context the *Last Instructions* was written, we may surmise, to influence the debates on both sets of impeachment proceedings and, according to the Popple manuscript, it was completed on 4 September 1667, a date whose very specificity must carry some weight. Marvell's intentions were clearly to remove the blame for the Chatham disaster from military administrators like Peter Pett, whose insignificance in the political structure is demonstrated by the ironic proposition that he had total responsibility for the entire war:

> All our miscarriages on Pett must fall:
> His Name alone seems fit to answer all.
> Whose Counsel first did this mad War beget?
> Who all Commands sold thro' the Navy? Pett.
> Who would not follow when the Dutch were bet?

Who treated out the time at Bergen? Pett.
Who the Dutch Fleet with Storms disabled met,
And rifling Prizes, them neglected? Pett.
Who with false News prevented the Gazette?
The Fleet divided? Writ for Rupert? Pett.
Who all our Seamen cheated of their Debt?
And all our Prizes who did swallow? Pett.
Who did advise no Navy out to set?
And who the Forts left unrepair'd? Pett.
Who to supply with Powder, did forget
Languard, Sheerness, Gravesend, and Upnor? Pett.
Who all our Ships expos'd in Chathams Net?
Who should it be but the Phanatick Pett.

(ll. 767-784)

In this summative statement of all the accusations which the
*Second* and *Third Advice* had leveled at Clarendon, the
two Coventrys, Sandwich, Arlington, and others, it is worth
noticing where the rhetorical climax occurs. It is on the
"Phanatick Pett" that all these charges have, in a world of
inverted responsibilities, fallen; the suggestion is clearly
made that Pett is being made a scapegoat because of his
Nonconformity.

In contrast to these absurdist propositions, the *Last Instructions* fills in the parliamentary background to the
Chatham disaster by relating it to the issue of Supply. Here,
too, he is concerned to shift the blame from the Commons
to the Cabal, who he implied had themselves caused the
Commons' intransigence by proposing that the revenue
needed for the war should be raised by means of a general
excise tax, thereby alienating the country gentry who feared
for their own estates. Moreover, the self-interest of the
Country party's resistance is further exculpated by Marvell's assertion that funds already granted had not in any
case been spent on the war, but on maintaining the court's
luxury and debauchery; the sailors were rioting because
they had been paid by tickets in lieu of money, and the
fleet had been allowed to lie in disrepair:

159

Mean time through all the Yards their Orders run
To lay the Ships up, cease the Keels begun.
The Timber rots, and useless Ax does rust,
The unpractis'd Saw lyes bury'd in its Dust;
The busie Hammer sleeps, the Ropes untwine;
The Stores and Wages all are mine and thine.
Along the Coast and Harbours they take care
That Money lack, nor Forts be in repair.
Long thus they could against the House conspire,
Load them with Envy, and with Sitting tire:
And the lov'd King, and never yet deny'd,
Is brought to beg in publick and to chide.

(ll. 317-328)

In this formal inversion of a shipbuilding scene there lies a key to the satire's structure. The British fleet has been *unbuilt*; and in that situation there take place two parody battles, the only kinds of battle possible in such an anti-heroic world. In the first half of the poem the painter, "wanting other," is advised to draw the parliamentary debate over the Excise as if it were a real battle. "Old Waller" is converted to this new cause and, as one of the parliamentary fighters against the Excise, is sworn to "write / This Combat truer than the Naval fight" (ll. 263-264). And in the second half the assault of De Ruyter on the Thames is described in all the elevated language that English conduct so lamentably failed to deserve.

In accordance with this rational, if oversimplified, political argument, the *Last Instructions* continues and develops the topoi of an inverted pictorialism, and still further clarifies their theoretical appropriateness to a world of distorted and deceptive political behavior. Starting with a reminder of the Anacreontic source of the tradition, where advice to a painter referred to the portraiture of an admired woman, Marvell indicates that this poem is indeed the third in a series: "After two sittings, now our Lady State, / To end her Picture, does the third time wait." He then proceeds to list a number of alternative styles of "painting" appropriate to the political scene: painting without colors; sign-post daubing;[48] grotesque ale-house sketches; Indian feather paintings which, though skillful, imply both "luxury" and primitivism; scientific enlargements of insects, as in the illustrations to Hooke's *Micrographia*; and finally, the replacement of art by accident, in an anticipation of twentieth-century "action" paintings. For this last anti-ideal medium Marvell adapts one of Pliny's stories about ancient painters, and almost the only one that could be given negative implications. He recalls the story of Protogenes and how, during his painting of Jalysus, he had both relieved his frustration and completed his painting with a luckily thrown sponge. The story of the painting of Jalysus had, in earlier pictorial theory, functioned as an example of the *self-control* of painters, since while working Protogenes ate nothing but soaked lupins; Marvell, on the contrary, omits all reference to Protogenes' abstinence (which might have explained his moment of temperament) and instead exaggerates the anger in the episode, extending it to the dog, and linking dog and painter in a crazy celebration of the unintentional:

> The Painter so, long having vext his cloth,
> Of his Hound's Mouth to feign the raging froth,
> His desperate Pencil at the work did dart,
> His Anger reacht that rage which past his Art;
> Chance finisht that which Art could but begin,
> And he sat smiling how his Dog did grinn.
>
> (ll. 21-26)

By a curious coincidence, the relevance of this Plinean anecdote to Marvell's satirical activity was later confirmed by

[48] Dryden adopted this as a metaphor for his own satiric iconography in *The Medal* (1682), attacking Shaftesbury: "I must confess I am no great Artist; but Sign-post painting will serve the turn to remember a Friend by; especially when better is not to be had," *Works*, ii, 38.

one of the Anglican defenders of Samuel Parker. The author of *The Transproser Rehears'd* noticed Marvell's reference to the "Sponges" of the licensers in the *Rehearsal*, and remarked bitterly that "the Sponge has left little else visible in his Book more than what it did in the Figures of those two Painters, in the one of which it fortunately dasht the Foam of a mad Horse, and in the other, the Slaver of a weary Dog; the Sponges ruder Blot prevailing above all the light touches and tender strokes of the Pencil. And indeed for this inimitable Art of the Sponge, this of Expressing Slaver and Foam to the Life, I will not deny but this work deserves to be celebrated beyond the Pieces of either Painter."[49]

Later, Marvell names two other painters whose history had a special appropriateness to his subject. In describing Lady Castlemaine's affair with her groom, Marvell exclaims: "Ah Painter, now could Alexander live, / And this Camp-aspe thee, Apelles, give" (ll. 103-104). Pliny's famous story of Alexander's gift to Apelles of his beautiful naked model (*Natural History*, xxxv, xxxvi, 86) had functioned in pictorial tradition as an elevating example of royal generosity to painters. In Marvell's satire, the fact that the Countess of Castlemaine had for seven years been Charles's far from faithful mistress slides easily into the poem under cover of this venerable allusion. A rather different function is served by his suggestion, prior to the parliamentary section of the poem, that his painter "rest a little" before beginning his portrayal of the battle, "For so too Rubens, with affairs of State, / His lab'ring Pencil oft would recreate" (ll. 119-120). Rubens, court painter of the Spanish Netherlands, had been employed by the Infanta to negotiate both with England and Holland, and became Secretary of the Spanish Netherlands. He had negotiated under "pretence of pictures" with Buckingham, and in 1630 was knighted by

---

[49] Richard Leigh, *The Transproser Rehears'd* (Oxford, 1673), p. 131. Leigh has incorporated Nealces' "similar success" with a horse, which Pliny also recounts (xxxv, xxxvi, 104).

Charles I for the diplomatic services he had performed.[50] This devious use of his art for political purposes makes Rubens an excellent choice for the "painter" of the *Last Instructions*, and an appropriate transition from the satirical portraits of the opening section into the labyrinthine accounts of ministerial policy.

The battle of the Excise is, moreover, integrated with the theme of the grotesque announced in the opening lines of the poem, which in turn connects with the "Humano Capiti cervicem pictor equinam, / Jungere" motto of the *Advices*. The first portrait of the *Last Instructions* is virtually a translation of that program, since the artist is urged to represent St. Albans, ex-rake, ineffective ambassador to France, "with Drayman's Shoulders, butchers Mien, / Member'd like Mules, with Elephantine chine" (ll. 33-34), a brilliant condensation of indecorum on both the social and ontological scales. The Duchess of York, parodic member of the Royal Society, is to be portrayed with "Oyster lip . . . Chanc'lor's Belly, and so large a Rump. / There, not behind the Coach, her Pages jump" (ll. 61-64). Roger Palmer, Earl of Castlemaine, carries his cuckold's horns on pilgrimage to Pasiphae's tomb, thus connecting the theme of bestiality to the Minos myth introduced by Waller. Beyond these human monsters, there are allegorical ones. The day of De Ruyter's successful attack on Chatham is cursed as "the years monster." In the House of Commons "daring Seymour . . . / Had strecht the monster Patent on the Field" (ll. 257-258): but the main parliamentary battle is against "a Monster worse than e're before / Frighted the Midwife, and the Mother tore" (ll. 131-132). With her thousand hands, hundred rows of teeth, and revolting genealogy, enriched by echoes of Milton's allegory of Sin and Death, Excise is the logical conclusion of a grotesque pictorialism. It is significant that the poem's worst monster is an allegorical one, a product of man's brain rather than a picture of

[50] See R. H. Wilenski, *Flemish Painters 1430-1830* (London, 1960), I, 266, 270.

his exterior, in which monstrosity can only be represented up to a point.

For the *Last Instructions* also develops with some subtlety the expressive topoi of the *paragone*, one of which was that only poetry can represent interior reality or other abstract qualities. When, toward the end of the satire, the painter is asked to "Express" Charles listening in his chamber to the imaginary noises of a French invasion, there is a dry allusion to Leonardo's admission that not even the most realistic painting can convey its message to the ear:

> With Canon, Trumpets, Drums, his door surround,
> But let some other Painter draw the sound.
>
> (ll. 909-910)

Earlier, in the characterization of Turner, Speaker of the House, the poet needs metaphor (he swells like "squatted Toad") and Chaucerian analogue (he is as lecherous as Chanticleer) to deal with the disparity between his attractive appearance ("Bright Hair, fair Face") and his behavior, and the old mind–body distinction is invoked:

> Dear Painter, draw this Speaker to the foot:
> Where Pencil cannot, there my pen shall do't;
> That may his Body, this his Mind explain:
>
> (ll. 863-865)

The same distinction operates in the contrasting portraits of Archibald Douglas and Sir Thomas Daniel, in the burning of the fleet at Chatham. The painter is forced to represent Daniel as a conventional "Man of might":

> Paint him of Person tall, and big of bone,
> Large Limbs, like Ox, not to be kill'd but shown.
> . . .
>
> Mix a vain Terrour in his Martial look,
> *And all those lines by which men are mistook.*
>
> (ll. 633-638)

Douglas, on the other hand, presents an appearance of soft, feminine beauty, which at first deceives the eye (and the water-Nymphs) by its suitability for love rather than war. And yet it is Daniel who flees from the fire ships, and Douglas who is burned to death on his own. By denying expectations, however, Douglas becomes transformed by his heroism into a permanent image of value and brightness: "His shape exact, which the bright flames infold, / Like the Sun's statue stands of burnish't Gold" (ll. 679-680). Absorbed into the venerable tradition of classical heroism by an echo of the death of Nisus and Euryalus, he makes it possible for the two arts to cooperate again in a happy moment of idealism and historical certainty:

> Fortunate Boy! If either Pencils Fame,
> Or if my Verse can propagate thy Name;
> When Œta and Alcides are forgot,
> Our English youth shall sing the valiant Scott.
>
> (ll. 693-696)

It is to this world that the poet appeals in the envoy to the king. The last lines of the satire express the hope that Charles will be able to renovate the *ut pictura poesis* tradition and rescue it from its satirical phase:

> Painter adieu, how will[51] our Arts agree;
> Poetick Picture, Painted Poetry.
> But this great work is for our Monarch fit,
> And henceforth Charles only to Charles shall sit.
> His Master-hand the Ancients shall out-do
> Himself the Poet and the Painter too.[52]
>
> (ll. 943-948)

[51] Lord's text, which is based on Popple, reads "well" here. Margoliouth prints "will" from *State Poems* (1689), which is more interesting, but, alas, probably not correct.

[52] These lines may reflect Marvell's interest in Simon Ford's *The Conflagration of London: Poetically Delineated. Ut Pictura Poesis, Horat.*, an illegally published poem of which Marvell sent a copy to

The reforms which will make possible the reunification of poetry and painting, the concordance of exterior appearance with interior reality, and hence an idealized portraiture that is neither sham nor flattery, are then proposed in the final section of advice "To the King." These entail the replacement of most of the Privy Council who "about the Common Prince have rais'd a Fense" with country gentlemen who have both moral and financial independence, "whose Courage high / Does with clear Counsels their large Souls supply" (ll. 985-986), the same men who, in an earlier phase of the poem, were responsible for defeating the general Excise tax. Like Marvell himself, they are "to speak not forward" in the House; but when called upon in "Countryes Cause" they represent a composite and balanced political heroism, "in Action brave; / In giving Gen'rous, but in Counsell Grave" (ll. 291-292), which is far more truly supportive of the king than all the false heroics of royalist panegyric.

As in the former passage, Marvell has in the envoy managed to state positively what the three satires imply negatively, that the Dutch War is only the occasion of a far more serious constitutional battle over who should control the king's Supply. But apart from the elegant *double-entendre* on "gen'rous Conscience" and "large Souls supply" the advice given to the king remains at the level of generalization. As with the *Second* and *Third Advices*, specific remedies for the immorality of the court, the mistakes in naval strategy, the misuse of the Supply, the collapse of administration, the sinister diplomatic currents beneath the surface of events, do not appear in the "advice-to-the-King," because the world of ideal portraiture depends

---

Lord Wharton on 2 April 1667. He may have remembered Ford's urging his engraver to create

> A Nobler Draught, if thou'lt be rul'd by me.
> Take my Directions, and I'll shew thee how
> To act th'Engraver, and the Poet too.

(p. 25)

on abstractions. Even monarchy itself is finally only a symbolic relationship: "The Country is the King"; and without that most true of constitutional fictions it is, perhaps, not worth supporting.

The relationship between the *Second* and *Third Advices*, then, and the *Last Instructions* is not merely one of form, which could easily be copied, or of identity of attitude, which could, even in its details, be shared. It is the identity of a consistent theoretical program, which has a tight and timely relationship to both political and literary events. Intelligent exploitation of the pictorial tradition supports the impression made by coincidence of political sympathy and reference. These characteristics are not found in the *Fourth* and *Fifth Advices*, nor in any of the other imitations which were still to follow, despite Marvell's declared intention to be last. It is conceivable that more than one poet was involved, and that the *Advices* were a group project, a hypothesis which is supported by the publication of the *Second*, *Third*, *Fourth* and *Fifth Advices* in a single volume, and by the manuscript statement in an important copy of this edition that they were "written for the Company of Poets."[53] Even if more than one poet was involved, however (and the question will probably never be finally settled), Marvell's position in the group must have been at the innovative center.

### THE *Loyall Scot*

In the 1670s there appeared another group of satires of which Marvell's authorship has been more generally presumed. The *Loyall Scot*, ascribed to Marvell in two printed texts,[54] is theoretically interesting as an extension of the problem raised in the *Advices*, as to how political sympathies affect the tone of public poetry, and the distribution of heroic or satiric perspectives. Taking off from Cleveland's

[53] Bodleian Gough Ms. London 14, as described above.
[54] See *Poems and Letters* I, 384-385.

satire, *The Rebel Scot* (1647), the poem is presented as an act of "favourable Pennance" performed by Cleveland's ghost, a recantation of his "former satyr"; and the "praise" that constitutes Cleveland's apology is nothing else but the account of Archibald Douglas's death in the Chatham disaster, made newly relevant by the discussions in Parliament early in 1670 of a possible union between England and Scotland.[55] The "death soe Generous," which in 1667 had served as a measurement of the English disgrace, now serves to "Unite our distance, fill the breaches old," and to eradicate political distinctions based on nationality. The argument for international union is developed in such a way as to explain the generic device of retributive praise:

> The world in all doth but two Nations bear,
> The good, the bad, and those mixt every where.
> Under each pole place either of the two,
> The good will bravely, bad will basely doe;
> And few indeed can paralell our Climes
> For Worth Heroick or Heroick Crimes.
>
> (ll. 236-241)

This is a long way from the easy satire of national character with which, in the *Character of Holland*, Marvell had been almost satisfied. From the Dutch War he had learned that no nation has a monopoly of courage or treachery and, if Marvell wrote these lines, the recantation in question must have been consciously his own, as well as "Cleavland's."

What makes me think he did, apart from the presence of the longest version of the poem in the Popple manuscript, is the tone of classical and Christian humanism with which it draws to a conclusion. The concept of nation, we are told,

---

[55] Discussions of possible union took place in Parliament in the winter of 1669-1670; Col. Blood's attempt on the crown took place on 9 May 1671; and if Marvell was responsible for the anticlerical satire, the whole poem may not have been put together until he had become involved in research into church history for the *Rehearsal Transpros'd*.

is really only a language problem, a result of the breakdown in human communication caused by the Fall:

> In Paradice Names only Nature Shew'd,
> At Babel names from pride and discord flow'd,
>
> . . .
>
> Rationall mens words pledges are of peace,
> Perverted serve dissentions to increase.
> For shame extirpate from each loyall brest
> That senseless Rancour against Interest.
> One King, one faith, one language and one Ile:
>
> (ll. 248-249, 256-260)

But the biblical myth is complemented by another, equally important passage in which Charles is compared to "the prudent Husbandman" who knows how to resolve the "idle tumult of his factious bees" by sprinkling them with meal "till none discern their foes." The allusion is to Virgil's *Georgics* IV, 85-86 ("hi motus animorum atque haec certamina tanta / pulveris exigui iactu compressa quiescunt"), and part of Virgil's compliment, through this time-sanctioned metaphor for a well-run state, to Augustan politics. The effect is to place Charles, "our great soul," on the right side of Marvell's ethical system, aligning him with the Augustan Cromwell of the *Horatian Ode* who became the "Husbandman" of his country celebrated in the *First Anniversary* (l. 286).

It remains true, of course, that this rational appeal for a peaceful use of language is preceded by nearly 150 lines of anticlerical satire, that section of the text that Margoliouth was reluctant to accept as Marvell's. It seems wiser, given the testimony of the Popple manuscript, to accept the canonical status of this passage, and to conclude that Marvell, while recanting from national satire, had discovered a new, universal, enemy. In a letter to William Popple of July 1675 Marvell was to describe the bishops in the House of Lords as having grown "odiously ridiculous" (II, 343), while Lauderdale's oppression of the Scottish Nonconformists, as the same letter makes clear, should be seen as part of an international papist conspiracy. It would not be surprising, then, if in 1669-1670 Marvell had perceived the Anglican clergy, in their opposition to Scotland, as unnatural monsters of hate and ambition. The theme of monstrosity familiar from the *Advices* is here rather effectively integrated into an argument about what is natural in the body politic, a metaphor especially appropriate to the man-shaped island in question:

> Prick down the point whoever has the Art
> Where Nature Scotland doth from England part.
> Anatomists may Sooner fix the Cells
> Where life resides or Understanding dwells:
> But this wee know, tho' that Exceed their skill,
> That whosoever separates them doth kill.
>
> (ll. 75-80)

The bishops' confusion of spiritual with secular power has become so excessive that "in a Baron Bishop you have both / Leviathen serv'd up and Behemoth," biblical and Hobbesian monsters which Marvell was shortly to associate with Samuel Parker. The *Loyall Scot* reminds its audience of the prodigious "scotch Twin headed man" who was born in the reign of James IV: "Nature in Living Embleme there Exprest / What Brittain was . . . / Well that Scotch monster and our Bishops sort" (ll. 190-191, 198).

## THE "STATUE" POEMS

The next stage of Marvell's satirical activity was also partly generated by a two-headed monstrosity, the "Episcopal Cavalier Party," whose growth Marvell had described to Popple in the letter mentioned above. In the same letter there is a significant account of the accompanying exercises in political symbolism or "Pageantry" designed to strengthen royalist feelings in the public. Marvell records dryly that "the old King's Statue on Horseback, of Brass, was bought, and to be set up at Charing-Cross, which hath been doing longer than Viner's, but does not yet see the Light. The old King's Body was to be taken up, to make a perfect Resurrection of Loyalty, and to be reinterred with great Magnificence" (II, 341-342). There is an obvious connection between this remark, with its skeptical recognition of the iconographical issue, and the three "Statue" poems ascribed by different sources to Marvell, two of which appear in the Popple manuscript; but while they have generally been admitted into the Marvell canon, they have sometimes been rigorously excluded from that other indefinite corpus, "his poetry properly so called."[56]

The "Statue" poems are, however, not without theoretical interest. It has been suggested, for example, that their cheerful crudity deliberately inverts Baroque conceptions of monumental dignity,[57] and in this they could broadly be compared to the parodic "Painter" poems. But in their details the "Statue" poems make their own contribution to the problems of political image making, and suggest that their conceptual structure is considerably more sophisticated than their formal properties. *The Statue in Stocks-Market*, for example, uses Sir Robert Viner's unattractive statue of Charles II as a metaphor for satirical meiosis. The statue "shews him a monster more like than a king," and is thus more "scandalous" than all the "Dutch pictures that caused the war." Those supposedly provocative reminders of 1667 suggest to the poet another metaphor, an analogy between the torn sails of Charles's fleet and the canvas which has for weeks past shrouded the statue during renovations. Both come between the spectator and the idea of royal splendor which the monument was intended to celebrate. What was erected "out of modesty" to conceal the statue's inadequacies becomes instead a visual emblem of past humiliations.

[56] See Margoliouth's comment on ll. 265-273 of the *Loyall Scot* (I, 393).
[57] Nevo, *The Dial of Virtue*, p. 165.

Finally, the carver's attempts, under cover of canvas, to "reform" his portrait are wittily double-edged: "For 'tis such a king as no chisel can mend." The reader suddenly becomes aware that the real king may be no better than his image, and that the satirist's viewpoint may be no distortion.

*The Statue at Charing Cross*, though less developed, extends the discussion of political symbolism by relating it to political motives. Danby's erection in 1675 of an equestrian statue of Charles I was designed both to "comfort the hearts of the poor Cavaleer" and to improve his own popularity, considerably damaged by his closing of the Exchequer. Much play is therefore made of the fact that the statue was made of brass, and the main emphasis is financial, but the satirist delivers an unmistakable warning about the dangers of propaganda that is too far removed from the known facts:

Does the Treasurer think men so Loyally tame
When their Pensions are stopt to be fool'd with a sight?
And 'tis fourty to one if he Play the old Game
Hee'l shortly reduce us to fourty and eight.

(ll. 21-24)

Finally, the *Dialogue between the Two Horses* connects both statues, and both statue poems, by imagining a discussion between their mounts when their riders have, for their own purposes, disappeared. This comic reversal of expectations is carefully established as generically sound, an appropriate device to be used in an age of political repression and censorship. The "Magpyes and Parratts" of the "Introduction" recall Skelton's *Speke Parrot*, conceived as a vehicle for safe criticism of Cardinal Wolsey, and the two horses are presented as topical examples of "Beasts that have uttered Articulate words" when their human counterparts have not dared to speak openly. The catalog of contemporary evils in accentual verse is deliberately archaic. "Bondage and Begery," though resulting from a "Curst hous of Commons" and a "rabble of Rascally Lords," are the same as ever they

seemed to early Tudor satirists, and the two horses discuss
a very old dilemma:

> Сн.　Enough, dear Brother, for tho' we have reason,
> 　　　Yet truth many times being punisht for Trea-
> 　　　　son,
> 　　　Wee ought to be wary and Bridle our Tongue;
> 　　　Bold speaking hath done both man and beast
> 　　　　wrong.
> 　　　　．　．　．
>
> W.　　Truth's as Bold as a Lyon, I am not afraid;
> 　　　I'le prove every tittle of what I have said.
> 　　　Our riders are absent; who is't that can hear?
> 　　　Letts be true to ourselves; whom then need
> 　　　　wee fear?
> 　　　　　　　　　　　　(ll. 97-100, 105-108)

The conclusion of the poem both clarifies the theoretical
function of this conceit (a cross between beast fable and
prophetic portent) and relates it historically to the December 1675 edict against coffee houses, which the king is advised, in distinctly threatening tones, to recall:

> Tho' Tyrants make Laws which they strictly proclaim
> To conceal their own crimes and cover their shame,
> Yet the beasts of the field or the stones in the wall
> Will publish their faults and prophesy their fall.
> When they take from the people the freedome of words,
> They teach them the Sooner to fall to their Swords.

If these lines are indeed Marvell's, they provide a natural
transition to the themes of his prose pamphlets, where problems of validity in political iconography give place to a
more systematic defense of "truth" and "freedome of
words" and conscience; at the same time the "Statue" poems
are the last examples of a calculated indecorum. In the
*Second Part* of the *Rehearsal Transpros'd*, in *Mr. Smirke*
and its appended *Historical Essay*, and especially in *The*

*Growth of Popery and Arbitrary Government,* Marvell moved gradually away from a belief in the political necessity of satire. Eventually he arrived at a position where it was possible to define the "tyrants" in the king's executive council as the new libelers of their sovereign's reputation; while the modest "relator" of their disloyal proceedings was identified instead with political and societal respectability.

# 4

## "The dignity of the Churche's jester":
## Theory of Polemic I

In the last two decades of the seventeenth century Marvell's contemporaries began to ascribe anonymous satires to him, and from 1689 his name was used as an advertisement for editions of *Poems on Affairs of State*. This magnetic function was not, however, generated by his verse satires, but by the *Rehearsal Transpros'd*, which appeared in two parts, in the autumn of 1672 and the winter of 1673-1674. Both parts, but especially the first, quickly established his reputation as the leading political satirist of his day. Gilbert Burnet's description of the two parts of the *Rehearsal* as "the wittiest books that have appeared in this age,"[1] Anthony à Wood's hostile admission that Marvell was "a very celebrated wit among the Fanaticks, and the only one truly so,"[2] and Dryden's connection in the preface to *Religio Laici* between Marvell and Martin Marprelate, "the first Presbyterian Scribbler, who sanctifi'd Libels and Scurrility to the use of the Good Old Cause" all tell the same story, that the *Rehearsal Transpros'd* was perceived, albeit grudgingly by his enemies, as an outstanding achievement in political satire. Twentieth-century critics who have been interested in the *Rehearsal* have usually directed their attention also to the satirical strategies and/or the political context of this unusually readable essay in propaganda, and in this one area of Marvell's canon there has been an admirable concurrence of literary and political inquiry.[3]

[1] Burnet, *History of My Own Time*, ed. O. Airy (Oxford, 1897), I, 467.
[2] Wood, *Athenae Oxonienses* (London, 1691), p. 620.
[3] The study of the satirical strategies of the *Rehearsal Transpros'd* was initiated by John S. Coolidge, "Martin Marprelate, Marvell and

Nevertheless (which is often a strategic conjunction in Marvell's debating style), to concentrate only on the satirical skills or the political doctrines of the *Rehearsal Transpros'd*, or indeed to concentrate upon the *Rehearsal* to the exclusion of the later pamphlets, is to lose sight of the essential difference between the verse satires and the prose. *The Character of Holland*, the "Painter" poems, the "Statue" poems, even the *Loyall Scot*, are recognizably "poems on affairs of State," with their focus on contemporary events and the behavior of public figures. The prose pamphlets, with the exception of the *Account of the Growth of Popery and Arbitrary Government*, are linked by their focus on church policy and doctrine, and with their more or less successful attempts to deal with longstanding ideological issues. It is important to remember that, from 1672 to 1678, when he published his *Remarks* in defense of the moderate Nonconformity of John Howe against a more adamant Calvinist, Marvell had turned his attention not just to the actual situation of the Nonconformists under the revived Clarendon Code but to the whole mammoth problem of the relationship between church and state, and to the validity of different structures of belief. It is easy to forget how much research he did into the opinions of the medieval Church Fathers and early ecclesiastical historians; it has consequently not been noticed that in these pamphlets Marvell was facing a different theoretical problem, not merely extending his newly developed satirical stance. In place of his focus on validity in public images, institutions, and forms

*Decorum Personae* as a Satirical Theme," *PMLA* 74 (1959), 526-532. It has since been skillfully developed by Raymond Anselment in "Satiric Strategy in Marvell's *The Rehearsal Transpros'd*," *MP* 68 (1970), 137-150; and " 'Betwixt Jest and Earnest' : Ironic Reversal in Andrew Marvell's *The Rehearsal Transpros'd*," *MLR* 66 (1971), 282-293. The political arguments of *The Rehearsal . . . The Second Part* were interpreted by John M. Wallace in *Destiny his Choice: The Loyalism of Andrew Marvell* (Cambridge, 1969); and see also D.I.B. Smith, "The Political Beliefs of Andrew Marvell," *UTQ* 36 (1966), 55-67.

of communication, Marvell discovered, as he worked on the problems of ecclesiastical polity, that in this area form could actually invalidate content. The dilemma confronting the church polemicist was that he too, like the satirist, was needed to correct or refute the errors of others; but how was he to dispute at all about the operating terms of Christianity without himself committing an offense, without betraying the definitively Christian values?

As always, Marvell's discovery of this permanent problem, and his gradual evolution of an acceptable rhetorical response, was the result of his commitment to topicality. What caused his entry into polemics was the combined occasion of Charles's Declaration of Indulgence in March 1672, which suspended all penal laws against both Roman Catholics and Nonconformists, and the appearance of an energetic campaigner for enforced religious conformity, in the person of Samuel Parker. The contrast between the king's apparent intentions and the published statements of a rising member of his church establishment was striking, and any suspicions Marvell may have had about the real meaning of the royal Declaration only made Parker more of a menace. It was not that his advice was likely to influence Charles (whom it seems he only succeeded in annoying)[4] but rather that his intolerance might give fuel to the persecuting spirit in the House of Commons, which was in fact shortly to enforce the retraction of the Declaration as exceeding the limits of royal prerogative.

What needed to be done, therefore, was that Parker should be discredited, and his views shown to be unacceptable to any rational being. John Owen, an Independent minister, had tried to answer Parker (and indeed gave Mar-

[4] D.I.B. Smith, ed., *The Rehearsal Transpros'd and the The Rehearsal Transpros'd: The Second Part* (Oxford, 1971), cites from *HMC Report* 7, p. 518a, Lord Anglesey's message to Roger L'Estrange that the king would not have the *Rehearsal Transpros'd* suppressed "for Parker has done him wrong, and this man has done him right" (xxii).

vell a number of strategic hints as to how he might be answered) but was partly disqualified by his role as a recognized spokesman for the Nonconformists. And so Marvell came in and, with the first part of the *Rehearsal Transpros'd*, not only demolished Parker's "Importance comfortable," as Rochester put it,[5] but made his own reputation. What he came to see, however, in the course of his intense exposure to Parker's style and methods, was that satire itself was a form of aggression, a version of the intolerance he despised and was attempting to refute. In Marvell's articulation of the opposite virtues as they ought to be exercised in church polity, he worked his way gradually toward a new theory of polemical style, not entirely devoid of wit, but more compatible with an ideal of moderation. Abandoning the methods of his personal success, he moved deliberately toward a polemic which was "not in the merry part so good as the Rehearsall Transpros'd," as he wrote to Sir Edward Harley about the reception of *Mr. Smirke* (II, 346). In this he was clearly directed by the fact that Parker himself had raised the theoretical issue, rejecting the norms of style historically associated with his own church party, and asserting his right to make use of satire and personal abuse. He thus encouraged Marvell to reconsider the whole tradition in England of Anglican-Puritan debate, and to work out for himself a somewhat more acceptable compromise position. In this situation there was no impulse to turn to classical models, and not only because the distinction between pagan and Christian thinking was central to Marvell's arguments. In the theory of polemical style, Englishmen had developed their own traditions, and the authority of the recent past was not to be ignored.

The initial stage of the Anglican-Puritan logomachy had been recognized by Parker himself as the historical context of his dispute with Marvell. He accused his opponent of

[5] John Wilmot, Earl of Rochester, "Tunbridge Wells," in *The Miscellaneous Works of the Right Hon. The Late Earls of Rochester and Roscommon* (London, 1707), p. 39.

adopting the strategies of the notorious Martin Marprelate pamphlets of the 1580s,[6] an accusation which Dryden repeated in reverse by calling Martin "the Marvell of those times." Initiated by Thomas Cartwright and the Cambridge Puritans, the Marprelate or Admonition Controversy had focused on the issue of vestments, the symbol of the impurity of the Elizabethan church settlement. Elizabeth's wily regime was never seriously incommoded by this voluble protest, but it was unpleasant enough to have motivated one of the most influential documents in Marvell's own development. In 1589 Francis Bacon wrote, apparently for private circulation, a pamphlet mediating between Anglicans and Puritans and calling for a cessation of hostilities. His purpose was not only to point out where each side was at fault but to emphasize what was or should be the common ground between them ("one Faith, one Baptisme, and not one Ceremonie, one Policie"), and to suggest some ground rules for the style and conduct of religious polemic conducted in the public press. Both sides were exhorted to drop the tone of abuse and mockery which had characterized the Marprelate pamphlets, and to discourse together in reason and charity. The open-mindedness familiar to readers of Bacon's essays, which can sometimes seem irritatingly inconclusive, here appears to its best advantage, a dignified objectivity which is yet capable of emotional force:

> Indeed bitter and earnest writing is not hastily to be condemned: for men cannot contend coldly and without affection about things they hold deare and pretious. A politicke man may write from his braine without touch or sense of his heart, as in a speculation that pertaineth not unto him; but a feeling Christian will expresse in his words a character either of zeale or love: the latter of which as I would wish rather to be embraced, as being more fit for the times; yet is the former

[6] Samuel Parker, *A Reproof to the Rehearsal Transpros'd* (London, 1673), pp. 105, 113.

warranted also by great examples. But to leave all reverend and religious compassion toward evils, or indignation toward faults, to turne religion into a Comedy or
Satyr, to search and rip up wounds with a laughing
countenance, to intermix Scripture and Scurrility sometime in one sentence, is a thing farre from the devout
reverence of a Christian, and scant beseeming the honest regard of a sober man.[7]

The significance of Bacon's protest, from a theoretical point
of view, lies in its capacity to amalgamate different levels of
reference. The surface of his statement is concerned with
rhetorical decorum, since the polemicists have muddled their
genres, treating the gravest of all subjects in the style of
comedy and satire; but this issue is both included in and
transcended by the criterion of Christianity itself, and the
behavioral implications of the doctrines under dispute.
Mockery, abuse, and *ad hominem* strategies are aesthetically
"low," destructive of the public peace, and intellectually
suspect, since they replace refutation by denigration. Furthermore, beyond such faults, which should be apparent
to any "sober man," they are incompatible with Christian
reverence and Christian charity.

This formulation of the polemicist's dilemma was central
to the next stage of Anglican–Puritan conflict. The Smectymnuan Controversy of the 1640s was, at more than one
level, a dispute over style. Vestments, liturgy, the episcopal
hierarchy itself could be and indeed were read as language,
a "style" of Christianity now far more seriously threatened
by an alternative decorum; on both sides rhetorical equivalents were formulated which matched the opposing polities.
On the left the Presbyterians, with Milton as their most
memorable spokesman, stood for change, and justified it by

[7] Cited from the first printed edition, *A Wise and Moderate Discourse* (London, 1641), pp. 7-8. See R. W. Gibson, *Francis Bacon, A
Bibliography of his Works and of Baconiana to the year 1750* (Oxford, 1950), Nos. 207a, 207b.

the language of zeal and enthusiasm. Milton's "vehemence," as he called it, included satire and abuse, for which he provided an elaborate rhetorical and scriptural defense.[8] On the right the Anglican clergy were represented most eloquently by Bishop Joseph Hall, for whom "decency" of ceremony and "moderation" of speech were the signs of an established church and a reasonable mind. Each set of terms had its negatives: to a Puritan, Anglican moderation was the luke-warmness rebuked in Revelations 3:15, and Anglican decency, itself authorized by 1 Corinthians 14:40, was a love of dress, the sign of a church still encrusted with Romish externality. To an Anglican, Puritan zeal was a form of madness, or at least bad temper. The author of *A Modest Confutation* defended Bishop Hall against Milton in terms which made explicit this exchangeability:

> Must he therefore be luke-warm, because his zeal burns not as hot as hell? Will Grace mix with nothing but adust choler, or lowring morose peevishnesse? Cannot Grace and Nature consist? When we deny ourselves, must we deny humanity? Doth Gods Spirit now inspire Christians, as the Devill did his Priests of old, by putting them out of their wits? . . . Why else cannot a sober, modest, humble, orthodox Prelate go for a Christian among us?[9]

The balance between these rival decorums was further symbolized by the use of the contradictory texts from Proverbs 26:4, 5 ("Answer not a fool according to his folly, lest thou also be like unto him. Answer a fool according to his folly,

---

[8] See Thomas Kranidas, *The Fierce Equation: A Study of Milton's Decorum* (The Hague, 1965); Irene Samuel, "Milton on Comedy and Satire," *HLQ* 35 (1971), 107-130; D. P. Speer, "Milton's 'Defensio Prima': 'Ethos' and Vituperation in a Polemic Engagement," *Quarterly Journal of Speech* 56 (1970), 277-283; my own "The Civic Hero in Milton's Prose," *MS* 8 (1975), 71-101; and James Egan, "Milton and the Marprelate Tradition," *MS* 8 (1975), 103-121.

[9] Anon., *A Modest Confutation* (1642), p. 18.

lest he be wise in his own conceit"). In *Animadversions* Milton had laid himself wide open by asserting that "it will be nothing disagreeing from Christian meeknesse to handle such a one in a rougher accent. . . . Nor to do this are we unautoritied either from the morall precept of Salomon."[10] Needless to say, the Modest Confuter made good use of the opposing text.

A further sign of the theoretical sophistication of this phase was the use of the defining terminology in the titles of pamphlets. Hall wrote a *Modest Offer* to the Westminster Assembly and a handbook on *Christian Moderation*, in which he formulated "rules" for religious debate. Milton wrote a set of *Animadversions*, which came to be the name for a certain type of aggressive, step-by-step destruction of someone else's argument. He also objected strenuously to the improper use of the term "modest" in the title of *A Modest Confutation*: "this officious epithet so hastily assuming the modesty which others are to judge of by reading is a strong presumption that this his modesty set there to sale in the frontispice, is not much addicted to blush . . . 'tis manifest his purpose was only to rub the forehead of his title with this word *modest*, that he might not want colour to be more impudent throughout his whole confutation."[11] One of the most striking of all such declarative titles was that under which Bacon's pamphlet was now published: *A Wise and Moderate Discourse, concerning Church-affairs. As it was written, long since, by the famous Author of those Considerations, which seem to have some reference to this. Now published for the common good* (1641). The title defines both the tone of Bacon's pamphlet, and the role its publishers hoped it would play. At the same moment as the original Marprelate tracts were themselves being reissued,[12] Bacon

[10] Milton, *Complete Prose Works*, ed. Don M. Wolfe *et al.* (New Haven, 1953-    ), I, 662-663.

[11] Milton, *Apology for Smectymnuus* (1642) in *Complete Prose Works*, I, 876.

[12] Coolidge, "Martin Marprelate, Marvell and *Decorum Personae*," p. 529.

was being summoned up as a voice of wisdom and sanity from the past, to argue against extremism of thought or violence of language.

The mediatorial function designed for Bacon's pamphlet can be partly distinguished from another source of attitudes to polemical style which also cut across party lines, replacing them by something we may call formal Christian ethics. In 1615, for example, the Puritan William Perkins had published *A Direction for the Government of the Tongue according to Gods word*, which frequently cites Augustine on the concept of holy silence, and defines the virtues of Christian communication as "Wisdom, Truth, Reverence, Modesty, Meekness, Sobriety, Urbanity, Fidelity, Care of others good name" (pp. 17-18), all of which are later extended to the government of the pen. Similarly, St. Ambrose's depaganized version of Cicero's *Offices*, translated in 1637, contains several chapters on restraint and modesty of speech, and at one point illustrates its criticism of contentiousness by Christ's rebuke of Peter for cutting off Malchus' ear (Matt. 26:51-53),[13] a text which was to become topical in both Anglican and Puritan disputes about passive obedience. The impact of this neoclassical approach to the ethics of rhetoric cannot be underestimated, and it even found its way, via John Wolleb's Christian Aristotelianism, into Milton's *De Doctrina Christiana*, which was probably being written in the 1640s.[14] Despite the strength of his tactical arguments to the contrary, Milton in the *De Doctrina* makes obeisance to a very different set of rhetorical virtues, *simplicitas, fidelitas, gravitas, taciturnitas, comitas, urbanitas, admonitio*.[15] Whatever the process of transmission, Marvell himself was clearly aware of this tradition. The *Second Part* of the *Rehearsal Transpros'd* makes mention of the

[13] *Christian Offices Crystal Glasse*, trans. Richard Humphrey (London, 1637), p. 13.

[14] See Maurice Kelly, "Milton's Debt to Wolleb's *Compendium Theologiae Christianae*," *PMLA* 50 (1935), 156-165.

[15] Milton, *Complete Prose Works*, VI, 766-770.

"Homileticall Conversable Virtues, *Veritas*, *Comitas*, and *Urbanitas*" (p. 265).

The clear polarities of the Smectymnuan Controversy were, in any case, inevitably blurred in subsequent stages of the Civil War, when the Presbyterians became the proponents of their own brand of orthodoxy, to be opposed by Independents, Levellers, and other subcultures of Puritanism. The challenge to a complex church polity by a would-be simple one was replaced by the issue of religious toleration, and the impossible search for a new structure broad enough to absorb the sectaries. Meanwhile the range of polemical styles expanded to include such diverse forms of reformism as Lilburne's appeals to popular sympathy (*England's Miserie, and Remedie*, 1645), Richard Overton's satirical allegory (*The Araignement of Mr. Persecution*, 1645), and the classicism of Milton's *Areopagitica*. Until there was once again an established church with a king at its head, polarization was impossible; and when, after twenty years of political chaos and a regicide, these conditions were fulfilled, and the Act of Uniformity drew the line between the two sides, there was naturally considerable anxiety about reopening hostilities. The farewell sermons of the ministers ejected from their pulpits on St. Bartholomew's Day were far from militant, emphasizing the duties of love, peace, and patience under persecution. John Collins reminded his parishioners of St. Ambrose's famous motto, "The Arms of the Church are prayers and tears,"[16] a topos which had been used in the previous generation by John Donne in articulating the defensive position of the Anglican church,[17] and by the author of *Eikon Basilike* in presenting Charles I as a Christian martyr.[18] The position of the con-

[16] John Collins, *Farewell Sermons of Some of the Most Eminent of thé Nonconformist Ministers* (London, 1816), p. 310.

[17] Donne, *Sermons*, ed. E. M. Simpson and G. R. Potter (Berkeley, 1953-1962) IX, 342; X, 122.

[18] *Eikon Basilike* (1648) presented "Charles's" deliberately pathetic statement that "My chiefest Armes left Me, were those only, which

forming ministers was probably fairly represented by Edward Stillingfleet, who published at the end of 1660 a plea for moderation and prudence in the settlement of church polity, under the title of *Irenicum. A Weapon—Salve for the Churches Wounds*, which resembled in tone and methodology Richard Hooker's *Lawes of Ecclesiastical Polity*, written in the 1590s to pacify the Admonition controversialists. When Edmund Calamy forgot himself and preached an inflammatory sermon on the spur of the moment, at Aldermanbury in December 1633, he was rebuked by O. Udall in the language of Hooker's preface: "Well Master Calamy, there will come a time when three words uttered with meeknesse and charity shall receive a far more blessed reward, then three thousand Volumes written with disdainfull sharpnesse of wit, and with malicious partiality."[19] As Milton withdrew into the poems of passive fortitude, the Nonconformists discovered a new spokesman in John Owen, whose response to the Clarendon Code was significantly (and accurately) entitled *A Peace-Offering in an Apology and humble Plea for Indulgence and Libertie of Conscience* (1667). Anthony à Wood impartially concluded that Owen "was one of the most gentile and fairest writers, who have appeared against the Church of England, as handling his Adversaries with far more civil, decent and temperate language than many of his fiery Brethren, and by confirming himself wholly to the cause without the unbecoming mixture of personal slanders and reflection."[20]

---

the Ancient Christians were wont to use against their Persecutors, Prayers and Teares" (p. 67). This was effectively parodied by Milton in *Eikonoklastes*, revealing its pacifism as nothing more than a rationalization of defeat: "were they Praiers and Teares that were listed at York, muster'd on Heworth Moore, and laid Siege to Hull for the guard of his Person?" (*Complete Prose*, III, 452.)

[19] O. Udall, *Perez Uzza. Or. A Serious Letter sent To Master Edm. Calamy January the 17th 1663, Touching His Sermon at Aldermanbury, December the 28th, Intimating his Close Design, and dangerous Insinuation against the Publick Peace* (London, 1663), p. 29.

[20] Wood, *Athenae Oxonienses*, II, 558.

Even in the period of disillusionment following the Dutch War and the fall of Clarendon, when Nonconformity flourished and the "terrible Bill against Conventicles" was in the making, the Puritans exhorted each other (and were exhorted) to behave in the spirit of the Beatitudes. Simon Patrick's *Friendly Debates* and Bishop Gilbert Burnet's *Modest and Free Conference Betwixt a Conformist and a Nonconformist . . . By a Lover of Peace* (1669) both exemplify, if rather speciously, Anglican desire for rational discussion. Burnet's "Conformist" reproaches his "Nonconformist" for his contentiousness by recalling the story of Malchus' ear: "Do you think that God cannot maintain his own right, but the wrath of man must work his righteousnesse? nay, we see the contrary, for from the beginning till this day, God hath made the sufferings of his people, the chief mean of propagating Religion; whereas fighting hath been ever fatal to it. And Christ did begin the Gospel with his suffering, though he could have commanded Legions of Angels for his defence. . . . Since then he forbade his Disciples to draw a sword for him, with so severe a threatning, as 'whosoever will draw the sword, shall perish by the sword' " (pp. 7-8).

It is all the more startling, therefore, to read the preface to Samuel Parker's *Discourse of Ecclesiastical Politie* (1669), in which he set out to justify the violence of his own polemic style by an account of Nonconformist writing which is partially obsolete and certainly exaggerated, but which recalls the terminology of the Smectymnuan Controversy in an unpleasing rearrangement. He asked:

Let any man, that is acquainted with the Wisdom and Sobriety of True Religion, tell me how 'tis possible not to be provoked to scorn and indignation against such proud, ignorant, and supercilious Hypocrites; who though they utterly defeat all the main Designs of Religion, yet boast themselves its only Friends and Patrons; signalize their Party by distinctive Titles and

Characters of Godliness, and brand all others, howso-
ever Pious and Peaceable, with bad Names, and worse
Suspicions? . . . Thus the only hot fit of Zeal we find
our Saviour in, was kindled by an Indignation against
the Pride and Insolence of the Jews, when he whipt
the Buyers and Sellers out of the outward Court of
the Temple. . . . Now to lash these morose and churlish
Zealots with smart and twingeing Satyrs is so farr from
being a criminal Passion, that 'tis a Zeal of Meekness
and Charity. . . . If you will ever silence them, you
must be as vehement as they: nothing but Zeal can en-
counter Zeal.[21]

In other words, Parker asserted, the moderation formerly
associated with the Anglican position was no longer an
adequate response to enthusiasm; he identified himself with
the position defined and defended by Milton, the Juvenalian
satirist and scourge who nevertheless believes that his anger
is not incompatible with "Meekness and Charity." Parker's
choice of decorum therefore matched his advice to the
king, whom he urged to employ his prerogative in a vigorous campaign to eradicate Nonconformity, and to employ
persecution where necessary as an instrument of political
stabilization.

The implications of both style and argument were immediately perceived by John Owen, who temporarily suspended his own pacifist stance, and so indicated on the title
page of *Truth and Innocence Vindicated* (1669): "Non
Par[t]um studiis agimur; sed sumsimus arma, Consiliis
in[n]imica tuis, Discordia Vaecors" ("We are not a little
driven from our studies; but we take up arms hostile to
your counsels, you crazy figure of Discord"). Owen's re-

---

[21] Samuel Parker, *A Discourse of Ecclesiastical Politie, Wherein
The Authority of the Civil Magistrate Over the Consciences of Sub-
jects in Matters of External Religion is Asserted; The Mischiefs and
Inconveniences of Toleration are Represented, And All Pretenses
Pleaded in Behalf of Liberty of Conscience are Fully Answered* (Lon-
don, 1669), iii-ix. Parker's title adequately represented his thesis.

sponse to Parker's belligerence was of enormous importance
for Marvell, for he perceived that the language of aggression could be turned against itself. Absorbing the achievements of Cervantes and Butler,[22] Owen created a mock-
heroic persona for his opponent which took the sting out of
conflict. Violence was defeated by good humor. Parker
was recognized as "some great Commander, In *Campis Gur-
gistidoniis / Ubi Bombamachides Cluninstaridysarchides /
Erat Imperator Summus* . . . such expressions *animi gladia-
torii* doth he march withall." And Owen wondered why
"such a Man of Arms and Art as he is, should harness himself with so much preparation, and enter the Lists with so
much pomp and glory, to combat such pittiful poor baffled
Ignoramus's as he hath chosen to contend withall." It would
have been more appropriate for him "to have sought out
some Giant in Reason and Learning, that might have given
him at least *par animo periculum,* as Alexander said in his
conflict with Porus, a danger big enough to exercise his
Courage, though through mistake it should in the issue have
proved but a Wind-mill" (pp. 13-14).

But it was not enough to make Parker look foolish. His
arguments had to be countered by logic and revealed as
suspect by a more fundamental criterion. Parker was reproached for irreverence in citing the precedent of Christ's
anger at the moneylenders: "Let any sober man judge . . .
whether those expressions he useth of the *hot fit of zeal* . . .
do become that Reverence and Adoration of the Son of
God which ought to possess the hearts, and guide the
Tongues and Writings of men that profess his Name" (p.
38). He was accused of theological error, of a radical confusion between pagan morality and Christian grace. In
Parker's account of human nature since the Fall there is
"neither Supposition, nor Assertion of Sin, or of a Re-
deemer" (p. 204), the result being "the rudest, most imper-

---

[22] The first two parts of *Hudibras,* published in 1663, and containing a satirical caricature of Nonconformity, made mock-heroic a
*topical* strategy.

fect and weakest Scheme of Religion" that Owen ever saw
(p. 198). And he represented, Owen suggested, a clergy
who had a history not only of unwarranted interference in
affairs of state but of an anti-Christian spirit of intolerance
and persecution:

> It is certain, for those in particular, who take upon them
> . . . to be Ministers of the Gospel, there are commands
> for meekness, patience and forbearance, given unto
> them. And it is one of the greatest duties incumbent on
> them, to express the Lord Jesus Christ, in the frame of
> his mind and Spirit unto men; . . . I know not therefore
> whence it is come to pass, that this sort of men do prin-
> cipally, if not only, stir up Magistrates and Rulers to
> Laws, Severities, Penalties, Coercions, Imprisonments,
> and the like outward means of fierce and carnal power,
> against those, who in anything dissent from them in
> Religion.
>
> (p. 403)

## THE *Rehearsal Transpros'd*

There is no question but that Marvell was deeply indebted to Owen's pamphlet for the tone and method of the
first part of the *Rehearsal Transpros'd*. Marvell's mockery
of Parker as crazy Quixote, false Crusader and "Buffoon-
General to the Church of England" (p. 22) derives directly
from Owen, sometimes with specific echoes of phrase. Marvell, for example, tells his audience not to underrate Parker's
crusading zeal by thinking he will "enter the Lists where he
hath but one man to combate . . . Hungary, Transylvania,
Bohemia, Poland, Savoy, France, the Netherlands, Den-
mark, Sweden, and a great part of the Church of England,
and all Scotland . . . may perhaps rouse our Mastiff, and
make up a Danger worthy of his Courage" (p. 21). A
glance back at the quotations from Owen will show where
this passage originated but, in addition to the mock-heroic

strategies which Marvell developed and expanded, and which made the *Rehearsal Transpros'd* an instant success, the influence of Owen's arguments is also apparent. Like Owen, Marvell was twice provoked to comment on the irreverence of "that most unsafe passage" in Parker's preface where a "hot fit of zeal" was attributed to Christ (pp. 76, 144); like Owen, Marvell attacked Parker for his inability to distinguish between Grace and mere morality, and remarked acidly that "all Astragon appear'd . . . the better Scheme of Religion" (p. 143); and, following on Owen's initiative, Marvell developed the hypothesis that the Anglican clergy whom Parker represents have a record of propagating "the most precipitate, brutish and sanguinary Counsels." They are defined by the "*Rationem ultimam Cleri*; Force, Law, Execution. . . . You would think the same day that they took up Divinity they divested themselves of Humanity, & so they may procure & execute a Law against the Nonconformists, that they had forgot the Gospel" (pp. 106-107). In the context of the Declaration of Indulgence, Marvell was able to develop Owen's criticism into a fundamental contrast between Charles and his ecclesiastical advisors: "God be prais'd his Majesty is far of another temper" (p. 60). The effect is similar to the distinction between king and council in the satirical *Advices*; the implication is that the Declaration of Indulgence, however unconstitutional, imitated in spirit the New Dispensation. Marvell's reliance on Owen, to whose defense he came but to whom he gives no scholarly credit, did not go unnoticed. As Parker himself observed in *The Reproof to the Rehearsal Transpros'd*, "This is very shrewd, but then it is none of your own, J. O. had it before you, and in truth you are so given to purloining, that I expect ere long to hear of you among the Advertisements at the bottom of the Gazet."[23]

This substantial act of borrowing contributes to the confusions of attitude, the rather muddled decorum, which

[23] Parker, *Reproof*, p. 28.

characterize the first part of the *Rehearsal Transpros'd*. On the one hand, the need to discredit Parker has clearly directed Marvell to satiric and comic strategies which have been proven successful elsewhere. The title page identifies Marvell's pamphlet as belonging to the combative genre of animadversions, to which Milton had given a certain polish in his contest with Bishop Joseph Hall. Attention is also drawn to the Marprelate rationale for satire: "not to be grave with a Buffoon" (p. 49). More importantly, the sustained allusion to Buckingham's dramatic burlesque, *The Rehearsal*, allows Marvell to capitalize on Buckingham's deflation of Dryden, while at the same time, perhaps, exploiting the king's fondness both for the theatre and for Buckingham himself. The connection between all these precedents, of course, is not just the value judgment that Parker's work is itself "part Play-book and part Romance" (p. 12). It is that all of them had been directed against the enemies of the Nonconformists. Marvell makes this very point about his assimilation of Parker to the name and character of Bayes, Buckingham's parody of a poet-Laureate gone crazy with self-importance:

> ... Mr. Bayes and he do very much Symbolize; in their understandings, in their expressions, in their humour, in their contempt and quarrelling of all others, though of their own Profession ... And ... because both their Talents do peculiarly lie in exposing and personating the Nonconformists.
>
> (pp. 9-10)

On the other hand, Marvell seems genuinely offended by Parker's lack of "modesty," which is from the very first page a key word in the pamphlet; he attacks him vigorously for his "railing" style, claiming to replace it by raillery, but constantly asserting the absolute values of pacifism and restraint. The result is a radical inconsistency, which had been partially apparent in Owen's model but is fully developed in the *Rehearsal Transpros'd*. In regretting the Civil War, Marvell recalled St. Ambrose's aphorism that the "Arms of the Church are Prayers and Tears" (p. 135). In the very act of answering Parker, however, he had necessarily abandoned that pacifist ideal; and the more successfully he attacked Parker's personality, the closer he came to committing Parker's own offenses. The last paragraph of the *Rehearsal Transpros'd* seems to me to betray uneasiness on this score. Marvell professes that he will be "recompensed" for the labor of pursuing Parker from one disgraceful statement to another *if* his own polemical methods have seemed to the reader to be appropriate to the task: "if any one that hath been formerly of another mind, shall learn by this Example, that it is not impossible to be merry and angry . . . without profaning and violating those things which are and ought to be most sacred" (p. 145). The negative syntax of this appeal is more suggestive of anxiety than satisfaction, and it leads directly into the *Second Part* of the *Rehearsal Transpros'd*, where the tensions in Marvell's polemical theory are made explicit.

It has been observed that the *Second Part* of Marvell's response to Parker is a fully premeditated work of epic proportions,[24] announced by Marvell in a letter to Sir Edward Harley, in which he described being "drawn in . . . to intermeddle in a noble and high argument." If that is indeed an epic proposition, Marvell's remarks to Harley about the work in progress suggest an undertaking which has affinities with *Paradise Lost*, whose "Argument" Marvell may have been reading at this time, in preparation for his own contribution to the 1674 edition. The lines *On Mr. Milton's Paradise Lost* focus on the problem of the writer who tackles a great theological subject, and acclaim Milton's style as being so equal to his material that no one could accuse him of irreverence:

[24] Wallace, in *Destiny his Choice*, pp. 196-207, greatly increased the respect of all subsequent readers for Marvell's argument while, to my view, underemphasizing its theological aspects.

That Majesty which through thy Work doth Reign
Draws the Devout, deterring the Profane.
And things divine thou treatst of in such state
As them preserves, and Thee inviolate.
At once delight and horrour on us seize,
Thou singst with so much gravity and ease;
And above humane flight dost soar aloft,
With Plume so strong, so equal, and so soft.

(I, 138)

Similar preoccupations appear in the letter to Harley. "I will," he wrote, "for mine own private satisfaction forthwith draw up an answer that shall have as much of spirit and solidity in it as my ability will afford & the age we live in will indure. I am (if I may say it with reverence) drawn in, I hope by a good Providence, to intermeddle in a noble and high argument which therefore by how much it is above my capacity I shall use the more industry not to disparage it" (II, 328). It is much to the point that Marvell's praise of Milton focuses on the blend of apparently irreconcilable opposites, "delight and horrour," "gravity and ease," which makes for an acceptable theological poem; for consciousness of a mixed decorum, as well as an almost obsessive concern with the problem of reverence, is everywhere apparent in Marvell's second pamphlet.

The *Second Part* begins (after a few pages of scurrilous jokes at Parker's expense) with Marvell's response to the charge that he has been disrespectful toward Parker's office as representative of the church, that he has offended against "the Gravity of his Profession" (p. 159). What follows is, in effect, an apology for, and defense of Marvell's satirical strategies. He begins by stating that all writing is an "envious and dangerous imployment" because one's motives are invariably open to misinterpretation, and "not to Write at all is much the safer course of life." But while all writing is dangerous, satirical writing is doubly so, since it may very

193

likely endanger one's own reputation, but it will certainly damage that of one's victim, and hence the structure of mutual confidence on which society is based:

> For 'tis better that evil men should be left in an undis-
> turbed possession of their repute . . . then that the Ex-
> change and Credit of mankind should be universally
> shaken . . . how can the Author of an Invective, though
> never so truely founded, expect approbation . . . who,
> in a world all furnished with subjects of praise, in-
> struction and learned inquiry, shall studiously chuse
> and set himself apart to comment upon the blemishes
> and imperfections of some particular person?
>
> (p. 161)

Furthermore, beyond the writer's duty to support societal ideals in general, there is a pressing reason why "the Clergy certainly of all others ought to be kept and preserv'd sacred in their Reputation. For . . . few Men will or can be perswaded by his Doctrine, whose practice they conceive to be opposite" (p. 162). Marvell has carefully constructed a hierarchy of reasons, from personal through social to religious, as to why one should *not* do what he has recently and most successfully done.

Then, with a remarkable reversal, and a characteristic conjunction, Marvell revokes all three general objections in the particular case: "And yet *nevertheless*, and all that has been said before being granted, it may so chance that to write, and that Satyrically, and . . . this too even against a Clergyman, may be not only excusable but necessary" (p. 163). A clergyman who leaves his pulpit to commit himself to the public press, Marvell asserts, has given up his right to sanctuary, has himself destroyed "the Gravity of his Profession": "In this Case . . . a Clergy-man is laid open to the Pen of any one that knows how to manage it; and every person who has either Wit, Learning or Sobriety is licensed, if debauch'd to curb him, if erroneous to catechize him, and if foul-mouth'd and biting, to muzzle him" (p. 164). Since

Parker's superiors in the church have neglected either to catechize or to curb him, to correct either his style or his doctrine, it has been left to Marvell, a "private man" and amateur theologian, to undertake this double duty. Rhetorically, it is the "nevertheless" at the crucial moment which reverses our expectations, and turns self-accusation into self-defense.

However, Marvell goes out of his way to emphasize that the task remains unattractive, and that he is temperamentally unsuited to the satirist's role. Forced out of a lifetime of "modest retiredness" (p. 169), he claims a special kind of shyness: "For I am too conscious of mine own imperfections to rake into and dilate upon the failings of other men; and though I carry always some ill Nature about me, yet it is I hope no more than is in this world necessary for a Preservative" (p. 165). Admittedly "modest retiredness" is an unusual description of the life of a Member of Parliament, and charitable humility is a disingenuous claim for the author of the *Last Instructions*. But, disingenuously or not, Marvell manages to give this apology a convincing tone of weariness and distaste. "It hath been thus far the odiousest task that ever I undertook, and has look't to be all the while like the cruelty of a Living Dissection, which, however it may tend to publick instruction, and though I have pick'd out the most noxious Creature to be anatomiz'd, yet doth scarse excuse or recompence the offensiveness of the scent and fouling of my fingers" (p. 185). The effect is therefore very different from Milton's *Apology for Smectymnuus*, which bears the same kind of relationship to his *Animadversions* as Marvell's second pamphlet does to his first. Both are self-defenses but, whereas Milton's *Apology* is at least as aggressive as what it justifies, Marvell's is so negatively constructed as to be virtually self-conviction.

Despite this clear awareness of the polemicist's dilemma, Marvell declares himself committed to finishing the unpleasant task, which he proposes to manage by a mixture of rhetorical strategies:

Yet I will not decline the pursuit, but plod on after him
in his own way, thorow thick and thin, hill or dale, over
hedge and ditch wherever he leads; till I have laid hands
on him, and deliver'd him bound either to Reason or
Laughter, to Justice or Pity. If at any turn he gives me
the least opportunity to be serious I shall gladly take
it: but where he prevaricates or is scurrilous (and
where is he not?) I shall treat him betwixt Jest and
Earnest.

(p. 187)

As Marvell was later to discover, this was no real solution
to the fundamental clash of values defined in Bacon's *Wise
and Moderate Discourse*, and he was shortly to move much
closer to the Baconian position. For the moment, however,
the proposal to alternate satire with serious argument, and
the suggestion of a point of compromise "betwixt Jest and
Earnest" allowed Marvell to develop his critique of Parker's arguments with a new seriousness, while pausing from
time to time to hit below the belt.

Even the most blatantly satirical parts of the new pamphlet, however, have been given a certain coherence and
moral authority. The defamation of Parker's personality
depends on three propositions, between which, it seems,
Marvell has been careful to establish links. Firstly, Parker,
having unwisely referred in his *Reproof to the Rehearsal
Transprosed* to a "distemper" which had delayed his response, is by his own admission diseased. He suffers certainly from "Abelteria, a Greek discomposure," meaning
stupidity, but which may also be the symptom of "a more
active and stirring Disease" which "derives its name from a
Countrey much nearer" (p. 152), the French pox which
was also rampant in the world of the Dutch War satires.
Venereal disease has, of course, madness as one of its consequences, and it continues to be part of Marvell's purpose
to suggest that Parker's zeal is a form of insanity, though

196

he is also by this time suffering from jaundice, the jealousy disease, brought on by the literary success of Marvell's first pamphlet. He seems in more than one sense, "sick of the *Rehearsal Transpros'd*": "The great little Animal was on a sudden turn'd so Yellow, and grown withall so unwieldy, that he might have past currant for the Elephant upon a Guinny" (p. 156).

This last quotation provides one of the several connections Marvell makes between the theme of disease and the theme of bestiality, a conventional but nonetheless effective procedure for dehumanization. Parker's distempers, we are later told, are liable to infect the entire ecclesiastical system:

> Yet then if our great Pastors should but exercise the Wisdom of common Shepheards, by parting with one to stop the infection of the whole Flock, when his rottenness grew notorious; or if our Clergy would but use the instinct of other creatures, and chase the blown Deer out of their Heard; such mischiefs might quickly be remedied.
>
> (p. 164)

The same passage identifies Parker also as a mad dog, "foul-mouth'd and biting," which it is Marvell's duty to muzzle, and as the traditional goat-man, a "Satyr out of his own bounds," who ought to be hunted "thorow the woods with hounds and horn home to his harbour" (p. 165). The juxtaposition of these images reveals that the bestialization of Parker is intelligibly related to Marvell's generic purpose, and that his own hunting of Parker is to be justified by his victim's loss of human status. It is to be distinguished, however, from the antisocial forms of satire which Parker himself practices, symbolized by the figure of the mad dog, which recalls the Blatant Beast of Spenser's *Faerie Queene* VI, an image of irrational slander and detraction let loose upon the world. And at the very end of his pamphlet Marvell confirms his source and repeats the charge:

> You are a Blatant Writer and a Latrant; and for lesser crimes, though of the same nature, was Gnevoski, the Polander, sentenc'd to lye barking underneath the Table.

(p. 327)

It is through the hunting metaphor, also, that Marvell's generic intentions are connected to his political message. If hunting the beast might, for society's protection, be justified, it was also potentially a metaphor for tyranny, by association with Nimrod, the first hunter in Christian history (Genesis 10: 8-9), whom generations of commentators had established also as the first of absolute rulers. Part of Marvell's serious strategy is to advise the king against political theory derived from the Nimrod precedent, and to warn him that "Princes, whose dominion over mankind resembles in some measure that of man over other creatures," cannot expect to prosper, "if by continual terrour they amaze, shatter, and hare their People, driving them into Woods, & running them upon Precipices." Rather they should cultivate a pastoral mode of government, for the "wealth of a Shepheard depends upon the multitude of his flock, the goodness of their Pasture, and the Quietness of their feeding" (p. 234).

Political meaning continues to assert itself in other sections of Marvell's bestiary. Parker at one stage is being hunted as a whale (p. 198); a few pages later we are shown that this connects him with Hobbes, whose theoretical absolutism, indeed, Parker has outdone: "I do not see," remarks Marvell, "but your Behemoth exceeds his Leviathan some foot long" (p. 214). Still later, we perceive that the whale image signifies Parker's fatal distortion of scale and proportion. As a whale is to a fly, so Parker's arguments make the ceremonial issue "at once stupendiously necessary and at the same time despicably little" (p. 308).

198

The intellectual coherence of Marvell's bestiary depends, however, on levels of meaning more profound than those of politics. As with the theme of disease, Parker himself had given Marvell an opening. In his *Free and Impartial Censure of the Platonick Philosophie* (1667), Parker had suggested that the controls exerted by virtue and religion might cause a backlash, and that "when the man is divided from the Beast" by those imperatives, his "inferiour and brutish appetites" will often fight back. This passage proves, Marvell asserts with glee, that the man in Parker's own composition "may at some time have been obliged to carry the brute a pick a pack" (p. 154). But beyond this easy victory, it is Parker's denial of spirituality in book after book which justifies his bestialization. It is in this context that we can understand the long quotation from Donne's *Progress of the Soul* which, as Marvell must have discovered to his delight, unites in one cynical passage all the components of his own bestiary, and grounds them firmly, if absurdly, on the story of the Fall. In Donne's poem, the soul, or principle of *evil*, began its life cycle in a "chast and innocent Apple," became at one stage a lustful cock sparrow, and at another a little fish who grew up to be "the great Leviathan." Contraction and expansion were repeated in the stages of mouse and elephant, and then the soul moved into more destructive forms, spending some time both as a dog and as a wolf who harassed the flock of Abel, the first shepherd. Eventually, "after this Soul had passed thorow so many Brutes, & been hunted from post to pillar," it took refuge in a human, female form, and was married to Cain, the first murderer (pp. 176-177).

There is, finally, a natural connection between seeing Parker as brute, and presenting him as a reincarnation of the persecuting Roman emperors, Nero, Caligula, and Julian the Apostate. Marvell devotes several hilarious pages to working out this analogy, which is formally linked to the theme of brutalization by the story of Caligula's horse, an apt metaphor for Parker the place-seeker:

This same Caligula was he that took so great affection to Incitatus, a fleet and metall'd Courser, that beside a Stable of Marble, a Manger of Ivory, Housing-cloaths of Purple, and a Poictrell of precious stones, he furnish'd him an house very nobly, and appointed him a family to entertain those who render'd visits to his Equinity and his Hinnibility. . . . Nay, so far did he carry on this humour, that 'tis said, had he not been prevented, he design'd to have made this race-horse Consul; as fit however for that Office, as his Master to be Emperor. What pity 'tis, Mr. Bayes, that you did not live in that fortunate age, when desert was so well rewarded and understood, when preferments were so current! Certainly one of your Heels and Mettle would quickly have arrived to be something more then an Arch-Deacon.

(p. 219)

From being an emperor's horse, however, Parker grows gradually indistinguishable from Nero in "Savage cruelty" (p. 216), Caligula in egomania, and Julian in mockery of the Christians. This deft application of ecclesiastical history is, furthermore, integrated into the formal structure of Marvell's attack; for it serves as the subject matter or "plot" of "Debauchery Tolerated" and "Persecution Recommended," two of the six "plays" attributed to Bayes in the overall theatrical metaphor, and previously sketched out in the first part of the *Rehearsal Transpros'd*.

The heart of Marvell's new profundity lies, however, in his elaboration of the first three "plays," the self-contradictory notions of an "Unlimited Magistrate," "Public Conscience," and "Moral Grace." To judge from Marvell's own emphasis, the most dangerous of Parker's theses, in its possible effects on the religious and political life of England, was that an unlimited royal prerogative in ecclesiastical matters was not only established by divine authority but actually required for the safety of the state. As Parker him-

200

self had complained in his *Reproof*, Marvell had initially avoided this tricky theoretical issue; but in the new pamphlet, and the different political circumstances of 1673, it was essential to confront it directly. The Declaration of Indulgence, now withdrawn, could be recognized as a sop to Nonconformist opinion to make more palatable Charles's renewal of hostilities against the Protestant Dutch. The Test Act against Catholics, passed by the Commons in reaction and suspicion, had made an avowed Catholic of the heir presumptive, James, Duke of York, who promptly confirmed his intentions by marrying "the most bigoted and francophile Catholic available,"[25] the Italian Duchess of Modena. In Scotland, Lauderdale, maintaining a standing army, was actively persecuting the Presbyterians; the Roman Catholics in Ireland had agents at court, one of whom was discovered, as a result of a coaching accident, to be in close contact with the Treasurer Clifford;[26] and, perhaps as a consequence of Clifford's resignation under the Test, rumors were circulating about the secret clause in the Treaty of Dover whereby Charles had committed himself, as part of his alliance with Louis XIV, to announce his own conversion, and to support his position if necessary with the assistance of French troops. A situation which, in November 1673, drove Shaftesbury, only recently appointed Chancellor, into the Opposition, could scarcely have failed to affect Marvell; and in refuting the idea of a monarch with unlimited power over the religious life of his subjects he extended, I think, a subtle warning to Charles against any further interference in ecclesiastical matters. The issue of persecution had broadened to the point where it was possible to see a whole nation out of conformity with the religion practiced at court. It was not merely the spirit of

[25] J. P. Kenyon, *The Stuarts* (Glasgow, 1958, 1970), p. 121.

[26] Margoliouth, *The Poems and Letters of Andrew Marvell*, rev. ed., ed. Legouis (Oxford, 1971), I, 422, provided a summary of the events of 1673 as part of his commentary on the *Advice to a Painter to Draw the Duke by*.

exaggeration which dictated Marvell's response to Parker's proposition that the "Magistrate hath Power to bind his Subjects to that Religion that he apprehends most advantageous to publick Peace and Tranquillity": "So that he may if he chuse his Religion," Marvell wrote, "chuse his God too . . . and if he begin to think as you say he does, 'that Christianity is an enemy to Government,' he may make use of Paganism" (p. 213).

Rhetorically, Marvell's refutation of Parker's central thesis is extremely subtle. His strategy was to replace his opponent's all-or-nothing approach with a set of finer distinctions, in which the sources, sanctions, and uses of power are carefully separated and analyzed. Similar arguments in the Cromwell poems are, perhaps deliberately, recalled. He begins, in a long elegiac passage, by reminding his audience that magistracy itself is less than an ideal institution. It "were desirable," of course, "that men might live in perpetual Peace, in a state of good Nature, without Law or Magistrate"; but prelapsarian society is gone for better or worse, and in its place we experience, as part of our punishment for the Fall, "intermitting seasons of Discord, War, and publick Disturbance." "Nevertheless," Marvell continues, "it is most certain, that Tranquillity in Government is by all just means to be sought after" and, a moment later, "The Power of the Magistrate does most certainly issue from the Divine Authority" (pp. 231-232). Without admitting any Hobbesian reasoning, some sense of causation is implicit in the *placing* of these arguments; the concept of divinely authorized power has already been limited by its seeming to be one of the consequences of the Fall.

Marvell then proceeds to what he calls "the modester Question . . . how far it is advisable for a Prince to exert and push the rigour of that Power which no man can deny him" (p. 233). It is in this section that he emphasizes the prudential value of clemency and moderation,[27] going so far as to

[27] According to Wallace, this pragmatic approach is the whole of Marvell's argument.

suggest that a wise patience on the ruler's part will have the effect of depoliticizing his subjects, who will out of gratitude and security themselves abrogate their constitutional rights: "I will not say what one Prince may compass within his own time, or what a second, though surely much may be done: but it is enough if a great and durable design be accomplished in the third Life, and, supposing an hereditary succession of any three taking up still where the other left, and dealing still in that fair and tender way of management, it is impossible but that even without reach or intention upon the Princes part, all should fall into his hand, and in so short a time the very memory or thoughts of any such thing as Publick liberty would, as it were by consent, expire and be for ever extinguish'd" (p. 234). This passage is in flagrant contradiction both of Marvell's private views as expressed in his letters[28] and his future defense of civil liberties in the *Account of the Growth of Popery and Arbitrary Government*; but we will be less likely to misinterpret its function if we recognize that it is also a parody of part of the *First Anniversary*. There, Marvell attacked the hereditary monarchs who, unlike Cromwell, fail to accomplish anything of value in a single generation, "For one Thing never was by one King done." In place of that "wondrous Order and Consent" when Cromwell reestablished constitutional government, anticipating the "great Designes kept for the latter Dayes," Marvell now suggests that "a great and durable design" to subvert the constitution might be completed, "as it were by consent," in the reign of James's successor. The irony of this encouraging proposal is matched by the sardonic quality of Marvell's warnings. "A Prince that goes to the Top of his Power," he remarks, "is like him that shall go to the Bottom of his Treasure" (p. 235). So

[28] Compare the letter to Popple of 14 April 1670, in which Marvell described a proposed addition to the Conventicles Act as one which would have restored to the king "all civil or ecclesiastical Prerogatives which his Ancestors had enjoyed at anytime since the Conquest . . . a Piece of absolute universal Tyranny" (*Poems and Letters*, II, 317).

long as Parliament retained its fiscal sanctions, the political prudence of the monarch could, to some extent, be enforced.

However, as in the political situation there had begun to be apparent a level of crucial religious significance, so in Marvell's rhetorical strategy the argument from expediency gives way to a more profound criterion. What is advisable in the pragmatics of power is distinguished from what is actually required of a king by the source from which his power derives. For "as it is the Wisdom and Virtue of a Prince" to rule with moderation, "so he hath that advantage that his safety herein is fortified by his Duty, and as being a Christian magistrate, he has the stronger obligation upon him to govern his Subjects in this Christian manner" (p. 235). Indeed, Marvell's conclusion to this argument happily unites the duties of both subject and magistrate and, translating into more acceptable terms his advice as to how "Publick liberty" might be made obsolete, he anticipates the withering away of all laws and secular structures, not excepting monarchy itself:

> [Christ] by the Gospel gave Law to Princes and Subjects, obliging all mankind to such a peaceable and gentle frame of Spirit as would be the greatest and most lasting security to Government, rendring the People tractable to Superiors, and the Magistrate not grievous in the exercise of his Dominion: And he knew very well that *without dethroning the Princes of the World at present*, yet by the constant preaching of that benevolous and amiable Doctrine . . . all opposition would be worn out, and all Princes should make place for a Christian Empire.
>
> (p. 236)

In the argument as a whole, this carefully manipulated sequence of moods, tenses, and epistemological signposts ("it were desirable," "it is most certain," "it is advisable," "it is solemnly commanded") recalls, with some difference, the method of the *Horatian Ode*. There syntax was used to distinguish between attitudes to power which were clearly the responses of a single mind, divided by conflict of loyalties and the limitations of historical perspective. Here the shifts in language are used hierarchically, to distinguish between different types of argument and to arrange them in order of value. The moving but useless elegy for preinstitutional innocence is clearly replaced by functional political theory, and this in turn is transcended by the imperatives of belief. In the last phase, in fact, the analogy with the *Horatian Ode* ceases to be relevant, and we find ourselves back with the millennial aspirations of the *First Anniversary*, from which all trace of irony has disappeared.

This is not only the most important section of Marvell's advice, through Parker, to the king; it is also, despite its warnings, the most hopeful. In refuting the other absurdities of Parker's position he sometimes comes close to identifying Charles with Parker, despite the governing fiction carried over from the first part: that it is only his ecclesiastical advisers who stand between Charles and a golden age of religious concord. Marvell's constant connections between Parker and the anti-Christian Roman emperors were all too easily transferable; under the appropriate heading of "Debauchery Tolerated," he happily reintroduces the whole text of Parker's parody of the Declaration of Indulgence, while in the same breath rebuking "Bayes R[ex]" for the impertinence of his analogy (pp. 277-278).

There is, further, a natural connection between Parker's role as a surrogate for Charles as potential ecclesiastical tyrant and his function as a catalyst in Marvell's thinking about the style and methods of polemic. As before, a great deal of Marvell's attention in the *Second Part* is directed to Parker's faults of style, and much is made of his irreverent use of scripture. At the same time his position in the dispute reveals him to be unduly concerned with form at the expense of content. A man who could formulate notions of "moral grace" or "public conscience" was clearly unable to grasp the essential inwardness of Protestantism; he had even "expounded the Fruits of the Spirit to be meer Moral virtues, and the Joy, Peace, and Faith there spoken of to be only Peaceableness, Chearfulness and Faithfulness, as if they had been no more than the three Homileticall conversable Virtues, *Veritas, Comitas,* and *Urbanitas*" (p. 265). In Parker's mind, the ceremonial differences between churches were *merely* a question of style, and Nonconformity was merely an irrational stubbornness. What Marvell had to do was toe a delicate line between this kind of superficiality and any overt rejection of the doctrine of things indifferent to salvation. He wished to support the position of the Nonconformists, that conscience was truly involved in their stand against the Anglican liturgy; but at the same time, in order to justify toleration, he needed to argue that ceremonial issues were not worth fighting or, more importantly, persecuting for.

In a long and carefully personalized passage, which is remarkable both for its precision and its intentional vagueness, Marvell delivered his own conclusions on the ceremonial dispute:

> In this one matter only of the Ceremonial Controversie (as it is managed) in our Church, I must confess my want of capacity, which I have reason in all other things to acknowledge; and though indeed our Ecclesiastical Governours have the Law herein upon their side, it befitted them however to have seen that the dispute should have been managed even on their part with more humanity: which having been otherwise, has drawn me as it might any man else beyond mine own diffidence to say what I thought expedient. Even the Church of Rome, which cannot be thought the most negligent of things that concern her interest, does not, that I know of, lay any great stress upon Rituals and Ceremonials, so men agree in Doctrine: . . . I have as much as possible disingaged my mind from all Bias and

Partiality, to think how or what prudence men of so
great Piety and Learning as the Guides of our Church
could find out all along, it being now near an Hundred
and fifty years, to press on and continue still imposi-
tions in these matters. On the Non-conformists part it
is plain that they have persisted in this dispute, because
they have, or think they have the direct authority of
Scripture on their side, and to keep themselves as re-
mote as might be from the return of that Religion, from
which they had reformed. . . . But whatever design
the Ecclesiastical Instruments managed, it is yet to me
the greatest mysterie in the world how the Civil Magistrate could be perswaded to interess himself with all
the severity of his power in a matter so unnecessary,
so trvial, and so pernicious to the publick quiet. For
had things been left in their own state of Indifferency,
it is well known that the English Nation is generally
neither so void of Understanding, Civility, Obedience,
or Devotion, but that they would long ago have volun-
tarily closed and faln naturally into those reverent matters of Worship which would sufficiently have exprest
and suited with their Religion.

(pp. 241-242)

Without any specification of what "those reverent matters
of Worship" might be to which the national majority would
naturally have given assent, Marvell has managed to imply
that he speaks, without "Bias and Partiality" for the whole
body of English Protestantism. Christianity itself, "the most
short and plain Religion" (p. 238), is symbolically endangered by Parker. Behind him the "Episcopal Cavalier party"
is once again endeavoring to subvert "the great Charter of
Christian Liberty," which "aims all at that which is sincere
and solid and having laid that weight upon the Conscience
. . . it hath not pressed and loaded men further with the
burthen of Ritual and Ceremonial traditions and Imposi-
tions" (p. 246). And Marvell looks forward to a time when

"it would please God to inspire the hearts of Princes to curb that sanguinary and unchristian Spirit of those that for their own corrupt ends make Government so uneasie to Princes; so that we might once come to an experiment how happy a Prince and people might be under a plain and true Christian administration" (pp. 246-247). The *content*, in other words, of "Christian Moderation" (p. 242) has been defined in terms of all those values that Parker has not only failed to exhibit but patently fails even to comprehend: civility, reverence, simplicity, sincerity, charity. In this identification of style with theological substance, as distinct from a mere formalism, the "Homileticall conversable Virtues" can be reabsorbed into a system of Christian ethics.

It is in this context that we can understand what Marvell was up to in the final section of the *Rehearsal Transpros'd*, particularly in his remarkable use of Francis Bacon's *Wise and Moderate Discourse*. He has throughout been at some pains to indicate the catholicity of his sources, to support his case that Parker's is actually the minority position. He refers, for example, to the *Tract Concerning Schisme and Schismatiques* (1642) of his Anglican friend John Hales, whose advice against the unnecessary imposition of ceremonies had displeased Archbishop Laud. He refers to Stillingfleet's *Irenicum*, the ideal statement of Conformity at the Restoration (pp. 295, 325). We are also reminded (p. 304) that a bevy of Anglican bishops, John Morton, John Davenant, and Joseph Hall, had collected their thoughts "concerning reconciliation of Protestants among themselves" under the title *De Pacis Ecclesiasticae Rationibus* (1634); and Marvell makes good use of the similarity in title between Parker's work and Richard Hooker's infinitely more judicious *Lawes of Ecclesiastical Polity*.[29] Wherever possible Marvell refutes Parker by using against him the

---

[29] *Rehearsal*, p. 256: "Reverend Mr. Hooker ought to have serv'd you for a better example. . . . You might have done wisely to have imitated his Modesty." See also pp. 269, 295, 303.

authority of members of his own church, and his choice of documents shows him familiar with all phases of the ceremonial dispute. No authority, however, is produced with more deliberation than Bacon, whom Marvell had threatened to quote in the first part of the *Rehearsal*, to refute Parker's arguments for a satirical polemic:

> Nor is it worth ones while to teach him out of other Authors, and the best precedents of the kind, how he, being a Christian and a Divine, ought to have carried himself. But I cannot but remark his Insolence and how bold he makes . . . with the Memories of those great Persons there enumerated, several of whom, and particularly my Lord Verulam, I could quote to his confusion, upon a contrary and much better account.
>
> (p. 75)

In the *Second Part*, having been challenged to make good his claims, Marvell offers several mock-anticipations of his grand denouement. A piece of folly on Parker's side about pork and Bacon has allowed him to create a form of comic suspense: "What remains, Mr. Bayes, is to serve in your Bacon, but because I would do it to the best advantage, I shall add something else for your better and more easie digestion";[30] but the tone in which Bacon's *Wise and Moderate Discourse* is finally introduced is not lighthearted at all. Although he used the recent edition of Bacon's papers known as the *Resuscitatio*,[31] Marvell's language echoes the title of the 1641 edition in its evocation of wisdom from the past: "I the rather quote him because a wise man is as it were eternal upon earth; and he speaks so judiciously and impartially, that it seems as if these very times which we now live in had been in his present prospect" (p. 323).

[30] Ibid., p. 322. See also pp. 302-303, 307-308.
[31] *Resuscitatio, or, bringing into public light several pieces of the works Civil, Historical, Philosophical, and Theological, Hitherto Sleeping, of the Right Hon. Francis Bacon*, 3rd. ed., 1671. This collection was edited by William Rawley, the royal chaplain.

So impartially, in fact, does Bacon speak that he is not to be used, like the other authorities, to bolster Marvell's case. Rather he is presented as the voice of judgment before which Marvell must plead guilty alongside his prisoner:

> Pray, Mr. Bayes let us both listen, for I assure you, before he has done, he will tell us many a wiser thing then is to be met with either in *Ecclesiastical Politie* or *Rehearsal*.
>
> (p. 323)

The passages which Marvell has selected to condemn himself as well as Parker are those in which Bacon recommended the "virtue of Silence and Slowness to speak, commended by St. James"; in which he urged an end to the "immodest and deformed manner of writing . . . whereby matter of Religion is handled in the stile of the Stage"; and asserted that the use of satire and mockery in religious polemic "is a thing farre from the devout reverence of a Christian, and scant beseeming the honest regard of a sober man." Bacon's latitudinarianism about ceremonies as things indifferent was obviously helpful to Marvell's case, as were his observations on the misuse of censorship, a point to which Marvell was to return in the *Growth of Popery and Arbitrary Government*. But the significance of Bacon's comments lay in their relevance to the problem of expression with which, it seems, Marvell had been so earnestly grappling. Carefully omitting Bacon's qualified defense of "bitter and earnest writing" when a man is inspired by genuine zeal, Marvell in effect admits his own failure to find an acceptable tone. Raillery is ultimately subject to the same criticisms as railing, not least because it may be more effective. There is, perhaps, no viable poise "betwixt Jest and Earnest," and the originator of a new style of banter can only, finally, reject the whole enterprise: "truly our sport is . . . unfit for serious Spectators. However I have spit out your dirty Shoon" (p. 327).

## *Mr. Smirke* AND THE *Remarks*

In the pamphlets that followed the *Rehearsal* Marvell continued his withdrawal from satire, and moved gradually towards a style and method that conformed more closely to the Baconian position. In the first place, his later pamphlets present for their justification a defensive rather than an aggressive occasion. Whereas the *Rehearsal* was a piece of public execution forced upon Marvell by the negligence of others, *Mr. Smirke: Or, The Divine in Mode* (1676) defended Herbert Croft, Bishop of Hereford, against the only one of his three respondents who answered him satirically.[32] Similarly, Marvell's *Remarks upon a late Disingenuous Discourse* (1678) were written in defense of John Howe's *Letter* against the attack of his fellow Nonconformist, Thomas Danson. In the case of Croft, Marvell explains how he had been drawn into his defense by the circumstances and title under which his work appeared. Not written for publication, and intended only for circulation to Members of Parliament, Croft's pamphlet had apparently been marketed without his consent by a "covetous printer."[33] Also its title, *The Naked Truth: Or, the True state of the Primitive Church*, along with Croft's pseudonym, "an Humble Moderator," and the biblical quotations included on the title page (Zach. 8:19, "Love the truth and Peace." Gal. 4:16, "Am I therefore become your enemy, because I tell you the truth?") sufficiently indicated its pacific and constructive in-

[32] Francis Turner, Master of St. John's College, Cambridge, in *Animadversions Upon a Late Pamphlet* . . . (London, 1676). The other two respondents were Bishop Peter Gunning, whose *Lex Talionis: or, the Author of Naked Truth Stript Naked* (1676) was not so much a personal attack as an exposé of Croft's ignorance of church history; and Bishop Gilbert Burnet, whose *Modest Survey of the* . . . *Naked Truth* was indeed a modest and dignified work.

[33] *Complete Works*, ed. A. B. Grosart (New York, 1875, reprinted 1966), IV, 19-20. All subsequent quotations in this chapter are from this edition.

tentions. By contrast, Francis Turner's pamphlet identified itself with a genre Marvell had by now learned to dislike: *Animadversions upon a late Pamphlet*. In the *Historical Essay* appended to *Mr. Smirke* Marvell was to equate animadversion with persecution, in the figure of the Emperor Julian, who added "to his other severities" to the early Christians "that sharpness of his wit, both 'exposing' and 'animadverting' upon them, at another rate than any of the modern practitioners . . . can ever arrive at" (p. 136). Moreover, in the case of Croft, Marvell undoubtedly came to the rescue of someone who was incompetent to defend himself. The preface of *The Naked Truth* presents him as an astonishingly simple-minded person, wide open to the charges of poor scholarship and faulty reasoning leveled by *Lex Talionis*: "I am a weak man, of great Passions, not able to bear Commendations or Reproach, my small ability puts me out of danger of the first, but in great fear of the later . . . it is now above two years since I had these thoughts, in which time I have read and conferred all I could to discover if I were in an error, but for all yet I could meet with, do not find it so, but hope all I say is truth . . . I am sure I found it so very long before I could master them, and that of education most difficult." In a letter to William Popple dated 15 July 1676, shortly after the appearance of *Mr. Smirke*, Marvell observed: "I doe not perceive the foole hath any harme nor that although they talk of it they will or can answer him according to his folly"; there follow transcripts of his recent correspondence with Croft, who has thanked him fulsomely for his intervention (II, 347). If this letter to Popple indeed identified Croft as the fool of Proverbs 26: 4,5, Marvell's championship of weakness is all the more interesting, for he chose to define it in terms of one of the central texts of the Smectymnuan Controversy. Even if "the fool" is an ironical reference to Marvell himself, the pamphlet itself leaves us in no doubt as to which of the two conflicting proverbs he preferred.

Secondly, Marvell intervened in both these later disputes on points of theological principle. In one sense he was being more impartial than in the *Rehearsal*, since *Mr. Smirke* defends an Anglican bishop against an Anglican bishop, and his defense of John Howe is of one Nonconformist against another. But it would be a mistake to assume that, because his later pamphlets cannot be suspected of alignment with any confession, the framework of his belief was weakening or, as has been suggested,[34] that he was moving under rationalist influence toward Deism. His denial that "General Councils" of any kind have authority over belief, and his rejection of an uncompromising theory of predestination, are based on the same broad convictions which had opposed Parker: a latitudinarianism safely founded on Luther's definition of Christian liberty, for "a good Christian will not, cannot atturn and indenture his conscience over, to be represented by others" (pp. 126-127); and a belief that violence or coercion in any form, whether in the behavior or dogma of the church, is incompatible with the message of the Gospel. The most effective passage in Marvell's case against predestination occurs as reaction against the concept that Adam's Fall was itself predetermined, and that God's will directed his hand to the apple as a writing-master directs his scholar's hand. "If the cause be not to be defended upon better terms than so," Marvell exclaims, "what Christian but would rather wish he had never known writing-master, than to subscribe to such an opinion; and that God should make an innocent creature in this manner to do a forbidden act, for which so dreadful a vengeance was to issue upon him and his posterity?" (p. 229).

But, as his emotional response to Danson's metaphor suggests, Marvell remained deeply concerned about the act of writing itself. The title of this chapter is derived from a passage in *Mr. Smirke*, in which Marvell deftly summarizes

[34] Legouis, *Andrew Marvell*, pp. 206-208, 221-223.

his new theory of polemical style in any issue where the "Churche's credit" is involved. "The Churche's credit," he writes, "is more interested in an ecclesiasticall drole, then in a lay chancellor":

> It is no small trust that is reposed in him to whom the bishop shall commit *omne et omnimodum suum ingenium, tam temporale quam spirituale* [absolutely all his wit, both temporal and spiritual]: and however it goes with excommunication, they should take good heed to what manner of person they delegate the keys of Laughter. It is not every man that is qualified to sustain the dignity of the Churche's jester.

All potential polemicists, therefore, should submit to a four-part qualifying examination, to determine:

> first, whether they have any sense; for without that how can any man pretend,— and yet they do,—to be ingenious? Then, whether they have any modesty; for without that they can only be scurrilous and impudent. Next, whether any truth; for true jests are those that do the greatest execution. And lastly, it were not amiss that they gave some account too of their Christianity; for the world has always been so uncivil as to expect something of that from the clergy, in the design and stile even of their most uncanonical writings.

(pp. 8-9)

The four principles here enunciated are in ascending order of importance. Starting with that vital Ciceronian *ingenium* (for he who tries to be witty had better be clever) the polemicist must also know how to control his wit according to the principle of modesty, which operates simultaneously in ethical and rhetorical behavior. But even a modest wit fails if not backed up by facts, if engaged, perhaps, on a wrong cause; and, finally, the church's jesters must make it clear to their audience that they understand and indeed practice the principles of their own creed.

Similarly, in his introduction to the *Remarks*, Marvell stated that they were partially intended as an essay in "how the unruly quill is to be managed . . . as Mr. Howe's Letter may serve for a pattern of what is to be imitated, so The Discourse may remain as a mark (the best use it can be put to) of what ought to be avoided in all writing of controversies, especially by Divines, in those that concern Religion" (p. 174). The *Remarks* are actually organized under a series of headings of "what ought to be avoided," and so provide a negative theory of polemic, somewhat resembling the "rules" of Bishop Joseph Hall's *Christian Moderation*, but in reverse.

One sign that Marvell's practice has altered in accordance with his theory is that the late pamphlets show obvious strategies of depersonalization. In place of the dialog with Parker-Bayes and the other *ad hominem* techniques of the *Rehearsal*, the speaker in *Mr. Smirke* deals in the third person with "the Animadverter" or "the Exposer." In the *Historical Essay* there appears a new persona, "the Historian," through whom, be it the author of the biblical Acts, Eusebius, or Socrates Scholasticus, Marvell can speak with an objectivity greater than his own. In the *Remarks* on Danson's *Discourse* this process of depersonalization is not only extended but explained. Since the offending pamphlet appeared only under the initials T. D., implying that its author wished to remain incognito, Marvell offers to "so far observe good manners, as to interpret them only 'The Discourse,' heartily wishing that there were some way of finding it guilty, without reflecting upon the Author; which I shall accordingly indeavour, that I may both preserve his, whatsoever, former reputation, and leave him a door open to ingenuity for the future" (p. 174). By the standard of this wry charity, *ad hominem* arguments are ruled out; in neither pamphlet are there any reflections upon the life of the opposing author, or upon his character, except as that is expressed in his style. It is on this issue that Marvell's wit is employed, in developing metaphors to express the "character," both of the books he is defending and those he is defending them against.

The *Discourse*, for example, which was not satirical at all but merely pedantically technical, is personified as a *miles gloriosus*, "dreadfully accoutred and armed cap-a-pe in logic, categorical and hypothetical syllogisms, majors, minors, enthymems, antecedents, consequents, distinctions, definitions . . . terms that good Mr. Howe as a meer novice is presum'd to be unacquainted with, and so far from being able to endure the ratling of The Discourse's armour, that as those Roman legions once bragg'd, even the sweaty smell of Its armpits would be sufficient to rout him" (p. 198). More serious is a metaphor common to both *Mr. Smirke* and the *Remarks*, in which Marvell distinguishes between "humane" and subhuman character, as expressed in language. Croft "speaks like a man, a creature to which modesty and reason are peculiar: not like an Animadverter, that is an animal which hath nothing humane in it but a malicious grinne" (p. 22). John Howe's *Letter* is similarly, but with more justice, described as "a manly discourse, resembling much, and expressing the humane perfection; in the harmony of language, the symmetry of parts, the strength of reason, the excellency of its end, which is so serious, that it is no defect in the similitude with man, that the Letter contains nothing in it suitable to the property of laughter" (p. 173). In this extended metaphor for style as the image of man, as man is the image of God, Marvell in effect provides the positive ideals of polemic which must replace the *Discourse*'s many faults.

However, the most important development of the later pamphlets is Marvell's discovery of a symbolic center for the issue which he is in each case confronting, and which allows him to focus his intellectual and emotional energies with some economy. In the title of Bishop Croft's *Naked Truth* he perceived an opportunity to renovate an old Puritan trope, and make it his own credo. The personal preference for simplicity in worship which had emerged in the

*Rehearsal Transpros'd* is now enlarged into a complete persona, Andreas Rivetus, whose name stands for the naked truth, as *The Divine in Mode* represents all who favor ornament and obfuscation. The stagey allusion to Etherege's fop is not a weak imitation of the earlier transprosal from Buckingham, but a new metaphor relevant to the ceremonial dispute; the implications of subtitle and pseudonym continue to expand as the argument of the pamphlet develops. Truth tellers, like St. Stephen and St. Paul, have historically met with abuse; nevertheless, "the Naked Truth, Christianity, hath made a shift, God be thanked, to continue till this day; and there will never want those that bear testimony to it" (p. 22). (There is an echo here of another truth teller, the Duchess of Albemarle, whose response to the "vain Pomp" of the court is to "make a Shift" of her own prophetic candor. *Third Advice*, ll. 322-323.) In the *Historical Essay* Marvell makes a familiar appeal to the clergy for greater toleration and, though he cannot count on any genuine desire for peace among them, "it is no unreasonable request that they will be merciful unto themselves, and have some reverence at least for *The Naked Truth* of History, which either in their own times will meet with them, or in the next age overtake them" (p. 156). In the *Growth of Popery and Arbitrary Government* this metaphor was, as it turned out, finally validated by extension into method, the almost total replacement of argument by bare fact.

Similarly, in his *Remarks* on the *Discourse*, Marvell took issue with Danson's title, and its claim to speak "De Causa Dei":

Who would have thought that T.D. should have become the defender of the faith, or that the cause of God were so forlorn, as to be reduced to the necessity of such a champion? . . . The cause of God! Turn, I beseech you, Its whole book over, and show me anything of that decorum with which that should have been managed. What is there to be found of that grav-

ity, humility, meekness, piety or charity requisite to so
glorious a pretence? (graces wherewith God usually
assists those that undertake His quarrel . . .)

(p. 234)

The image of a false Crusader, occurring incidentally in
Marvell's responses to Parker and Turner, has now become
central, thanks to Danson's own presumption. It has also
now become completely clear in Marvell's mind that the
cause of God must not be undertaken in a militant manner,
that the Cross and the Sword are indeed opposed symbols.
Even St. Peter's defense of Christ, despite its personal heroism, is to be rejected, as it was by Christ himself: "our Sav-
ior though [it was] done in His defence, rebuked him;
adding, 'They that take the sword, shall perish by the
sword'; . . . and the taking of the pen hath seldom better
success, if handled in the same manner" (p. 174). The topos
of Malchus' ear and Peter's sword, which had been used by
Bishop Burnet to persuade the Nonconformists to passive
obedience, and by Croft to deny the exercise of the magistrate's sword in imposing conformity,[35] is here fused with
the more venerable topos of sword and pen, and so becomes
part of Marvell's religious aesthetic.

It is now possible to see the whole process by which
Marvell worked out his own response to the Christian polemical dilemma. Starting with Owen's handy model and
the experience of his own satires, the last lines of the *Rehearsal* and the opening defense of the *Second Part* showed
him growing self-conscious about the disparity between
jest and earnest, when the only method of separation was
alteration, and there was no real ground "betwixt." By the
end of the *Second Part* Marvell seemed to have rejected his
own mixture of "Reason" and "Laughter" for a wiser and

[35] Bishop Herbert Croft, *The Naked Truth* (London, 1675), p. 8.
For Burnet's application, see p. 186 above. See also Christopher Love,
*The Zealous Christian* (London, 1657), p. 22; and Richard Baxter,
*The Cure of Church-divisions* (London, 1670), B 2v.

more moderate discourse, and the opening of *Mr. Smirke* offered a positive schema of that negative conclusion. Although *Mr. Smirke* itself retained a satirical title and sometimes the tone of satire, it was noticeably more restrained (and hence, alas, less readable) than either part of the *Rehearsal*. The *Historical Essay touching General Councils* provided Marvell with a different medium, an opportunity to escape completely from satirical strategies into the impersonality of the historian; he concluded it with a quotation from the preface to Hooker's *Ecclesiastical Polity*, which had looked forward hopefully to a time "when three words uttered with charity and meekness, shall receive a far more blessed reward, then three thousand volumes written with disdainful sharpness of wit."

Finally, Marvell completed his defense of John Howe by urging him not to continue the argument with Danson if he really had the welfare of the church at heart: "lest, as David, for having been a man of blood, was forbid to build the temple . . . so he, as being a man of controversie" (p. 242).[36] A great Puritan metaphor for the construction of the new church polity and doctrine was thus transferred from the *First Anniversary* celebrating Cromwell to the pacifist prose where it more properly belonged, and Marvell himself stepped lightly out of the arena, with his sense of dignity as the "Churche's jester" clearly restored: "As for myself, I expect in this litigious age, that some or other will sue me for having trespassed thus far on theological ground: but I have this for my plea, that I stepped over on no other reason than (which any man may legally do)

---

[36] For this topos, compare Bishop John Davenant, *De Pace Ecclesiastica* (London, 1638), p. 49; and, perhaps more to the point, Richard Baxter's address of loyalty to Richard Cromwell, cited by Margoliouth (*Poems and Letters*, I, 335): "Many are persuaded that you have been strangely kept from participating in any of our late bloody contentions, that God might make you the healer of our breaches, and employ you in that Temple work which David himself might not be honoured with . . . because he had shed blood abundantly and made great wars."

to hinder one divine from offering violence to another" (p. 242).

It was ironic that Marvell's developed dignity was noticed but not appreciated by his readers. In an unsigned letter to Sir Edward Harley written 1 July 1676 he commented upon the reception of *Mr. Smirke*: "The book said to be Marvels makes what shift it can in the world but the Author walks negligently up & down as unconcerned. The Divines of our Church say it is not in the merry part so good as the Rehearsall Transpros'd, that it runns dreggs." The letter ends with a verbal shrug of the shoulders: "Who would write?" (II, 346.) Possibly Marvell was thinking back to the apologetic opening of the *Second Part* of the *Rehearsal*, and his own discarded proposition that "not to Write at all is much the safer course of life." In any case, the ironic use of the third person, and the stance of wry detachment which the letter maintains, provide him with a kind of serenity, unusual in writers contemplating a bad review of their work. Apparently the "dignity of the Churche's jester" stood him in good stead.

# 5

# "The Naked Truth of History":
# Theory of Polemic II

The different focus of Marvell's penultimate pamphlet removes it from its chronological position, between *Mr. Smirke* (June 1676) and the *Remarks* (1678). Published with a false "Amsterdam" imprint sometime shortly after 3 December 1677, when the Speaker Seymour for the third time broke parliamentary rules by adjourning the House on his own authority, *An Account of the Growth of Popery and Arbitrary Government* suggests by its title an equal focus on church and state. In fact in this pamphlet the threat of Roman Catholicism is primarily a matter of foreign policy, the sinister understanding between Charles (or his ministers) and Louis XIV, the "most Christian" king of France. As a threat it is clearly subordinate to the real subject, the development of arbitrary government in England by peaceful but insidious methods: an unnatural extension of the original Restoration Parliament, combined with long and frequent prorogations; the corruption of both Houses of Parliament from within, by direct and indirect bribery; rigorous eradication of all political opposition by various forms of censorship; and constitutional improprieties on the part of government ministers that revealed their contempt for law.

Theoretically, however, the *Account* occupies a position in Marvell's work which is clearly compatible with the later religious prose. As a result of his experiences in the *Rehearsal* and *Mr. Smirke*, Marvell had broadened his stylistic options, and when he returned to the kind of material which had previously generated the Dutch War satires, he did not return simply to his earlier methods. The pamphlet combines the forthrightness of the *Advices to a Painter* with the uprightness of *Mr. Smirke* and the documentary plainness of the *Historical Essay touching General Councils*; as usual, Marvell's new method is generated out of the historical situation itself. As compared to the 1660s, when the satirist was inevitably an outsider, the 1670s offered no panegyrical temptations or optimistic norms. In a world in which the guardians of public order had themselves inverted the standards of decency, it was no longer necessary for the truth teller to identify himself by satirical impropriety. At one moment the authorities were blatantly licensing the abusive *Pacquet of Advice to the Men of Shaftsbury*,[1] which appeared anonymously in 1676, "not out of any spark of *modesty*," as Marvell observed, but so that its author "might with more security exercise his impudence . . . against all publick truth and honesty."[2] At another Dr. Nicholas Cary was fined £1,000 and committed to the Tower by the House of Lords, on the grounds that he had merely carried to the printer a book questioning the validity of the Long Prorogation, and had refused to give evidence about its author.[3] The same manipulation of standards had been apparent in spoken debate. When Charles rebuked the House of Commons, on 28 May 1677, for encroaching on his prerogative of making all foreign

[1] *A Pacquet of Advices and Animadversions, Sent from London To the Men of Shaftsbury*, which had three separate printings in 1676, was in fact a response to a pamphlet probably commissioned by Shaftesbury, *A Letter from a Person of Quality to His Friend in the Country* (London, 1675), which described the crucial debate in the Lords over a proposed Test for all Members of Parliament. It was followed in May 1677 by *A Second Pacquet* of the same nature.

[2] *Complete Works*, ed. A. B. Grosart (New York, 1875, reprinted 1966), IV, 317. For consistency, I have used Grosart's edition for all references to the *Account*, despite the appearance of a facsimile edition, intr. G. Salgado (Farnborough: Heppenheim Press, 1971).

[3] See *Account*, p. 333, and *The Poems and Letters of Andrew Marvell*, rev. ed. Pierre Legouis (Oxford, 1971), II, 182-183, 187.

policy decisions, several members of the House "offered *modestly* to have spoken," but were cut off by the Speaker, who "had the confidence, without any question put, and of his own motion, to pronounce the House adjourned till the 16th of July, and stept down in the middle of the floor, all the House being astonished at so unheard of a violation of their inherent privilege and constitution" (pp. 405-406). The meaning of this behavior became clear when the confrontation between king and Commons was reported to the public, and the humiliation of the parliamentarians completed; for, "while none of their own transactions or addresses for the public good are suffered to be printed, but even written copies of them with the same care *as libels suppressed*; yet they found this severe speech published in the next day's news book, to mark them out to their own, and all other nations, as refractory disobedient persons, that had lost all respect to his Majesty" (p. 406).

It was in these circumstances, when the normal meanings of satire and libel had been distorted by the tactics of a repressive administration, that Marvell perceived the opportunity and the necessity for a new form of political commentary. As compared to the military incompetence, the lack of proper Intelligence, the personally motivated misconduct of the Dutch Wars, the country now faced, he believed, a well-organized, highly coordinated threat to its most cherished institutions; and in place of the isolated targets, the individually venal office holders, whom the satirical *Advices* had held up for recognition and hopefully for removal, there was now a powerful group of unknown size, with a coherent strategy of muzzling both press and Parliament, of destroying history as they gained control over its media. What was needed, therefore, was not satirical attack, the weapon of minority opinion, but a style and genre that could be readily identified with decorum, with rectitude, and especially with the constitutional principles and public institutions that were now at stake.

It is for this reason that the *Account* begins by defining
the values inherent in the English system, in a manner
subtle enough to require our close attention; but this introduction can best be understood if we turn first to Marvell's
description of the *Account* itself, and the procedures he
intends to use in bringing the conspiracy to public notice.
"And now," Marvell wrote (immediately after his definition
of the English state and church):

> should I enter into a particular retail of all former and
> latter transactions, relating to this affair, there would
> be sufficient for a just volume of History. But my in-
> tention is only to write a naked narrative of some of
> the most considerable passages in the meeting of Par-
> liament the 15th of February 1676: such as have come
> to my notice, which may serve for matter to some
> stronger pen, and to such as have more leisure and
> further opportunity to discover and communicate to
> the publick. . . . Yet, that I may not be too abrupt, and
> leave the reader wholly destitute of a thread to guide
> himself by thorow so intriguing a labyrinth; I shall
> summarily, as short as so copious and redundant a mat-
> ter will admit, deduce the order of affairs both at home
> and abroad, as it led into this Session.
>
> (pp. 263-264)

Marvell's proposal, then, is to identify himself with history,
but within certain limitations. His "naked narrative" may
be compared with the "Naked Truth of History" invoked
in his defense of Bishop Croft; but instead of "the Historian" who features in the *Essay touching General Councils*, the author of the *Account* is more modestly defined.
He is merely a "relator" (we would call him a reporter) of
events which have come to his own "notice," and particularly of the parliamentary session which followed the Long
Prorogation. The relator is needed to collect and preserve
basic records, especially at a time when large amounts of

public documentation were disappearing into the fire; but his work is seen as preparatory to a complete or "just volume of History," to be undertaken in the future by "some stronger pen."

This is both a fine example of a modesty topos, and a genuine contribution to historical genre-theory. There is a striking analogy to it in Francis Bacon's *Advancement of Learning* (1605). Bacon, whose views on the writing of polemic had figured significantly in the *Second Part* of the *Rehearsal Transpros'd*, was no less authoritative on the question of historiography; it would appear that both his views and his terminology have contributed to Marvell's position.

Bacon, as always, divided and subdivided his topic. To begin with, civil history must be distinguished from other categories, and one can then distinguish between "preparatory" and "just and perfect history," each of which can be further analyzed. Preparatory history includes both "commentaries," or accounts of "*naked* events and actions," without interpretation of "the motives or designs, the counsels, the speeches, the pretexts, the occasions"; and "registers," or collections of public documents, "without a perfect continuance . . . of the *thread* of the narration." Just and perfect history, on the other hand, includes "chronicles," "lives," and "*narrations* or *relations*," which can be distinguished both by subject and by value:

> Of these, although the first be the most complete and absolute kind of history, and hath most estimation and glory, yet the second excelleth it in profit and use, and the third in verity and sincerity. For . . . *narrations* and *relations* of actions, as the war of Peloponnesus, the expedition of Cyrus Minor, the *conspiracy* of Catiline, cannot but be more purely and exactly true than histories of times, because they may choose an argument comprehensible *within the notice* and instructions of the writer: whereas he that undertaketh the story of a

time, especially of any length, cannot but meet with many blanks and spaces which he must be forced to fill up out of his own wit and conjecture.

It appears, moreover, that "relations" (what we might today call documentaries) are, in Bacon's system, closer to preparatory than to "absolute" history. He urges his contemporaries to show more diligence in the limited form, in order to provide the raw material for larger endeavors:

> for there is no great action but hath some good pen which attends it. And because it is an ability not common to write a good history, as may well appear by the small number of them; yet if particularity of actions memorable were but tolerably reported as they pass, the compiling of a complete history of times mought be the better expected, when a writer should arise that were fit for it: for the collection of such relations mought be as a nursery garden, wherby to plant a fair and stately garden, when time should serve.[4]

The relationship between these pronouncements and Marvell's statements of purpose can scarcely be accidental; and the connection is further strengthened when Marvell returns to questions of method in the *Account*'s closing paragraphs. Having brought his narrative further than he originally intended, to include the third occasion on which the House of Commons was illegally adjourned without its own consent, Marvell concludes it by emphasizing (as had Bacon) the sincerity and veracity of his procedure. "Thus far hath the conspiracy against our Religion and Government been laid open, which if true, it was more than time that it should be discovered, but if anything therein have been falsely suggested, the disproving of it in any particular will be a courtesie both to the publick and to the relator; who would be glad to have the world convinced of the

---

[4] Francis Bacon, *The Advancement of Learning*, ed. G. W. Kitchin (London, 1973), pp. 73-78.

contrary, though to the prejudice of his own reputation" (p. 411).

So impersonal has he managed to be, in fact, that he expects to be reproached for obscuring the issue by those who actively oppose the government. "Some will expect, that the very persons should have been named; whereas he only gives evidence to the fact, and leaves the malefactors to those who have the power of inquiry. It was his design indeed to give information, but not to turn informer" (p. 413). This provision of anonymity, not only for himself but for those "to whom he hath only a publick enmity, no private animosity," is, of course, partly a fiction, since in most cases the conspirators could be identified by their offices; but as a fiction it is a more serious version of the notion that Thomas Danson's *Discourse* had written itself, and it appears to proceed from the same generous motives. Marvell's offer to Danson to "preserve his, whatever, former reputation, and leave him a door open to ingenuity in the future" (IV, 174), exactly corresponds to his present hope that the conspirators "might have the privilege of statesmen, to repent at the last hour, and by one signal action to expiate all their former misdemeanours." If they should fail to do so, and if others insist on justice, the relator has given adequate directions for their discovery; and "if any one delight in the chase, he is an ill woodman that knows not . . . the beast by the proportion of his excrement" (p. 413). The metaphor of the satiric hunt, momentarily recalling those of the *Rehearsal Transpros'd*,[5] underlines by its very unexpectedness how generally Marvell had been avoiding that brutalizing exercise.

This implicit rejection of satire is finally explained, as

[5] Compare *The Rehearsal Transpros'd: The Second Part*, ed. D.I.B. Smith (Oxford, 1971), pp. 164-165: "Rather, wheresoever men shall find the footing of so wanton a Satyr out of his own bounds, the neighbourhood ought, notwithstanding all his pretended capering Divinity, to hunt him thorow the woods with hounds and horn home to his harbour." See also pp. 171, 187.

Marvell considers what is likely to be the fate of his *Account*, which he fully expects to be treated like the "late printed book" described in a letter to Hull in November 1675. The Lords themselves "voted it a Libell: and to be burnt by the hands of the Hangman & to inquire out the Printer and Author" (II, 172). Only in a perverse society, Marvell asserts, could books like these, written in the interest of open public discussion, be suppressed as libelous. In reality, it is the tyrants in Council who are *the living libels against the government.*" The *Account* should be recognized as a statement of loyalty, "written with no other intent than of meer fidelity and service to his Majesty, and God forbid that it should have any other effect, than that 'the mouth of all iniquity and flatterers may be stopped', and that his Majesty, having discerned the disease, may with his healing touch apply the remedy." The *Account* thus concludes with the same formula of "advice" to the king, the same fiction of the king's personal immunity from criticism, that had redirected the Dutch War satires toward constructive thinking; "for so far is the relator himself from any sinister surmise of his Majesty . . . that he acknowledges, if it were fit for Caesar's wife to be free, much more is Caesar himself from all crime and suspicion." We, being familiar with the ironies with which Marvell's Cromwell poems had endowed the name of Caesar and the royal power of healing, may be suspicious of this conclusion; but without such special knowledge the pamphlet returns with this gesture to the level of ideal political theory and the hope of reformation.

The *Account*, then, has been offered to the public as documentary history, with all of its consequences for accuracy, objectivity, and starkness—a "naked narrative" of events uncolored by the bias or the rhetoric of its author. What Marvell claims to have done, however, and what he has actually done are not the same. As any reader of the pamphlet quickly discovers, there are sections which bear no resemblance to "facts," and cannot possibly be described as candid or impartial reporting. Truth and modesty topoi are themselves, of course, warnings that we may be manipulated, and we certainly are. There is also a constant evaluative pressure, especially of the "motives or designs, the counsels, the speeches, the pretexts," which Bacon had excluded from a genuinely naked preparatory history. The total effect is one of powerful tension between fact and suasion, the facts themselves being of so shocking a nature as to justify evaluative fervor; and the *Account* thereby leans backward toward a more old-fashioned historiography, the didactic, humanist, rhetorical tradition, founded on *the* classical definition of the historian's task. As Roger Ascham, for example, had translated them from the *De Oratore* (II, xv, 62-63), Cicero's rules of historiography were themselves a compromise:

> First . . . to write nothyng false: next, to be bold to say any truth, wherby is avoyded two great faultes, flattery and hatred . . . Then to mark diligently the causes, counsels, actes, and issues in all great attempts: And in causes, what is just or unjust: in counsels, what is purposed wisely or rashly: in actes, what is done couragiously or fayntly: And of every issue, to note some generall lesson of wisedome & warines, for lyke matters in time to come.[6]

With this understanding, we can look again at the opening pages of the pamphlet, where Marvell sets out to define the institutions endangered by the conspiracy. Beginning with the threat to the state, he describes the English constitution in a long passage already recognized as crucial to Marvell's intentions. The difference between my reading and others is only a matter of emphasis,[7] but it is the empha-

[6] Roger Ascham, in his preface to *A Report . . . of the affaires and state of Germany* (London, 1552), Aiiiv.

[7] In *Destiny his Choice* (Cambridge, 1968), pp. 207-231, John M. Wallace follows Caroline Robbins, *The Eighteenth-Century Com-*

sis which, I think, Marvell's *language* carries. It is the difference between political theory in the abstract, and political theory subject to particular expression. Unlike less fortunate nations who suffer from arbitrary monarchies, Marvell explains:

> here the subjects retain their proportion in the Legislature; the very meanest commoner of England is represented in Parliament, and is a party to those laws by which the Prince is sworn to govern himself and his people. No money is to be levied but by the common consent. No man is for life, limb, goods, or liberty, at the Soveraign's discretion: but we have the same right (modestly understood) in our propriety that the prince hath in his regality . . . His very Prerogative is no more than what the Law hath determined. His Broad Seal, which is the legitimate stamp of his pleasure, yet is no longer currant, than upon the trial it is found to be legal. He cannot commit any person by his particular warrant. He cannot himself be witness in any cause: the balance of publick justice being so delicate, that not the hand only but even the breath of the Prince would turn the scale. Nothing is left to the King's will, but all is subjected to his authority; by which means it follows that he can do no wrong, nor can he receive wrong; and a King of England keeping to these measures, may without arrogance, be said to remain the onely intelligent Ruler over a rational People.
>
> (pp. 248-249)

One can pause here, in the middle of Marvell's definition, because the rhetoric allows it, and note the following points. Firstly, that if Marvell intends to provide an orthodox description of the balance of powers in the mixed state, he has not started in the orthodox manner, by defining the

---

*monwealthman* (Cambridge, Mass., 1959), pp. 53-54, in reading Marvell's "prolegomena" as political orthodoxy, free from any suspicious taint of contract theory.

king's prerogative, and then its limitations. Rather, he has begun with what the king may not and cannot do to his subjects, in an astonishing series of *negative* propositions which must have given Charles, if he read them, rather a start. Secondly, there is no mention of the House of Lords in the balance of power. The Commons' jealously guarded sole right over financial legislation, and the individual's rights of liberty and property are stated and restated; but nothing is said of the judiciary powers vested in the Lords, which had recently been so sadly abused. And the effect of this omission is fortified by the sense of verbal balance between two, not three powers, a highly serious use of alliteration, parison, and homeoteleuton. England has an "intelligent Ruler" matched by a "rational People," an exact equation of "his regality" and "our propriety." Roger L'Estrange, who focused much of his attack on what he called *The Growth of Knavery* on Marvell's opening statements, was not deaf to the implications of this rhetoric. The balance between regality and propriety carried with it, he warned, "an Innuendo, that the King may as well Forfeit his Crown, as the Subject his Free-hold."[8] At the same time Marvell has incorporated into his hypothesis a denial that this is unusual or improper doctrine. The subjects "retain their *proportion* in the Legislature"; their rights are to be "*modestly* understood." The result is an eloquent definition of the limited monarchy which goes far beyond the corresponding passage in the *Rehearsal Transpros'd*. The statement of the king's immunity from error and its repercussions is consistent with the previous negations: "by which means it follows that he can do no wrong, nor can he receive wrong." A ruler whose hands are tied cannot be blamed for arbitrary government. L'Estrange's response reveals Marvell's strategy with considerable acuteness: "Let us suppose that this Charge of a Popish, and Arbitrary Design, does neither Intend nor Reflect any Imputation upon

[8] L'Estrange, *An Account of the Growth of Knavery* (London, 1678), p. 46.

THEORY OF POLEMIC II

his Majesty; . . . It is yet a worse Libel Another Way . . .
For he employes his Utmost Skill to represent his Majesty
only Passive in all his Administrations."[9]

In the second half of his statement, Marvell proceeds to
define what remains to the king after these restrictions have
been understood. The rhetorical strategy is to deny in order
to affirm, but even in his affirmations Marvell demands wary
reading:

> In recompense therefore and acknowledgment of so
> good a Government under his influence, his person is
> most sacred and inviolable; . . . He hath a vast revenue
> constantly arising from the hearth of the Householder,
> the sweat of the Labourer, the rent of the Farmer, the
> industry of the Merchant, and consequently out of the
> estate of the Gentleman: a large competence to defray
> the ordinary expense of the Crown, and maintain its
> lustre. And if any extraordinary occasion happen, or
> be but with any probable decency pretended, the whole
> Land at whatsoever season of the year does yield him
> a plentiful harvest . . . He is the fountain of all honours,
> and has moreover the distribution of so many profitable
> offices of the Household, of the Revenue, of State, of
> Law, of Religion, of the Navy and (since his present
> Majestie's time) of the Army, that it seems as if the Na-
> tion could scarce furnish honest men enow to supply
> all those imployments . . . In short, there is nothing
> that comes nearer in Government to the Divine Per-
> fection, than where the Monarch, as with us, injoys a
> capacity of doing all the good imaginable to mankind,
> under a disability to all that is evil.
>
> (pp. 248-250)

If this description of the prerogative were to be read as acceptable loyalism, it could only have been by some predis-
position in the audience. The *effect* of loyalty is certainly
created, but with magnificent imprecision, by the use of

[9] Ibid., pp. 43-44.

metaphor and myth rather than legal statement. The king's person is "most sacred and inviolable," although (as L'Estrange observed)[10] his father had discovered the contrary. The controversial Supply becomes a cornucopia of natural blessings, a "plentiful harvest" yielded by benevolent abstractions. His right of appointing officers, which was in fact balanced by Parliament's right of impeachment, is the "fountain of all honours"; and political idealism acquires in the last lines a tone not unworthy of James I, who was much in favor of the analogy between kingship and the rule of God Himself. If one looks more closely, even these abstractions become less reassuring. Nothing is said of that area of prerogative, the king's right of making war and peace and forming alliances, which was the cause of the present governmental stalemate. The sense of a grateful country yielding up extra revenues for some "extraordinary occasion," such as the war with France, is somewhat qualified by the possibility that such occasions might be only "pretended," and that "probable decency" might have to do for truth. Even stronger is the irony informing the king's right of appointment, since "it seems as if the Nation could scarce furnish honest men enow" to fill all the positions he has to bestow. As Marvell was shortly to accuse the Commons of widespread conflict of interest, approximately one-third of its members holding one of those "profitable" offices, his statement is patently a thinly disguised reproach.

The directions of Marvell's irony may be partly confirmed by a letter he wrote to "a Friend in Persia" in August 1671, which describes how "the King having, *upon Pretence* of the great Preparations of his Neighbours, demanded three hundred thousand Pounds for his Navy, (tho in Conclusion he hath not set out any,) . . . our House gave several Bills . . . all Men foreseeing that what was given would not be applyed to discharge the Debts, which I hear are at this Day risen to four Millions, but diverted as

[10] Ibid., pp. 42-43.

formerly." The same letter explains the Commons' weakness, its agreement to the pretense, in terms of multiple bribes: "such was the Number of the constant Courtiers, increased by the Apostate Patriots, who were bought off, for that Turn, some at six, others ten, one at fifteen, thousand Pounds in Mony, besides what offices, Lands, and Reversions, to others, that it is a Mercy they gave not away the whole Land, and Liberty, of England" (II, 324-325). Even earlier Marvell had written to William Popple, describing the opening session of February 1670, when the king, "being exceedingly necessitous for Money, spoke to us *Stylo minaci & imperatorio*," thereby abandoning the pretense of constitutional decency. This letter ended with the unhopeful conclusion that Charles "was never since his coming in, nay, all Things considered, no King since the Conquest, so absolutely powerful" (II, 314-315).

Even without such guides to its interpretation, Marvell's constitutional statement is significantly different from the political orthodoxy. The document that best expressed the Stuart constitution was probably Charles I's answer, in June 1642, to the Nineteen Propositions of Parliament[11] which, even allowing for the Crown's point of view, provided a far more substantial account of the Crown's prerogative at a moment when it was about to be denied in practice. It is much to the point that, in 1677, Charles's statement was quoted in full by the author of *A Second Pacquet of Advices . . . to the men of Shaftsbury*, on the grounds that "a better Description of Kingly and Parliamentary Interest of Government cannot be had than what was described by the Pen of his Majesties Royal Father."[12] In Charles's speech,

[11] According to J. P. Kenyon, in *The Stuart Constitution 1603-1688* (Cambridge, 1966), pp. 21-22. The centrality of the royal *Answer* in English constitutional theory thereafter is documented by Corinne Comstock Weston, "The Theory of Mixed Monarchy under Charles I and After," *EHR* 75 (1960), 426ff. See also her *English Constitutional Theory And the House of Lords* (New York and London, 1965) pp. 24-123.

[12] *A Second Pacquet of Advice . . . to the men of Shaftsbury* (London, 1677), pp. 63-65.

which really was a definition of a mixed state, the division of power between king, Lords and Commons is stated without any equivocation. The actual government of the state, that is, "power of treaties of war and peace, of making peers, of choosing officers and councillors for state, judges for laws, commanders for forts and castles, giving commissions for raising men, to make war abroad, or to prevent and provide against invasions and insurrections at home, benefit of confiscations, power of pardoning, and some more of the like kind are placed in the King." By contrast, the House of Commons, "an excellent convener of liberty, but never intended for any share in government, or the choosing of them that govern," is legally entitled to nothing more than a watchdog function. In order "that the prince may not make use of this high and perpetual power to the hurt of those for whose good he hath it, and make use of the name of publick necessity for the gain of his private favourites and followers," the Commons is "solely entrusted" with the powers of impeachment and of initiating financial legislation. Finally, the judicatory powers of the Lords are explicitly defined as the mediatorial factor, "an excellent screen and bank between the prince and people, to assist each against any encroachment by the other, and by just judgments to preserve that law which ought to be the rule of every one of the three." The total effect of Charles's speech is of actual, rather than rhetorical balance. The qualifications of power are all on the surface, and beside these circumspect propositions Marvell's statement is revealed as a model of ingenuity.

The *Account of the Growth of Popery*, then, opens with a "praise" of the English constitution which manages to suggest two contrary propositions: the first, sustained by high-sounding catalogues of abstractions and linguistic equilibrium, asserts the ideal theory of a mixed state which imitates "the Divine Perfection"; the second, implied by negatives, inversions, omissions, and innuendoes, raises the questions which the surface of the statement begs, and is consistent with Marvell's criticisms of the real state of affairs, both in his private letters and in the pamphlet itself. The technique draws attention to the fact that the constitution, like all constitutions, is a fiction, "the balance of publick justice being so delicate" that it cannot exist outside the area controllable by language and defined by good intentions. This tension is comparable to that developed in the *Horatian Ode* between Justice and Fate, the "antient Rights" and the necessary impact of "greater Spirits"; but it is strikingly apparent that Marvell withholds from the definition of the Restoration State the sanction of his earlier metaphors. We do not find the images of music and building with which he had dignified Cromwell's far less balanced Instrument of Government; the king is no Amphion of constructive harmony; and we miss the positive sense of design, of workmanship and cooperation, with which Marvell had been able to inform a Parliament of which he had no personal experience. In the *First Anniversary* "the most Equal still sustein the Height, / And they as Pillars keep the Work upright." The "resistance of opposed Minds" is perceived as the outward pressure of the supporting arches, which in turn are "Knit by the Roofs Protecting weight." In the *Account* the only building to be found is the result of our "hacking and hewing one another, to frame an irregular figure of political incongruity," a metaphor which occurs in a later and very different statement of constitutional theory, where the difference between ideal and real is made explicit. In a fallen world, Marvell then admits, human institutions will necessarily appear "irregular" beside the "straight line" of Christianity. "Nevertheless because mankind must be governed some way . . . the vigour of such humane constitutions is to be preserved"; and no "publick person," however good his motives, may suspend the laws, as the king had done in his Declaration of Indulgence which, Marvell is now prepared to say, was an illegal extension of the royal prerogative (pp. 280-282).

Between these two contrasting definitions of the political principles which are now in jeopardy lies an equally subtle definition of the imperiled religious freedoms. "As we are thus happy in the constitution of our State," Marvell observes, "so are we yet more blessed in that of our Church; being free from the Romish yoak" (p. 250). But where we might reasonably expect a praise of the English *via media* in church doctrine and polity, we get instead an attack on the Roman church, which is described as "monstrous," "this last and insolentest attempt upon the credulity of mankind," "the pranks and ceremonies of Juglers and Conjurers"; and the Pope himself takes over the negative terminology of Samuel Parker, whom he resembles in his spiritual arrogance, political interference, and persecuting spirit (pp. 253-255). Marvell's strategy here is doubly indirect. Rhetorically he is engaged in praise by negative comparison, the dominant technique of *Upon Appleton House*. But, as with Fairfax's retirement, we must infer the complex values of the English church from the abuse of her major rival and, as with Fairfax's retirement, we may perhaps deduce that Marvell would have been hard pressed to praise directly, given a church which maintained its dubious integrity by harassing both Catholics and Nonconformists. He is, however, quite explicit about the tone of this passage. Since "Popery is such a thing that cannot, but for want of a word to express it, be called a Religion: nor is it to be mentioned with *that civility which is otherwise decent to be used*, in speaking of the differences of humane opinion about Divine matters" (pp. 250-251), satirical abuse is permitted; the relator is here exempted from the rules of procedure which govern the pamphlet as a whole.

In the survey of Restoration politics leading up to the Long Prorogation, the Pope's role as the focus of satire is occasionally taken over by Louis XIV, whose combination of spiritual presumption and political ambition were at this point in history far more directly responsible for the "growth of popery" in England. Marvell's characterization of Louis is also reminiscent of Parker, whose dangerous crusading instincts had been mocked by association with

French romances. When Louis declared war on the Netherlands in 1672, giving no other reason than that the Dutch
had caused a "diminution of his glory," Marvell's question
about the style of his declaration characteristically stands for
bigger things: "Was ever, in any age or nation of the world,
the sword drawn upon no better allegation? a stile so far
from being 'Most Christian,' that nothing but some vain
French romance can parallel or justify the expression" (p.
285). The threat to a Protestant country was combined with
an offense to international conventions of justice, as represented by Grotius' *De Jure Belli et Pacis* (since declarations
of war must be accompanied by reasons); both were conveniently symbolized by Louis' self-identification with a
world of fictional extravagance. Similarly, Marvell claims,
it was the sinister romance between Louis and Charles's
ministers that best explained the Long Prorogation. Although it was supposedly caused by the quarrel between
the Lords and Commons over the Shirley-Fagg case, the
silencing of Parliament from 22 November 1675 to 15
February 1677 allowed the French more than a clear year
to harass English ships, while being supplied with English
soldiers and ammunition. When Parliament finally met,
"that very same day the French king appointed his march
for Flanders. It seemed that his motions were in just
cadence, and that, as in a grand balet, he kept time with
those that were tuned here to his measure. And he thought
it a becoming gallantry to take the rest of Flanders our
natural out-work, in the very face of the King of England
and his *petites maisons* of Parliament" (p. 319). International
conspiracy was all the more alarming for being represented
as a courtly dance.

In contrast to this colorful villainy, the *Account* proceeds to develop the idea of true political heroism. Since
the death of Cromwell, Marvell had found himself short of
major heroes, and had had to make the best of General
Monck's slightly absurd adventures, the sacrificial gesture
of Archibald Douglas, and the scarcely disinterested vic-

tory of the Country party over the Excise. However, in the 1670s the question of courage became associated in his mind with resistance to royal, ministerial, or clerical despotism. He admired and wrote Latin poems about the daring of Colonel Thomas Blood, that "most bold, and yet sober, Fellow" (II, 326) who, as a political protest, had tried to seize the crown from the Tower, and that of James Mitchell who, in reenactment of C. Mutius Scaevola's Roman heroism, had made an attempt on the life of a tyrannical Scottish bishop.[13] In April 1670 he had written to Popple describing the attempt by the Lords to restore to the king "all civil or ecclesiastical Prerogatives which his Ancestors had enjoyed at any Time since the Conquest." This "Piece of absolute universal Tyranny" was turned back by the Commons and finally withdrawn, but the experience provoked Marvell's bitter comment, "We are all venal Cowards, except some few" (II, 317). When Charles took the unprecedented step of attending sessions of the House of Lords, thereby inhibiting the freedom of debate, Marvell's comment was to recognize the courage of those who spoke out notwithstanding: "The Lord Lucas made a fervent bold Speech against our Prodigality in giving, and the weak Looseness of the Government, the King being present. . . . But all this had little Encouragement, not being seconded" (II, 322-323). It was characteristic of the general repression that Lucas' speech, delivered in February 1671, was voted by the Lords to be libelous, and was publicly burnt by the hangman. The meaning of the event was epitomized in a metaphor which was to appear in the *Account* in an expanded and more intelligible form. "I take the last Quarrel betwixt us and the Lords," added Marvell, "to be as the Ashes of that Speech." It is the ashes of burned books and speeches which become, as we shall see from the *Account*, a

[13] The poems are *Bludius et Corona* (I, 178) and *Scaevola Scoto-Brittannus* (I, 213-214), both of which appear in the Popple manuscript. Blood's attempt took place in May 1671, and Mitchell's punishment in January 1676/7.

symbol of the irrepressibility of honest civic rhetoric, and hence of the inevitable failure of political censorship.

In the *Account*, this theme of the courageous and outspoken few is carefully established, as the positive standard by which to measure upright political action, and as the last major preliminary to Marvell's real subject, the response of Parliament and government ministers to constitutional issues. The issue on which the heroic standard was now erected was the proposal of a new Test Oath to be administered to all Members of Parliament. In April 1675 Marvell had supplied his constituents with a text of the proposed oath, which differed from previous loyalty oaths by concluding "And I do sweare that I will not at any time indevour the alteration of Government either in Church or State" (II, 148-149). It was thus a blatant attempt to eradicate all political opposition or pressure for reform, and in a letter to Popple in July of the same year Marvell described it as a device of "their Episcopal Cavalier Party" for getting rid of Parliament if it 'proved refractory' (II, 341).

As distinct from *A Letter from a Person of Quality to His Friend in the Country* (1675), which also described the crucial debate in the Lords over the Test, Marvell's *Account* does not concentrate on naming the speakers or otherwise identifying specific contributions to the debate. He succeeds, rather, in generalizing, in replacing the details of political action with larger traditional models and ideal forms:

> those Lords, that were against this oath, being assured of their own loyalty and merit, stood up now for the English liberties with the same genius, virtue and courage, that their noble ancestors had formerly defended the great Charter of England, but with so much greater commendation, in that they had here a fairer field, and a more civil way of decision: they fought it out under all the disadvantages imaginable: they were overlaid by numbers: the noise of the House, like the wind,

was against them, and if not the sun, the fire-side was always in their faces; nor being so few, could they, as their adversaries, withdraw to refresh themselves in a whole day's ingagement: yet never was there a clearer demonstration how dull a thing is humane eloquence, and greatness how little, when the bright truth discovers all things in their proper colours and dimensions, and shining, shoots its beams thorow all their fallacies.

(p. 309)

What we may recognize here is not the mixed tone of Marvell's mock-heroic account, in the *Last Instructions*, of the debate on the Excise Tax, when "Ev'n Iron Strangeways, chafing yet gave back, / Spent with fatigue, to breathe a while Toback" (ll. 279-280). It is not even the tone of sober praise with which he celebrates the backbenchers of the Opposition in that earlier debate, the "Gross of English Gentry, nobly born . . . / To speak not forward, but in Action brave" (ll. 287, 291). What it really sounds like is the unabashedly heroic resonance of Milton's *Areopagitica: A Speech for the Liberty of Unlicensed Printing*, the greatest (and likeliest) precedent in any discussion of freedom of opinion. Milton himself had described political debate as military action, and the activities of the censors as an offense against the chivalric code: "When a man hath . . . drawn forth his reasons as it were a battell raung'd, scatter'd and defeated all objections in his way, calls out his adversary into the plain, offers him the advantage of wind and sun, if he please; only that he may try the matter by dint of argument, for his opponents then to sculk, to lay ambushments, to keep a narrow bridge of licencing where the challenger should passe, though it be valour anough in shouldiership, is but weaknes and cowardise in the wars of Truth."[14]

This interpretation of the debate on the Test, as a crucial battle in the defense of Truth against political repres-

[14] Milton, *Complete Prose Works*, ed. Don M. Wolfe *et al.* (New Haven, 1953——), II, 562-563.

sion, is confirmed by another allusion that may also con-
nect Marvell's pamphlet with Milton's. When Marvell
points out that the official records of the Lords' proceedings were burned in the next session by order of the House,
he adds a significant phrase: "but the sparks of it will eter-
nally fly in their adversaries faces." What he is doing is quoting one of Francis Bacon's own comments on censorship,
which in turn was an expansion of one of Seneca's apho-
risms: "*Punitis ingeniis gliscat auctoritas*": "The authority
of wise men is increased by persecution." In Bacon's *Wise
and Moderate Discourse* Seneca's aphorism was expanded
as an argument against political censorship of Puritan
pamphlets: "Indeed," Bacon wrote, "we ever see it falleth
out, that the forbidden writing is thought to be a certaine
Sparke of truth that flieth up in the faces of them that
seeke to choke and tread it out; whereas a booke authorized,
is thought to bee but *temporis voces*, the language of the
time."[15] In the *Areopagitica* Milton had quoted this passage
on two occasions;[16] and Marvell's allusion to it shows how
carefully he had planned the location of his own pamphlet
in the polemical spectrum. As he had already discovered in
the *Second Part* of the *Rehearsal Transpros'd*, an association with Bacon's *Wise and Moderate Discourse* was an association with an impeccable tradition of moderate authority and latitudinarianism.[17]

His standards of conduct and constitutional principles
well established, Marvell could finally turn to his real subject, the session of Parliament which followed the Long
Prorogation, and to his new role as parliamentary reporter.
His position was that both Houses should have declared the
session illegal and forced Charles to call a new election. In

[15] Bacon, *A Wise and Moderate Discourse* (London, 1641), p. 11.
[16] Milton, *Complete Prose Works*, ii, 534, 542.
[17] Perhaps he was not aware that Bacon, as government spokesman
in the Commons under James, had argued that Members did not have
freedom of speech to discuss the royal prerogative. See Kenyon, *The
Stuart Constitution*, p. 27.

a letter to Edward Thompson prior to the session, he spoke of attempts "to make the Parliament men believe . . . they are dissolved by this Long Prorogation and that therefore it will be unsafe for them to sit. But it seems to be a Cavill and if the Parliament will not believe them they may spare their turning for Statutes and Precedents" (II, 350). But the *Account* shows Marvell apparently convinced, if not by "Statutes and Precedents," at least by other positions held by Shaftesbury's opposition group. A common theme of Shaftesbury's pamphlets in 1675[18] and Buckingham's speech in 1676 was that the House of Commons had outlived its usefulness as a representative body. Marvell develops this theme (omitting Shaftesbury's attack on the extension of privilege) into a major "digression" on the weakness and corruption of the House. Its longevity is seen as a long-term strategy, by which the Government gradually accumulated men it could count on: "Where the cards are so well known, they are only fit for a cheat, and no fair gamester but would throw them under the table" (p. 331). Consciousness of its own guilt has deprived the Commons of one of its most important defenses, the right of impeachment, and even those who were not actually on the king's payroll had succumbed to another, more insidious kind of self-interest, the unwillingness of men who hold a comfortable seat to hazard it in an election.

On 1 July 1676 Marvell had described to Sir Edward Harley the arrest of one Francis Jinks for calling in public for "a new Parliament as the Right and Remedy of the Nation," and on 17 July he reported to Popple that "Mr. Jinks will not petition the king . . . but keeps his prison as his

[18] *A Letter from a Parliament Man to his Friend, concerning the Proceedings in the House of Commons this last Session* (London, 1675); and *The Debate or Arguments for Dissolving this Present Parliament, and the calling of frequent and new Parliaments. As they were delivered in the House of Lords, Nov. 20, 1675*. Printed in William Cobbett, *Parliamentary History of England* (London, 1806-1812), IV, Appendices VI, VII.

fort . . . & perhaps may be prisoner till michaelmas terme, noe matter he is a single brave fellow" (II, 345, 348). The Commons, however, when reassembled in February 1677, did nothing but haggle about procedure:

> The first day, instead of the question, whether the Parliament were by this unprecedented prorogation indeed dissolved; it was proposed, something ridiculously, whether this prorogation were not an adjournment? And this debate too they adjourned to the next day, and from thence they put it off till the Munday morning. Then those that had proposed it, yet before they would enter upon the debate asked, Whether they might have liberty? as if that had not been more than implied before . . . and as if freedom of speech were not a concession of right, which the King grants at the first opening of all Parliaments.[19] . . . And so all that matter was wrapped up in a cleanly question, which involving the legitimacy of the House's sitting, was carried in the affirmative, as well as their own hearts could wish.
>
> (p. 320)

The *Account* does not mention the particular demurral of Richard Temple, one of Marvell's heroes from the *Last Instructions* and now traitor to the Country party, who objected: "Because the legality of our meeting is questioned by libels without doors, must we therefore make it a question within doors";[20] nor that on 21 February Marvell had acted as teller for the Noes against Temple's chairmanship of the Supply debate,[21] which in taking place at all was the ultimate proof of the Commons' venality.

In the Lords, on the other hand, great events were taking place. Buckingham and the other peers who had asked for

---

[19] Marvell was overstating the case here. Compare Kenyon, *The Stuart Constitution*, pp. 25-27.
[20] Cobbett, *Parliamentary History of England*, IV, 833.
[21] *JHC*, IX, 386.

a dissolution in November 1675, on the grounds that Lords and Commons could no longer work together, now argued from 4 Edward III, c. 14, and 36 Edward III that continuing Parliaments were supposed to sit at least once a year, and that a thirteen-month gap constituted legal dissolution. Buckingham's speech rebuked the Commons for regarding themselves "as a standing senate, and as a number of men picked out to be legislators for the rest of their lives" but, more importantly, he argued that this legal point made all the difference between constitutional and arbitrary government: "The whole matter, my lords, is reduced to this short dilemma; either the kings of England are bound by the acts above-mentioned of Edward III; or else the whole government of England by Parliament, and by the laws above, is absolutely at an end: for if the kings of England have power, by an order of theirs, to invalidate an Act made for the maintenance of Magna Charta itself . . . then they may not only, without the help of a parliament, raise money when they please, but also take away any man's estate when they please, and deprive every one of his liberty, or life, as they please."[22] When debate was carried on at this level, it was perhaps not surprising that there should have been reprisals, and the four main speakers, on refusing to apologize, were sent to the Tower, thereby quickly justifying Buckingham's prognosis. And so Marvell comments, "a prorogation without precedent was to be warranted by an imprisonment without example. A sad instance! . . . for nothing but Parliament can destroy Parliament. If a House shall once be felon of itself and stop its own breath, taking away that liberty of speech, which the King verbally, and of course, allows them . . . to what purpose is it coming thither?" (p. 322). Marvell subsequently rebuked the Commons for failing to resent "that breach upon the whole Parliament," as he chose to consider the imprisonment of the four peers, but in his own capacity as a Member of Parliament he had apparently adopted a similar discretion. Reporting to his

[22] Cobbett, *Parliamentary History of England*, IV, 818-820.

constituents on the opening of the session, he remarked: "no mention appears in the Journall of any Question of the validity of the Prorogation which tendernesse of the House you will also do well to imitate, by not propagating what I confide to you about it" (II, 179). There is no record of any speech by Marvell on the legality of the prorogation and, apart from his minor gesture of disapproval toward the Supply debate, no version of Jinks's heroism. Had Marvell already concluded that his criticisms would be more effective in print? Or should he now have repeated that earlier comment to Popple: "We are all venal Cowards, except some few" (II, 317)?

There are, in fact, some indications that Marvell did not dissociate himself from the collapse of parliamentary integrity. In this context it is well to recall events already mentioned in Chapter 1. On 27 March Marvell spoke at length, and surprisingly, on the Act for Securing the Protestant Religion, and two days later he was involved in an undignified scuffle with Sir Philip Harcourt, which nearly caused his expulsion from the House. Both events, as recorded in the Commons Journals, reveal a man who is worried both about the state of the House, and his own role as a Member. The speech had opened with a rebuke to his audience for their frivolity ("He is sorry the matter has occasioned so much mirth . . . there was never so solemn and sad an occasion, as this bill . . . ; but he is glad the house is returned into that temper, which the gravity of the matter requires"), and ends with an exhortation ("He desires that, during the King's reign, we may apply *ourselves* to preserve the people in the Protestant Religion . . . *If we do not practise upon ourselves*, all these Oaths and Tests are of no use; they are but phantoms").[23] Even more confessional, it would seem, was Marvell's allusion to his own disgrace, when he incorporated into his attack on the now invalid

[23] Anchitell Grey, *Debates of the House of Commons, From the Year 1667 to the Year 1694* (London, 1769), IV, 321-325.

246

proceedings of Parliament the language of Sir Thomas Meres's reproach to him on the subject of his own unparliamentary behavior.[24] "By this long haunting so together," wrote Marvell in the *Account*, "they are grown too so familiar among themselves, that all reverence of their own Assembly is lost" (p. 331). Knowing the source of this language, it is hard not to believe that "they" signifies "we," and that Marvell did *not* include himself among the few good men remaining in the Commons, the "handful of salt" (p. 329) that he exempted from his general condemnation.

Both Houses of Parliament, then, had been complicit in their own silencing, and in the repression of individual protest outside Parliament. Nothing, however, justified the extraordinary humiliation suffered by the Commons in 1677, to which Marvell devotes the last part of his pamphlet. From 5 March they had been debating and formulating requests to Charles to take unequivocal action against France, and to ally with the United Provinces in defense of the Spanish Netherlands. These debates, which are reported with uncompromising fullness, though without attribution to particular speakers, reveal the care with which the addresses to the king were worded, and that the Members were fully cognizant of the delicate constitutional issue. The court party opposed the addresses as an invasion on the foreign policy prerogative, and even argued that, since Charles was involved as a mediator in the peace at Nimvegen, "it would be an indecent thing for him at the same time to declare himself a party . . . there must be publick decorum" (pp. 395-396). The Opposition replied that "the prerogative is not at all intrench't upon; we do not, nor do pretend to treat or make alliances; we only offer our advice about them, and leave it with the King . . . It is no more than other persons may do to the King, or doubtless the privy council may advise him in this particular, and why not his great council?" (pp. 396-397.) The *Account* suddenly be-

---

[24] See Chapter I, pp. 45-46, above.

gins to sound like the idealizing "advices" which concluded the Dutch War satires and begged for a more candid relationship between the king and his public advisers: "We hope his Majesty will declare himself in earnest, and we are in earnest; having his Majestie's heart with us, let his hand rot off that is not stretcht out for this affair; we will not stick at this or that sum or thing, but we will go with his Majesty to all extremities" (p. 367). At the same time Marvell has to admit, rather grudgingly, that in these debates the Commons has partially recovered its lost dignity. The "handful of salt," the "little, but solid, and unbiassed party" (p. 329), which he had formerly exempted from his general contempt, can now flourish in a context in which the self-interest of the majority happens to coincide with the interests of the nation.

Charles's response to this unexpected firmness was not in the least conciliatory. On 28 May the Commons received a sharp chastisement for their interference. "Could I have been silent," he announced, "I would rather have chosen to be so, than to call to mind things so unfit for you to meddle with . . . you have entrenched upon so undoubted a right of the crown, that I am confident it will appear in no age (when the sword was not drawn) that the prerogative of making peace and war hath been so dangerously invaded" (p. 404). The insult was completed by the Speaker in adjourning the House immediately without its own consent, an insult repeated on 16 July and again on 3 December. One further adjournment occurred after Marvell had published his pamphlet, but the others were primary evidence for his thesis. On 16 July, we are told, the Speaker made his announcement and "in the same moment stampt down on the floor, and went forth (trampling upon, and treading underfoot, I had almost said, the privileges and usage of Parliament, but however) without shewing that decent respect which is due to a multitude in order, and to whom he was a menial servant" (p. 408). The parenthesis and the withdrawn hyperbole are far more effective in suggesting the real meaning of such events than any plain assertion, and shortly afterward Marvell confirms both the thesis and the structure of his pamphlet with ironical finesse: "if neither one prorogation, against all the laws in being, nor three vitious adjournments, against all precedents, can dissolve them, this Parliament is then immortal" (p. 410).

Immortal in physical presence, perhaps (though its absences had been rather more noticeable), but in spirit Charles's long-lived Parliament was, to all effective constitutional purposes, thoroughly dead. Marvell did not live to see its revival, its victory over Danby, and the achievement on 21 April 1679 of what he had so often argued for: Charles dismissed the Privy Council and swore in a new group of thirty councilors, including ten peers and five commoners, committing himself to make no more major decisions without their advice.[25] Marvell spent the last year of his life watching the maneuvers of the same old Parliament. If the appearance of the *Account* "about Christmas" 1677 was designed to coincide with the reopening of Parliament in January,[26] one of the first debates it was intended to influence must have been that on the illegal adjournments themselves. But on 9 February Marvell reported to Hull a scene which showed that he had failed. The debate began well enough: "Many insisted" on the "ill consequences" of such a breach of privilege; but on this occasion too much was said, not too little. In an excess of rhetoric, "it grew late." People moved for adjournment, tiredness and hunger prevailed over decency, and "all ended without coming to any Resolution upon that great point" (II, 214). Marvell was also to experience a repetition of the same ineffectual attempt to bargain with the king about France, another prorogation (though a short one) to punish the Commons for noncompliance, and another quarrel with the Lords about jurisdiction. In this piece of folly the Commons, always sensitive about their sole right to legislate fi-

[25] See Kenyon, *The Stuart Constitution*, p. 278.
[26] As suggested by Wallace, *Destiny his Choice*, pp. 209-210.

nances, protested against the Lords' amendment to a clause in the Supply Bill for the disbandment of the army, on the grounds that it could not be done in the time proposed. In the face of all reason, the Commons fought the matter until their own deadline for disbandment had passed, and then, to conceal their ignominy, passed a resolution reaffirming their financial privileges.[27] It was this resolution which formed the subject of Marvell's last letter to his constituents on 6 July 1678, so that by the whims of fate his last recorded statement continued the theme of the *Account*:

> Resolved that all Aids and Supplyes granted to his Majesty in Parliament are the sole gift of the Commons . . . This is what I have at present materiall.
>
> (II, 245-246)

The gap between constitutional theory and practice could not have been more absurdly marked.

The unspoken ironies of this finale to his public career as Member for Hull are consistent with the tone of his last surviving personal letter, written to William Popple on 10 June 1678. "There have been great Rewards offered in private, and considerable in the Gazette," Marvell informed his nephew, to anyone who could give information as to the author or printer of the *Account*. Unofficially, however, the secret is out. "Three or four printed Books since have described, *as near as it was proper to go*, the Man being a Member of Parliament, Mr. Marvell to have been the Author; but if he had, surely he should not have escaped being questioned in Parliament, or some other Place" (II, 357). Apart from the dry indirection of the third-person approach, it is surely with a dark sense of the *mot juste* that Marvell invoked, as a possible protection against his enemies, the principle of propriety whose undermining he had recently made apparent. Since the letter begins with a reference to the continued persecution of the Scottish Presbyterians, the man who had so far "escaped being questioned

---

[27] Kenyon, *The Stuart Constitution*, p. 413.

in Parliament, or some other Place" writes also, contextu-
ally, under the inquisitorial shadow. It is also consistent with
Marvell's self-effacing brand of heroism that he died, apparently from natural causes, before the Surveyor of the
Press, Sir Roger L'Estrange, was prepared to act on the information he had received. L'Estrange himself, in his formal
refutation of what he called *The Growth of Knavery*, preferred to refer to its author obliquely as a "Merry Andrew"
and, though he imprisoned Marvell's printer, apparently
avoided a more direct confrontation, perhaps with some
consciousness of Seneca's opinion that the punishment of
genius enhances its authority.

Along with the disturbance caused by his news, Marvell's generic innovation apparently made some impact, at
least on "Tom Tell-Troth," the "Downright Englishman"
who attempted to match Marvell's candid persona with an
opposing directness. In his *Letter to the Earl of Shaftesbury*
this anonymous protester offered a rather garbled account
of Marvell's writings (for we must reject the tempting hypothesis of lost works), which suggests that he had not read
them but was merely reacting to Marvell's growing reputation: "I protest, my Lord, that after having read over
abundance of such ware as little Andrew Marvel's Unhoop-
able *Wit and Polity*, and the *Independent Comment*
amongst it, together with the *Growth of Popery*, etc., as
also the *Naked Truth*, Treatises about *French Interests*, and
the *Succession of the Crown*, and all this bustle they have
made among us. To say the truth, my Lord, I am Tom tell
Troth, and between your Lordship and I, I do not believe
there's any need of any such Books, or any such Jeal-
ousies."[28]

We probably have a better perspective on the need for
Marvell's pamphlet than was available to Shaftesbury's

[28] *A letter to the Earl of Shaftesbury this 9th of July, 1680. From
Tom Tell-Troth a Downright Englishman* (London, 1680), p. 4.
Marvell was subsequently defended in *Tell Truth's Answer to Tell
Troth's Letter to Shaftesbury* (London, 1680).

anonymous correspondent. Knowledge of the secret clauses in the Treaty of Dover has given some credibility to Marvell's conspiracy theory and, though he did not succeed in shaming Parliament into any real confrontation with Charles on the constitutional issue, the *Account* must have contributed to the climate of opinion that led to the fall of Danby and the reconstitution of the Privy Council. Whole sections of the *Account* have earned a place in the parliamentary histories of his period, suggesting that Marvell, despite his disclaimer, had indeed written a "just volume of History"; and from the literary historian's point of view, his "naked narrative" completes the pattern of Marvell's intelligence. It brings us full circle back to the verses to Lovelace, and to Marvell's earliest preoccupation with a lost age of candor and civic virtues, with the "barbed Censurers" and the "Houses Priviledge" which, at that earlier time, had seemed to be in conflict with the writer's freedom of self-expression. Nearly thirty years later, Marvell's efforts to restore an open political climate were still inextricably involved with the art of "speaking well," in the traditions of Roman civic eloquence. If we read it carefully, his *Account of the Growth of Popery and Arbitrary Government* demonstrates that he had not forgotten how "to be ingenious," in the best Ciceronian sense of that word.

*Arbor ut indomitos ornet vix una labores.*
Hortus

# Index

Renaissance texts are listed by both author and title; for Marvell's works, *see* main Marvell entry. For biblical and mythological figures, *see* symbolism.

ordinance, 18, 61; religious intolerance of, 15, 177, 201; sermons to, 25, 84; Shirley-Fagg dispute, 12, 42, 238. *See also* legislation; Long Prorogation; privilege, parliamentary

*House of Lords* bishops in, 31, 169; censorship by, 43, 222, 228, 239; Charles II's attendance, 36, 239; in constitutional theory, 231, 234n, 235; debate over Non-Resisting Bill, 240-45; judiciary powers of, 231, 235; over Long Prorogation, 243n, 244-45; Shaftesbury in, 40, 43, 240-41, 244-45; Shirley-Fagg dispute, 12, 42, 238

Paston, Sir Robert, 126

Patrick, Simon, 186

*Peace-Offering, A* (Owen), 185

Peacham, Henry, 129, 143

Pepys, Samuel, 124, 138, 146, 153n, 155

Perinchieffe, Richard, 96n

Perkins, William, 183

Persius, 116

Pett, Peter, 32, 158-59

Phillips, Edward, 31n

pictorialism, 8-9, 112-18, 124, 127-34, 142-45, 161, 165n

Piles, Roger de, 132

Plato, 54, 55n

Pliny, 129-30, 133, 135, 161-62

*Poems on Affairs of State,* 41n, 111n, 175

Pope, Alexander, 8

Popple, William, 35-37, 40, 48, 157, 169, 170, 203, 212, 234, 239, 240, 246, 250

prerogative, royal, 40, 44, 222-23, 230-33, 236, 239, 242n, 247-48

Presbyterians, 11, 15, 18-19, 23, 153; in Scotland, 170, 201, 251

privilege, parliamentary, 18, 31-32, 40, 48, 223, 248, 252

*Progress of the Soul, The* (Donne), 199

*Prospective of the Naval Triumph, A* (Higgons), 137

*Prospettiva del Navale Trionfo* (Busenello), 137

*Protecting Brewer, The,* 83

*Protector, The* (Wither), 73

Protogones, 130-31, 161

Prynne, William, 41

Puritans, *see* Independents; Levellers; Nonconformists; Presbyterians

Quintilian, 51

Raphael, 131

Rawley, William, 209n

*Rebel Scot, The* (Cleveland), 36, 168

*Reconcilableness of God's Prescience . . . In a Letter* (Howe), 8, 39, 113, 176, 211, 215-16, 219

*Rehearsal, The* (Buckingham), 191, 217

*Religio Laici* (Dryden), 175, 179

*Reliquiae Baxterianae* (Baxter), 96n

*Report . . . of the . . . state of Germany* (Ascham), 229

*Reproof to the Rehearsal Transpros'd* (Parker), 36, 38n, 179, 190, 196, 201

*Resuscitatio* (Bacon), 209

rhetoric: Christian, 179-84, 204-08, 214-19; classical, 9, 16-19, 59-60, 65-68, 72, 240, 252; epi-

LIBRARY OF CONGRESS CATALOGING
IN PUBLICATION DATA

Patterson, Annabel M.
  Marvell and the civic crown.

  Includes index
  1. Marvell, Andrew, 1621-1678—Criticism and interpretation.
I.  Title.
PR3546.P3      824'.4      77-85555
ISBN 0-691-06356-7